# DISCOUNT eTRADING
# - REVEALED -

# DISCOUNT eTRADING
# - REVEALED -

*Former Stock, Futures and Options trader for 20 years Reveals the Astonishing Secrets of How to Make Money as a Discount (online) Trader.*

Meg Nolasco-Brewer

Bloomington, IN
authorHOUSE®
Milton Keynes, UK

*AuthorHouse™*
*1663 Liberty Drive,*
*Suite 200*
*Bloomington, IN 47403*
*www.authorhouse.com*
*Phone: 1-800-839-8640*

*AuthorHouse™ UK Ltd.*
*500 Avebury Boulevard*
*Central Milton Keynes, MK9 2BE*
*www.authorhouse.co.uk*
*Phone: 08001974150*



*First published by AuthorHouse 1/12/2007*

*ISBN: 978-1-4259-8125-9 (sc)*

*Library of Congress Control Number: 2006910572*

*Printed in the United States of America*
*Bloomington, Indiana*

*This book is printed on acid-free paper.*

## ACKNOWLEDGEMENTS

I WOULD LIKE to thank the following for their notable contribution to the completion of this book:

**Tony Brewer,** my mentor and critic for not letting me give up.

**S. Pierce, K. Capener,** and **E.S. Del Rosario** for their invaluable assistance in preparing this book and its web site.

The AuthorHouse Team – **Ashley Eller, Zoe Ragland, Elaine Ward, Jolene Barber** and **Tim Davies** for their extra effort and efficient service.

The "Ladies Who Lunch" – **Fides Herrera- Lim, Rina Reyes, Stella Sutton, Cynthia Turner, Marge Webster** and **Marichel Waring** – for their encouragement, support and for providing me a refreshing distraction when I needed it.

Finally, special thanks to my Mom, **Loretto Nolasco,** for inspiring me to BE.

# CONTENTS

# FOREWORD

THE ADVENT OF the Internet has revolutionized the way people invest and manage their investments. Once strictly the purview of people, computers and software programs have taken over the process. No one could accurately predict the impact of the continuing expansion of the online investment community on the world economy

America has become a society of equity investors. The number of households that own equities has increased more than three-fold since the early 1980's. Half of the approximately one hundred million United States households own stocks directly or indirectly through mutual funds. The number of households holding equities since 1999 has increased by 7.1 million, and by 2.8 million since 2002, according to the Investment Company Institute and the Securities Industry Association. The majority of the growth has come from the increased availability of defined contribution retirement plans, particularly 401k plans, where the majority of investments are made in stock funds. There has been equally impressive growth in individual investment accounts.

# INTRODUCTION

THIS BOOK WILL introduce you to discount etrading (online investing) and provide you with the basic knowledge and understanding of how to do it. I will not provide investment advice and I do not purport be an expert stock picker or a fund manager. In the process of illustrating discount etrading, I will provide practical strategies on how to evaluate investment opportunities and how to form your own investment decisions.

I assume that you want to join the ranks of online investors, or that you already do some financial transactions online and want to maximize your returns. If so, bear in mind that online investing is not mystical; it is hard work, but fun and very rewarding. Therefore, you are likely to have some or all of the following goals:

- To take advantage of all the timely investment information available on the Internet.

- To get more research done efficiently using the Internet. Online investing and monitoring can be time consuming.

- To make your money work harder for you by collaborating with your computer and the Internet.

I invite you to enjoy this book with the understanding that it can only be a starting point on your journey to discount etrading success. I invite you to do your own research on companies; applying what you learn from this book as a platform to gain a better and full understanding of what is involved in discount etrading.

## ESSENTIAL ELEMENTS FOR SUCCESSFUL DISCOUNT ETRADING

THE PRIMARY TOOL for successful discount etrading is a good computer with a high-speed connection to the Internet. You should not rely on old technology or dial-up technology if you seriously want to trade online; in fact, you can not trade effectively online without a fast computer and a fast Internet connection. A dial-up connection is useless. A slower DSL connection - too far from the terminal - is almost useless. A cable connection is usually preferred, because of its great speed and ability to process massive memory in nanoseconds. I am not technically qualified to set firm minimum standards, however, I personally will not attempt discount trading without a computer with at least 512 MB of RAM, a 1.5 Ghz. processor, and a 40 Gig hard drive.

Another essential tool to establish is a list of sites to use for your research on new investment opportunities. This means an account at a discount trading web site, and perhaps as many as five other web sites that offer research service. In addition, you need to learn how to formulate your own unique stock screens (*refer to Stocks De-Mystified*), and you must have the time and the desire to discount trade.

Market movements provide investment opportunities, in both bull (up market) and bear (down market) environments. No one can accurately foretell the exact movement of the market. However, you can develop an information system to monitor indicators of potential changes in stock prices and market trends. You need this information to help you manage your portfolio effectively, whether to buy, sell or hold a certain stock. I strongly recommend that you develop your own personal information system.

Successful discount trading requires the following six steps:

1. Developing an investment plan
2. Identifying new investment opportunities
3. Analyzing investment possibilities
4. Buying investments
5. Monitoring your investments
6. Liquidating investments – for profit or loss.

Before you begin to investigate investment opportunities, you need to identify your personal investment goals, and more importantly, your investment risk tolerance. You may state your goal in terms of rate of return. For instance, you may only invest where you have the potential for a 30% per annum profit. Moreover, if you are searching for an investment opportunity for your retirement account or Individual Retirement Account (IRA), you would not want to look at tax-free bonds, because being tax-exempt twice is not an advantage.

You also need to know and understand the type of investment you are considering for your investment portfolio. In particular, is it a common stock, preferred stock, unsecured loan stock, convertible loan stock, or a mutual fund?

Common stocks are often referred to as voting stocks. This means that the holders of this type of stock have the right to vote on company matters. These may be issues such as, re-electing the board of directors of the company, incentive schemes for directors, and other issues presented to the shareholders.

Preferred stocks or preference stocks generally are non-voting stocks. This means that owners of these shares do not have the right to vote on company matters. However, holders of this type of stock have the right to dividends and have priority over common stock holders over the assets of the company in case of liquidation. Issued with a par or face value, preferred stocks are often referred to as "hybrids". This is because they have the characteristics of both stocks and bonds. Typically, current interest rates at the time of issue can dictate the amount of dividend paid to holders of preference shares. The schedule for dividend payment varies from company to company. There are quarterly, semi-annual or annual distributions. Preferred stocks do not have maturity dates.

The most important tool in discount trading is your own investment strategy. A unique strategy you personally researched and developed. With your computer and the Internet, you can use the data available to you to formulate your own strategy and investment parameters.

In order to do this, you should be aware of the different types of stocks; their characteristics, and how they behave in general and particular economic conditions. This applies to mutual funds as well. The following are the different types of stocks and mutual funds:

- Blue-chip stocks: These are usually the most prominent, big capitalized stocks in the market. Stocks that have been around the longest with a long-term history of earnings and dividend payments. The most common examples of this type of stock are some of the constituents of the Dow Jones Index.

- Cyclical stocks: As the name implies, the price of this type of stock fluctuates in conjunction with economic cycles. These companies are very likely to be in certain industries such as: the automobile, steel, cement, and machine tools.

- Seasonal stocks: Similar to cyclical stocks, the price of this type of stock moves with the commercial seasons. A good illustration of a seasonal stock is a company in the retail sector, whose core business in a financial year occurs around Christmas time.

- Defensive stocks: These stocks tend to be stable with minimal price fluctuations, and relatively safe in declining markets (bear markets). These are generally stocks of companies who provide essential services, i.e. utilities, drugs, food and any industry where sales remain stable when the economy slows-down.

- Growth stocks: Growth companies are those who are positioned for future growth. Stocks of these companies can be the most volatile in the market. These companies do not pay dividends, and reinvest their profits back into the business for research and development to fuel future growth. Historically, they achieve a higher return on capital than mature well-established companies.

- Income stocks: Those who are interested in regular income at higher rates than what is offered in a regular savings account, generally acquire this type of stock. If your investment goal is to develop a monthly income then you should look into income stocks.

- International stocks: Investors who invest in international stocks generally feel that domestic stocks are over-valued, and international stocks present a more lucrative alternative investment opportunity. International stocks have inherent risks that are not present in domestic stocks. For instance, currency risks, different laws, different accounting principles, and most importantly, political risks.

- Speculative stocks and Initial Public Offerings (IPOs): Speculative stocks are generally easy to recognize, because they have price/earnings (P/E) ratios much higher than other stocks in the same sector or industry. Price/earning ratio will be explained in detail in a later chapter (*Fundamental Analysis*). Initial Public Offerings (IPOs) have higher risk than publicly quoted stocks, because the company has no substantial track record. More often than not, especially in the initial few years, there is no relationship between the stock price and the actual earnings of a company.

- Value stocks: These are stocks that are often undervalued in comparison to the stocks of companies in the same sector or industry.

### Hybrids

Hybrid securities combine some of the characteristics of both debt and equity securities.

Preference or Preferred Shares: These shares form an intermediate class of security between equities and debt. In the event that the issuer is liquidated, holders of these shares have the right to receive interest and a return of capital in priority to ordinary shareholders.

Convertibles: These are bonds that can be converted into another form of security such as equities, at the election of the bondholder.

Equity warrants: Warrants are contractual entitlements to purchase shares on pre-determined terms. They are often issued with bonds or existing shares, but are detachable and trade independently of the bonds or shares.

### Other Methods of Owning or Controlling Shares

You do not necessarily have to own shares in a company to trade the stock of the company. There are other possibilities, such as the following:

Call option: An option contract that grants the buyer the right, but not the obligation, to buy the optioned shares of a company at a set price (called the "strike price") for a certain period of time. If the stock fails to meet the strike price before the expiration date, the option expires worthless. You buy a call option if you think the share price of the underlying security will rise, or sell a call option if you think it will fall. Selling an option is also referred to as "writing" an option. The option seller is called the "writer".

Futures/futures contracts: This security is a contract to buy or sell an amount of a commodity for a specific price on a specific date in the future.

Naked options: These are options that are sold on securities when the seller does not actually own shares of the underlying securities. Naked options are often referred to as "uncovered options."

Penny stock: A very low-priced speculative stock selling for less than $1 a share, although the term is sometimes applied to stocks selling for up to $5 a share.

Put: A put option is a contract that gives the buyer the right, but not the obligation, to sell the stock underlying the contract at a predetermined price (the strike price). The seller (or writer) of the put option is obligated to buy the stock at the strike price. Put options can be exercised at any time before the option expires. Buy a put option if you think the share price of the underlying stock will fall, or sell a put option if you think the share price of the underlying stock will rise. The underlying stock need not be owned to buy a put. You can buy a put, wait for the price to fall below the strike price, then buy the stock and immediately resell it for the higher strike price. The person who sold the put is obligated to buy the stock at the higher price.

Real Estate Investment Trusts (REITs): REITs are a specialized form of equity that allow investors to own a portion of a group of real estate properties. Some investors view it as a good alternative to bonds. This is mainly because, they are granted special tax status by the Internal Revenue Service. REITs pay out at least 95% of their earnings in the form of dividends to shareholders. They can offer healthy dividend of the same magnitude as bonds, or even better. As REITs acquire more property and as the value of the properties they own appreciates, the value of the equity increases as well, providing a nice total return for investors.

Unit Investment Trusts (UITs): An investment trust that purchases a fixed unmanaged portfolio of stocks or other securities. Shares in the trust are then sold – usually by brokers - to investors, normally in units of at least $1,000. Because they are unmanaged, unit investment trusts are somewhat like index funds. However, UITs typically have higher sales fees or annual operating expenses, so they do not share the low-cost advantage of index funds.

Warrant: A warrant is an entitlement to purchase a share of a company, at a predetermined price (usually higher than the current price) for an extended period. Typically, warrants are offered with a bond issue or an Initial Public Offering (IPO). An example of a warrant might be the opportunity for an investor to buy one share of ABC Company for $50 until September 1, 2010. Although the warrant accompanies a bond or an IPO share, it trades separately from both, after it is issued.

Mutual funds come in five general types. Within these types are several categories of funds. You can find mutual funds that correspond to your investment plan. The following is a brief description of the five types of mutual funds:

Equity funds. These mutual funds include stocks of publicly traded companies. Investing in equity funds can quickly generate a desired diversity, or simply broaden your portfolio. Why? Some equity funds offer stocks in one sector or industry only, while others offer stocks in a wider variety of sectors or industries, and therefore are more diversified.

Equity funds carry the highest risk of all the fund types. However, they can also achieve the highest return. Equity funds often specialize in growth stocks, income stocks, or sector stocks such as, utility, transport and telecommunication sectors.

Bond funds. These funds invest in bonds of corporations and governments. Investors who buy bond funds are generally seeking income with a certain degree of protection of principal. The income comes from the interest on the bonds. For the average investor, this may be the only way to invest in expensive bonds with high face values or issue values. Bond funds are conservative investments and are generally considered for the interest income. Investment grade bonds usually have less risk than equity funds, but they are not free of risk.

Municipal bond funds. Are mutual funds that invest only in local and state government bonds. The income from these funds is generally tax-free.

Hybrid funds. These funds invest in a combination of equities and bonds. Structured to achieve predetermined investment objectives, such as, rapid growth, matching a market benchmark's performance, or investing in one industry only.

Money market funds. These funds invest in short-term debts of corporations and the federal government. These funds often buy treasury bills, commercial paper, banker's acceptances, negotiable certificates of deposit, and short-term debts of U.S. governmental agencies. Money market funds provide less return and less risk than other types of funds.

### *Open-end and Closed-end Funds*

An open-end mutual fund has an unlimited number of shares. You can buy open-end funds through your broker or directly through the mutual fund's company. A closed-end mutual fund is a hybrid – part mutual fund and part stock. It is a publicly traded investment company with a limited number of shares. There are approximately six hundred closed-ended funds and hundreds of thousands of open-ended funds available in the market.

If you are looking at a closed-end fund, keep in mind that the investment company does not stand ready to redeem its own shares from shareholders, and it rarely issues new shares beyond its initial offering. These funds are only bought and sold through exchanges and brokers. Furthermore, these funds are not valued using the net-asset-value (NAV) method. Market fluctuations determine the price, just like any publicly traded investment.

Remember information is what will make or break you. The Internet provides a great deal of information, so much in fact, that it can be overwhelming. Every industry has its own jargon and the financial industry is no different. More likely than not, you will come across some terms that you are unfamiliar with. Fortunately, you can find definitions and explanations of financial terms quite easily on the Internet. The following are three of the most accessible online investment glossaries: http://www.investorwords.com/; http://www. prufn.com/learningcenter/glossary; and http://biz.yahoo.com/f/g/g.html.

# IDENTIFYING INVESTMENT OPPORTUNITIES

KNOWLEDGE IS FINANCIAL power. The first piece of knowledge you should seriously take into account is your personal investment goals. If you want long-term growth, you pursue different kinds of investment opportunities than if you want to make for instance, $1,000 a week trading securities.

For the beginner, discount trading can appear to be a myriad of unintelligible babble. Each security has its own fine print. Your job is to find it, read it, and understand it. That is not always easy. Fortunately, the Security and Exchange Commission (SEC) offers a wealth of information to help you understand the mechanics of investing and more importantly how you can avoid investment mistakes and fraud. You will find valuable information at http://www.sec.gov, on the following truths and realities of online trading, and investing in general:

The higher the return, the greater the risk: Do not spend your profit until it is safely in your bank account.

Some investments can not be liquidated or converted into cash easily: One example is municipal bonds.

If you want or need to sell an investment quickly, there may be penalties or transaction charges to be paid: The most commonly known is the penalty for cashing in a Certificate of Deposit or an Individual Retirement Account (IRA) early.

Investments in new companies that do not have a long track record may involve greater risk: One succinct example is the recent dot.com bubble. In the late 90's, investors' demand drove stock prices up. This demand for dot.com stocks was fueled mainly by rumors and speculations on the prospects of a phenomenal expansion in the Internet market. The Internet market did burgeon albeit gradually and a great many of the dot.com companies went bust.

There is no insurance on securities: Unlike standard bank account deposits, there is no Federal Depository Insurance Corporation (FDIC) insurance on securities. However most, if not all, brokerage houses offer account protection up to $500,000 through the Securities Investor Protection Corporation (SIPC).

The securities you own may change: This may happen due to corporate reorganizations, mergers, acquisitions, or third-party actions. On occasions, you will be asked to sell your shares, or surrender your shares for conversion to new shares. If you hear of a rumor of a possible merger in one of your stocks, monitor the development closely.

Past performance of a security is not a guarantee of future performance: A good example of this maxim is Google.com. Within a few years of Google's IPO, the stock increased by hundreds of percent to approximately $450 per share. Analysts and TV experts predicted it would go to $600 easily within a month. It did not! In fact, the stock price declined to approximately $340 per share within a month of the $600 per share prediction.

The Internet offers a number of web sites where a novice can learn about investing in general. Most of these web sites are about 80% content and 20% sales pitch, avoid the web sites that are the opposite. A few valuable examples of these web sites are:

> About Investing for Beginners: (http://www.beginnersinvest.about.com)

> Investing basics: (http://www.aaii.com/invbas)

CNN/Money 101: (http://www.money.cnn.com/pf/101)
NASD Investor Education:
(http://www.nasd.com/stellent/idcplg?IdcService=SS_GET_PAGE&nodeId=13&ssSourceNodeId=5)

Moreover, certain web sites on the Internet specialize in working with new investors. They are generally free to use. Two excellent examples of these sites are: MSN Money (http://moneycentral.msn.com/investor/research/wizards/SRW.asp), and SmartMoney University (http://university.smartmoney.com).

The following is a summary of the twelve most commonly used methods for researching and identifying new investment possibilities:

Stock recommendations: These can come from almost anywhere. They can be found on television programs about stocks, from newspapers, from the Wall Street Journal and many other financial publications.

Company profiles: Available on most web sites of publicly listed companies'.

Source directories: Investor source directories on the Internet can often provide overlooked financial information on companies.

Direct purchase plans: Some public companies offer the investor the opportunity to buy direct from the company, thereby dispensing with broker's commissions or trading fees on discount trading sites.

Dividend reinvestment plans: These plans are programmed to reinvest dividends to purchase additional stocks at a discount and without a broker.

Initial public offerings (IPOs): These are great investment opportunities. It is rare for a new offering's share price to crash as it hits the market. IPOs often double or triple in price at the opening, on their first trading day. If you are a sophisticated investor and have a large account with a discount broker, you may be able to secure pre-issue stock, which is even a better opportunity.

Investing e-zines: There are quite a few of these on the Internet that offer investors facts and information, as well as educational articles.

News reports: News on the Internet, newspapers, magazines, and television can be very helpful in providing vital investment information.

Newsgroups: Internet newsgroups can be valuable sources of information. However, information gathered from these sites should be viewed with a large dose of skepticism. You should always do your best to verify information found on newsgroups.

Online database: You can find historical stock prices, economic forecasts, and statistical information from online database that are available free or on a subscription basis.

Search engines: Search engines provide easy access to financial information of companies published on the Internet.

Stock and mutual fund screens: These software programs sort, filter and cull through the vast amount of information available, based upon the parameters you set to help find the appropriate investments for you.

The most visible and up-to-date source of investment news is just that, the news. However, your source of news can make a significant difference in the accuracy of the information.

For large news organizations discount traders rely on two web sites: Bloomberg Personal Finance (http://www.bloomberg.com), and CBS Market Watch (http://www.cbs.marketwatch.com). Both web sites are full of timely news, data and analyses of the financial markets. CBS Market Watch's web site also offers a variety of online investment tools free.

The financial news arena is well represented online. Discount traders' favorites include the following newspapers:

Financial Times: (http://www.ft.com). You can access the latest headlines, special financial reports, company news, market and industry data, and other financial information from this web site, free of charge.

Investor's Business Daily: (http://www.investors.com). This web site of a daily newspaper provides facts, figures, and objective news. The online edition also has an education section. It offers a two-week free trial.

The New York Times: (http://www.nytimes.com). The business section of this daily newspaper provides quotes, charts, business and financial news, and information about the most active stocks. Its online edition offers online portfolio functionality. This site charges a subscription fee.

The Wall Street Journal: (http://public.wsj.com/home.html). This is the grand daddy of financial news. Access to this web site is not free, but it provides valuable information and news. You can access research information and price quotes on any one of 8,500 publicly listed companies. Also available on this site are news and overviews on 20,000 companies.

The following are a few examples of what the magazine industry offers online:

BusinessWeek Online: (http://www.businessweek.com). If you subscribe to the magazine, you get the online edition free. You can have access to daily market briefings, quotes, portfolio tracking systems, and search their archive for information.

Do not discount the scholarly world of journals for financial information, especially if you want to use the most innovative stock analysis information online. There are several web sites of journals on the Internet; however, the following are the most remarkable examples:

Financial Economic Network: (http://www.ssrn.com/fen/index.html). This network allows you to search for information by the most requested article, topic, or author. You can download abstracts and working papers. Membership costs $80 and the cost per journal varies.

The Journal of Finance: (http://www.afajof.org/default.asp). This publication offers research across all the major fields of financial research. Online use is available for an annual membership fee of $80.

When it comes to e-zines and electronic newsletters there are over 9,000 available on the Internet. Two exceptional examples are The Wall Street Journal (http://public.wsj.com/home.html), and Ziff Davis Publications (http://news.zdnet.com).

If you want to find out about other sites that provide electronic newsletters, there is an extensive searchable directory of investment newsletters available at http://www.newsletteraccess.com/investments/index.html.

To practice or simulate discount etrading, the following three web sites could be very illuminating and fun:

Fantasy Stock Market: (http://www.fantasystockmarket.com). This web site is a free educational investment simulation game that enables players to build $100,000 portfolio by trading stocks and mutual funds on major U.S. exchanges.

Marketocracy: (http://www.marketocracy.com). Allows you to create your own mutual fund with a virtual $1,000,000. Membership is free. If you want access to research, you will have to pay an annual subscription fee.

Virtual Stock Exchange: (http://www.virutalstockexchange.com). This site is a free stock simulation game that enables you to trade stocks, as you would in a real brokerage account. The site also provides research reports, market news, charts and graphs. You can test your latest profit strategies on this site free and with no real consequence to your investment capital.

# WHO IS THE INVESTOR IN YOU?

ALL THE FINANCIAL information in the world has no value to you unless you are working with a plan, which you have personally formulated, to meet your personal financial goals. "I want to make a lot of money", is not a financial goal. To develop a viable personal investment strategy and plan, you need to start with analyzing your current financial position.

It may surprise you to know that your financial well being has little to do with how much money you make, but rather it largely depends on how much money you spend. If you do not know how much you are spending, you should start with a budget that tracks what you spend.

Deciding on your financial objective is a key to whether your experience with discount etrading will be pleasant or disastrous. Make your goals specific and measurable. For example, I want to buy a new house in this … area, worth … in five years time, or I want to have a net worth of $1,000,000 in ten years, and so on and so forth.

Having a distinct personal investment plan and strategy, will help you focus your attention on valuable investment opportunities, and filter-out irrelevant investment information. Several so-called television pundits offer "investment opportunities" every time they are on television. However, is this valuable advice? In my opinion, it is just a lot of hot air! Again, the best example is the case of the Google stock. In the beginning of 2006, Google was priced at about $450 per share. At that time all these media pundits were touting the stock and predicting that it would go to over $600 per share within a month. They even went as far as actually advising us – the viewers – to rush to our computers and buy as much of the stock as we can. Had we done so, we would have been very disappointed as a month later the stock was down to about $340 per share!

### *How Much Can You Invest?*

This decision should not be guesswork. You should thoroughly analyze your personal financial situation; create a budget to include, paying regular bills, purchasing essential items, putting money into savings, etc. All of these items need to be taken into consideration, before you can realistically decide on an amount to allocate for your trading investments. This is one of the most critical decisions you need to make before you begin discount etrading.

## WHICH DISCOUNT BROKER TO USE

THERE ARE LITERALLY hundreds of discount brokers and other types of brokerage firms that offer discount-trading services on the Internet. Your ultimate choice of broker will largely depend on the type of investment products you require, your anticipated frequency of trades, and the kind and level of customer service you expect from your broker. There are wide variances in all of these elements from broker to broker.

There is information available on broker ranking; however, unlike other things in life the cream does not always rise to the top. Your individual requirements are essential in the selection of a discount-trading site. I strongly recommend that you investigate as many discount brokers as possible before you open an account.

The following is a list of factors to consider when selecting brokers:

1. <u>Trading Commissions</u>: Cheaper is not always better. The price per trade at a discount broker may also indicate the level of customer service that comes with it. If you are not trading frequently, and you are not too concerned about whether your trade is executed within 15 seconds or 2 minutes; there really is not a significant difference among the brokers charging $7 to $20. Any cheaper than that and you may have trouble getting someone on the telephone to answer any questions you may have. Conversely, if you are paying much more than that, your service had better be perfect.

2. Other fees: Beyond the trading commissions, brokerage houses may charge other fees, including fees for transferring assets into the account, fees for closing an account, IRA custodian fees, wire transfer fees, account inactivity fees and annual fees. In addition to these, a brokerage house may also charge fees for not maintaining a minimum balance or a minimum number of trades for a particular period.

3. Minimum initial deposit: Not all brokers have minimum account deposit requirement, but some do, and some have high minimum requirements.

4. Customer service: This is a consequential part of the formula no matter how the service is delivered. Discount brokers should be totally involved in delivering online service and support, which is accessible, easy to use, and provide satisfaction and security to clients. The ability to communicate with discount brokers via telephone is also critical.

5. Traditional banking services: This may not be a priority for most investors, but some investors look for a brokerage account that can accommodate their trading as well as their banking needs. As a result, many brokers now offer: Money market sweeps; check writing; bill payment; Visa card; direct deposit; and Automated Teller Machine (ATM), services.

6. Research: All types of brokers use research as a marketing tool and some brokerage companies market their research as a real bonus service.

7. Mutual funds: No-load mutual funds may be purchased directly from mutual fund companies, and therefore generally have no impact on broker evaluation. However, no-load mutual funds are available from discount brokers as well as, from mutual fund companies. More often than not, discount brokers offer only a small part of the mutual funds available in the market.

8. Investment product selection: All brokerage houses offer stocks traded on the major exchanges, and most will offer equity mutual funds. Nevertheless, there are other investment vehicles that clients

may wish to utilize. The high-risk over-the-counter market is popular with investors who like to speculate and some brokerage firms readily provide this service.

9. Other methods of getting your trades executed: What if Internet connections breakdown? Investors should always verify if the broker they are considering also has a telephone trading system. It is important to know how this trading system works before starting to trade. There may be instances when you need to place an order through a real, live person, and many discount brokerage houses offer this option as well.

Since you are not necessarily looking for a trusting personal relationship with a discount broker as you would with a full-service broker – a live human being, selecting a discount broker is more a comparison of features, benefits and costs. The features and benefits that are important to you will ultimately dictate your choice of broker. It is also quite possible to have more than one discount broker for different kinds of trading. This is especially true if you get into trading commodity futures and options as well as securities.

### *Investigate Before You Open an Account*

The Securities Investor Protection Corporation (SIPC) provides account protection for brokerage accounts in a way that is similar to how the FDIC insures bank accounts. Each account is protected up to $500,000 and some brokerage companies offer higher protection. The SIPC covers you in case your brokerage house goes out of business. However, it does not cover your bad investment decisions.

You should thoroughly check the background of the brokerage firm that you intend to use for discount etrading. The Central Registration Depository (CRD) is a registration and licensing database used by regulators throughout the securities industry, (federal and state), to collect data about securities firms and their individual brokers. It is available at the National Association of Securities Dealers (NASD) web site at http://www.nasd.com/web/idcplg?IdcService=SS_GET_PAGE&nodeId=370&ssSourceNodeId=1092.

The New York Stock Exchange (NYSE) issues monthly reports on disciplinary actions taken against brokers and brokerage firms. You can find these reports at http://www.nyse.com by doing a search on the home page of this web site for "disciplinary actions".

You can also use the National Association of Securities Dealers Regulation (NASDR) web site at http://www.nasdr.com to request for background information on a broker. It is available through their NASD Regulation's Public Disclosure Program called "NASDBrokerCheck". Your state securities commission will likewise have information and background on brokers and brokerage firms.

As the Internet evolved, so have online brokerage services. Moreover, brokerage firms will continue to innovate to generate more business from clients. Those that do not offer research today would most likely offer it in the near future, as "research" has become another sales tool for numerous brokers. Considering which type of brokerage service best matches your requirement, is a vital part of your investment decision.

### *Selecting Brokers According to Your Needs*

It is imperative to conduct a background check on a brokerage firm. No matter how frequently I emphasized this idea, some of you would still want to jump right into trading. Fortunately, some brokerage houses specialize in helping beginners and novices. The following brokerage firms are especially accommodating to new investors:

> TD Ameritrade: (http://www.tdameritrade.com/index.html). This broker requires a $2,000 account minimum and a $1,000 minimum for IRA accounts. Market and limit orders are $10.99 per trade. Account maintenance fee is $15 per quarter. A trading demo (simulation) and an investor education center is available on their web site for novices. Ameritrade and TD Waterhouse merged in April 2006, to form TD Ameritrade.
>
> Note: Market orders are instructions for the broker to buy or sell immediately at the best possible price available in the market. Limit

orders are instructions to buy or sell at a specified price. Different types of orders will be explained in "*Increase Profits by Using Specific Orders*".

Harrisdirect: (http://www.harrisdirect.com). This web site is ideal for the beginner because it does not require a minimum amount in the account and the more you trade the lower the cost per trade becomes. It offers a variety of research sources and investors with accounts of $100,000 or more have direct access to IPO stocks. Customers can place orders via the Internet, telephone, or wireless devices (PDA's) with this broker's proprietary software program.

E*Trade: (http://www.etrade.com). E*trade is one of the top online brokerage houses. There is a minimum amount of $1,000 to open an account and trades cost $14.95 per transaction, up to 1,000 shares. Customers have unlimited access to shares of IPOs, real-time quotes versus time delayed quotes, charts, baseline reports, market news, and more.

Several brokerage firms cater for the more mainstream investors who are often defined by the number of trades they make, rather than by their knowledge of the markets, or by the amount of money in their accounts. By industry standards, a mainstream investor is one who makes from two to twenty trades per year and have portfolios valued between $25,000 and $75,000. Mainstream investors as a norm, want convenient and easy access to their money, are often concerned with split-second trading executions and finding their own research information. Some examples of good brokers for mainstream investors are:

TD Ameritrade: (http://www.tdameritrade.com/index.html). This firm's web site provides great portfolio monitoring tools. It is very efficient and user-friendly.

Fidelity: (http://www.fidelity.com). Offers a newly updated and easy to use web site functionality. Customers can access their cash in a number of ways and without difficulty. Fidelity requires a $2,500 minimum account balance.

Charles Schwab: (http://www.charlesschwab.com). With trading commission at only $9.95 per transaction and with 30 trades per quarter, or a household balance of $1,000,000, requirement, Charles Schwab offers good value for money. Moreover, you can access your account by any means of communication.

Active investors, who are defined as those who make between five and ten trades per week, may want to use brokerage houses that specifically cater for them by providing special software programs, information streams, and good commission rates. Most active investors want fast trades with cheap trading fees. The best examples of good discount brokerage houses that cater for active investors are:

A.B. Watley: (http://www.abwatley.com). This firm offers NASDAQ Level II quotes, which are detailed real-time quotes of the bid and ask prices, for each individual market maker. It also has standard real-time quotes and trading fees start at $10. A minimum monthly balance of $2,000 and a monthly maintenance fee of $50 are required to maintain an account with this firm. In addition, investors must qualify with a minimum annual income of $50,000 and a net worth of a minimum of $150,000. The more frequently you trade with this firm the cheaper the fees become.

TD Ameritrade: (http://www.tdameritrade.com/index.html). The TD Ameritrade system is quick and responsive and trading fees are $10.99 for market and limit orders.

BrownCo: (http://www.brownco.com). This brokerage house offers inexpensive fees at $5 per trade. In order to open an account with this firm, you need to have five years of investing experience. They also require an initial deposit of $15,000.

Scottrade: (http://www.scottrade.com). This firm has won numerous awards for investors' satisfaction. Trading fees start at $7 per transaction, and there are no account maintenance fees required. The minimum to open an account is $500. You need to have an account with this broker to receive free real-time streaming quotes and charts from their database.

### Rating Online Brokers

To help in the selection process for a broker, you may want to examine the rankings of online brokers. You should approach brokers with the perspective that you may not always get what you pay for. This is just the reality of life. There are web sites that provide ranking and evaluations of online brokers. The following are three examples of these web sites:

ConsumerSearch: (http://www.consumersearch.com/www/personal_finance/online_brokers/reviews). This web site offers free reviews on brokers based on articles written by others. One thing to take into account when viewing this site is how up-to-date are the reviews. Furthermore, take special note of how current are the articles used for the reviews.

Kiplinger.com Rates Online Brokerages. (http://www.kiplinger.com). Ranks online brokers on asset values, commissions, execution times, mutual fund programs, research, and tax information.

SmartMoney.com: (http://www.smartmoney.com/brokers/index.cfm?story=2005-intro ). This web site offers ratings for both online brokers and premium online brokers.

### Do Not Forget the Hybrids

The Financial Services Modernization Act of 1999 allowed banks and brokerage houses to offer a full menu of products and services. This deregulation means that a brokerage house can offer the same services as a bank, including FDIC insurance. Combining both your bank accounts and brokerage account in one place can lower the cost of doing your business, and the time you spend online managing your portfolio and finances.

Banking with a brokerage firm has many advantages. For one thing, it is easy to transfer money to and from your bank accounts and brokerage accounts. The following are other attributes of having a "bankerage" account:

Account aggregation: This enables you to view simultaneously all the different types of investments and accounts you have in one firm.

Low brokerage charges: Some "bankerages" offer low commissions as well as low mutual fund fees.

Wide range of services: Several brokerage firms offer a wide range of services including quality research free, while others provide cost-based research.

Bill-payment services: A few brokerage houses provide free bill-paying services.

Low banking fees: Banking fees can vary widely from one firm to another. Free use of ATM is fairly standard. The most beneficial feature of a "bankerage" account is what is commonly called as "sweep programs". These programs automatically transfer excess funds from your account to higher interest earning accounts, when your account balance exceeds a predetermined level at the end of a business day. Conversely, these programs automatically transfer funds from other accounts to your brokerage account when your account balance is below a predetermined level at the close of a business day.

Good rates: Some brokerage firms offer higher yields on certificates of deposits and interest bearing checking accounts.

The following companies offer practical "bankerage" services:

Fidelity: (http://www.fidelity.com). This web site wins for low banking fees, low brokerage fees for index mutual funds, and comprehensive research.

NetBank: (http://www.netbank.com). Offers online application; requires a Social Security (U.S.) number to apply for an account.

Citibank: (http://www.citibank.com). You will need a little more to apply for an account in this bank, including the proverbial mother's maiden name.

Wells Fargo Bank: (http://www.wellsfargo.com). With Wells Fargo's "Onelook" service, you can securely manage both your Wells Fargo and non-Wells Fargo accounts. You have access to bill-payment, checking, savings, credit card, mortgage, loans and investment accounts.

## Analysts: How They Can Benefit You and Your Plan

Research is the fundamental key to identifying profitable investment opportunities. Analysts do research. As an astute investor, you should be aware of the different types of analysts and their corresponding duties. This is crucial since an analyst's report may substantially influence your investment decision. The following are the different types of analysts:

Sell-side analysts: These analysts generally work for the investment bank that has underwritten the securities that they analyze.

Buy-side analysts: Normally advise mutual fund managers, hedge fund managers, investment advisors, and other institutional money managers who purchase securities for the accounts they manage. These analysts make money when they make good recommendations. If you can become privy to their research, you will likely have credible information.

Independent analysts: These analysts are not associated with any brokerage house or firm that underwrites the securities they cover. They make money by selling their recommendations in online investment columns sponsored by large organizations, or by writing newsletters that are sold on a subscription basis.

As you study analysts' reports, bear in mind that positive analysts' reports can generate brokerage commissions. Therefore, analysts may be under a lot of pressure to release positive reports on a company, because their compensation could possibly be linked to the number of investment deals or new investment clients, the brokerage firm acquires because of their reports. In addition, analysts may be under pressure to issue positive reports to help their own stock holdings. The Securities and Exchange Commission (SEC) restricts analysts from owning stocks personally; however, it is possible for analysts to own stocks indirectly, through employment retirement plans or through "nominees"; or even through derivatives.

You may want to join a "stock picking" or an investment community to help you ascertain investment opportunities. However, these communities were the haven of "pump and dump" schemes during the dot.com bubble. Hype for a particular stock was conducted for the sole purpose of driving the stock price to higher levels. This created an opportunity for the perpetrators of these exaggerations to liquidate their holdings at higher prices. Of late, serious investors use these sites to gain valuable information, investment wisdom, new strategies that work, and to discover stocks that are potential winners. A few notable examples of investment community sites are:

> ClearStation: (http://clearstation.etrade.com/). This is a free investment and analysis site. Members can receive free stock recommendations via email, customize and add annotations to graphs, create a watch list, and participate in stock discussions.

> Marketocracy.com: (http://www.marketocracy.com). Constantly analyzes and ranks the stock-picking ability of its members using a complex algorithm that incorporates long and short-term performances. Marketocracy also uses an attribution analysis that accounts for, market, sector, style, and trading contribution that can isolate comparative returns. The goal of this web site is to eliminate the probability of "being in the right place at the right time" in relation to stock picking performance.

> Value Investors Club: (http://www.valueinvestorsclub.com). Accepts a maximum of 250 value investors. Membership is free, however, only a select few, based on investment ability, are allowed to post long and short investment ideas. An investment manager with the best long-term investment track record judges your application.

Tracking stocks does not cost anything. The mere fact that you have been monitoring a particular stock for years does not obligate you to invest in that stock. The following are examples of web sites to help you start your Wall Street stock tracking system:

> BestCalls: (http://www.bestcalls.com). This web site helps investors to conveniently track events and schedules for thousands of publicly traded companies. It also allows investor relations' professionals to promote and disclose information about their investor events. Their "Calltracker" service provides automated and personalized email alerts of conference calls. It costs $49.95 annually to subscribe to this service.

> Reuter's Risk Alerts: (http://www.investor.reuters.com). With this web site's free registration, you can access useful analyses published on the Internet. Their reports fall into four categories: risk alerts, estimates, recommendations and research reports.

> StarMine: (http://www.starmine.com). This web site provides independent, objective ratings of securities analysts. It measures analysts' stock-picking performances and the accuracy of their earnings forecasts. This site can cut the time usually required for perusing for good research because they identify the analysts that consistently produce the best estimates. There are both free and fee-based services. Designed for individual investors, the free version rates only certain analysts.

The essential point to remember about research is that, a report may unravel a hot investment opportunity, or it may be flawed and therefore worthless. You need to validate your information with several analytical sources and do your own research before investing in a stock or a fund. If you do not, you will not get much solace from blaming other people for your bad investment decisions.

## CREATING YOUR INDIVIDUAL INVESTMENT PLAN

BEGINNER AND NOVICE investors must be cautious of creating implausible expectations from investing. It takes more than one day to become a millionaire for most people. The markets can have drastic upswings and downswings. Value investing is achievable through a prudent combination of speculative buys and savings. Applying this strategy to your investment plan will build wealth over time. Time is the key.

Start your plan with a realistic and sensible goal for return on your investments. Be realistic. Do not think in multiples, but in percentages. How do you calculate your return on investment (ROI)? Let us say that you invest $10,000 in stocks on January 1. By December 31, your account has a value of $14,332. To calculate your return start with the ending balance and subtract the beginning balance ($14,332 - $10,000 = $4,332). Then divide the result by the beginning balance. ($4,332 ÷ $10,000 = 0.4332). Then multiply the result by 100. (.04332 x 100 = 43.32) Your ROI is 43.32%.

Breakdown your long-term investment goal into, medium-term, short-term, 1 month and even daily goals. This will serve as your target list and will provide you with a map to your long-term goal. Sometimes a huge goal may appear impossible to achieve, but once broken down to smaller segments it would appear more feasible. Breaking your long-term goal into smaller milestones' also creates a powerful focus that will propel you into immediate action.

To track your progress, keep an investing diary. Record all your trades to include details of trade date, purchase price, trade exit date, sale price, profit or loss from trade and so on and so forth. Furthermore, you may find it useful to make notes of lessons learned from your trades; what worked and did not work in a particular transaction, so you can learn from your mistakes. With your investment plan in place, you will have the confidence and the discipline to follow your strategy. Your investment decisions will be based entirely on your investment plan and strategy, and not on your emotions.

## FULL-SERVICE BROKER VERSUS DISCOUNT TRADING

YOU SHOULD GIVE considerable thought to the suitability of a discount trading service for your particular investment strategy. Engaging the services of a full-service broker may prove to be a more practical option for you. Besides the obvious difference of dealing with a real person rather than only trading online, full-service brokers exist because of the services they provide. Services provided by a full service broker include the following:

Recommendations and advice: Broker's advice is supposed to be unbiased and geared towards the customer's best interest. However, take into account that brokers only make money when clients trade. Since this is how they make their money, it is easy for a full-service broker to encourage clients to trade more than necessary. This is of course a gross generalization, and there are honest and conscientious brokers in the market.

Quality service: One would think that big accounts get better service than small accounts. In fact, the level of service is the same for both big and small accounts, because the broker's goal is to trade. A busy broker can also easily forget the clients.

Help with taxes: Some full-service brokers will even help you with your tax figures, by determining the amount of tax liability you have accrued in your account in a fiscal year.

First choice for IPO shares: Traditional brokers can inform their clients of new initial public offerings (IPOs) so that they can get involved at the early stage of distribution. However, the availability of IPO shares depends largely on the broker's level of participation in what is commonly known as the IPO "syndicate". This is a group of brokers who elect to underwrite an offering. As in all other things in life, hierarchy within a syndicate determines the "pecking order" in an IPO. Hence, a lead syndicate generally gets the largest allocation of shares in an offering, and effectively controls the allocation of shares to the other members of the syndicate.

Access to other investment options: Many investors may require assistance managing their real estate assets, investments in private companies or partnerships, along with their stock and bond investments.

Peace of mind: Traditional brokers are paid to monitor the markets, so that the clients do not have to. Additionally, if something goes wrong, the investor can always attribute it to a bad broker's recommendation, although that is not much comfort once you have actualized your investment losses.

Branch offices: Some investors find the need to visit their brokers in person to feel secure about their investments. Having a branch office nearby can be comforting for some clients. AG Edwards is the best firm in terms of number of branch offices all over the U.S. However, they do charge higher fees than most brokerage firms do.

## ONLINE TRADING WITH HELP

A POSSIBLE COMPROMISE to the brokerage dilemma is to use a premium online brokerage firm, which offers you the ability to trade online, and still have the assistance of a live human being when you want one. Often premium brokers are divisions of full-service brokerage firms. The following are excellent examples of online premium discount brokerage firms:

Charles Schwab: (http://www.schwab.com). Schwab offers "AdvisorSource" service for clients with $100,000 or more in their portfolio. This service provides analysis of your financial situation and helps you to construct a plan for your financial future. Schwab has 72 branch offices in the US.

Fidelity: (http://www.fidelity.com). This brokerage firm offers the services of representatives who are happy to review your personal investment goals, objectives, and to assist you with any Fidelity investment products or related financial services.

Merrill Lynch Direct: (http://www.mldirect.ml.com). This worldwide leading company has offices in 35 countries and 600 branch offices in the United States. It offers the "Financial Foundation" service, which analyzes your current financial status and creates a financial plan based on your long-term financial objectives.

TD Ameritrade: (http://www.tdameritrade.com). Provides the "AdvisorDirect" service to clients with portfolios of $100,000 or more. This service refers you to a financial advisor within the firm who will assist you with your financial plan.

## SELECTING THE RIGHT ONLINE DISCOUNT BROKERAGE

MOST ONLINE INVESTORS want brokerage companies that are financially sound, provide excellent customer service, and offer a variety of products. The following is a list of criteria to consider when selecting an online discount brokerage firm:

Ease of use. Web sites need to be uncluttered, easy to navigate, offer fast downloads and useful tools.

Prompt customer service. Should you need to speak to your broker on the telephone, you should be able to get through as quickly as possible.

Reliability & responsiveness. Frequent system-wide crashes in a brokerage firm are not acceptable. Quick and accurate trade executions are critical.

Investing options, products, and tools. You want online access to IPOs, options, and other financial products. There is more to the investment world than just stocks and mutual funds.

Low fees. Beware of hidden fees. Read the fine print to discover if there are hidden fees. Some brokers not only charge high trading fees, but also numerous incidental fees that can significantly alter your profits or compound your losses. For example, annual service fees, a minimum service fee based upon the number of trades, and so on and so forth.

Reliable Administration. This is essential; portfolio valuations must be accurate, and statement of accounts must be easy to understand.

## INCREASE PROFITS BY USING SPECIFIC ORDERS

WHEN YOU TRADE, you will be issuing an instruction to buy or sell a specific amount of a certain security or commodity at a specific price. Efficient order execution is one of the various specializations that brokers use to justify their fees. When in fact, your order will be executed only as efficiently as specified in your order. For instance, you issue a limit order to buy 1000 shares of ABC Company at $25.00 per share, Good Till Cancelled. Your order clearly defines the conditions for the completion of your order; that you want to buy 1000 shares of ABC, that you are willing to pay a maximum price of $25.00 a share, and the order is open until the whole 1000 shares are executed or otherwise cancelled by you. Therefore, your broker can not come back to you and deliver less than 1000 shares, or at a higher price per share than $25.00, or worst 1000 shares of XYZ Company. Your broker can not charge you a higher brokerage fee either, for buying what you specifically asked for in the first place. Order specification defines the way your order is executed, and can save you valuable time and money. The following are the different ways to specify your order:

Day order: As the name indicates, this is valid only on the trading day on which the order was placed.

Good Till Canceled (GTC) order: This order is open until executed or cancelled. This order is often used when a buyer wants to buy a stock at a price that is below the current market price, or sell at a price higher than the current market price. This type of order will not only include the instruction to buy at a certain lower price or to sell at a higher price, but will likewise include an order expiration date. For a buy order, should the price of the stock drop to the level stipulated in the buy order before the expiration date, the buy order would be activated and executed automatically. Conversely, for a sell order, should the price of a stock rise to the level stipulated in the sell order before the expiration date, the sell order would be activated and executed automatically.

<u>Limit orders</u>: These are orders where the prices are specified for buying or selling a certain security or commodity. For a sell limit order, the limit price is the minimum price the seller is willing to accept for a stock. For a buy limit order, the limit price is the maximum price that the investor is willing to pay for a stock.

<u>Market order</u>: As the name implies, is executed immediately upon receipt of the order, at the best possible price available in the market.

<u>Stop order</u>: This is an order to buy at a price above, or sell at a price below, the current market price. This type of order gives the investor more control over the execution price than market orders. The most efficient use of stop orders is to lock-in profits or cut losses on trading position. For example, to cut the loss on a certain stock holding you issue a sell-stop order say 10% below the current price level. Should the stock price decline to the price level you specified in your order, your order to sell will be triggered and automatically executed, and you contain your losses to the level you planned when you issued the order.

<u>Stop-limit orders</u>: As soon as the price of a stock reaches the investors limit price, the order is activated. This type of order can only be executed at the set price or better, for the order to be completed. Generally, stop-limit orders are used in realizing profits on stock holdings.

A limit order is more valuable when dealing in amounts that are less than full-lots of any stock. Full-lots are generally expressed in hundreds, units of 100 shares, or thousands, units of 1,000 shares. Odd-lots are less than 100 shares of any stock. A limit order increases the chance of getting an odd-lot order filled at a specific price. Odd-lots rarely get the best price in market orders and stop orders, because they must be bundled with other orders to create a full-lot.

## UNDERSTANDING THE INNER WORKINGS OF EXHANGES AND ECN'S

YOU MAY NOT want to know all about the inner workings of the various stock exchanges and markets; however, it is important to have a basic understanding of the mechanisms of the major markets. One trading system you should at least have a fundamental understanding of is the Electronic Communications Network (ECN) of the NASDAQ exchange. Remember the National Association of Securities Dealers (NASDAQ) does not physically exist. Unlike the New York Stock Exchange (NYSE) with its trading floor and specialist traders, NASDAQ is an electronic exchange.

On both NYSE and NASDAQ, stocks are actually traded by specialist traders. NASDAQ only requires a minimum of two market makers for each listed stock. This requirement is enough to create a market and liquidity for a stock. A market maker is the underwriter and manager of a stock.

On the ECN, computer programs replaced the human specialists. Anyone can purchase NASDAQ traded equities through a brokerage house that has access to the ECN. Investors buy stocks through an online broker, and if the broker's computer finds a seller in the ECN, the investor's order is executed with no human intervention. Because computers do not have to sleep, this innovation led to after-hours trading.

To appreciate the value of the ECN, as an alternative exchange, let us take a quick look at how transactions occur on the NYSE and NASDAQ.

Buying stocks on the NYSE involves the broker sending your buy order to a specialist on the exchange floor. The specialist then looks for sellers on the trading floor or on an electronic order book. If the specialist finds enough sellers to match your bid price, the specialist completes the transaction.

Buying stocks on the NASDAQ involves the broker consulting a trading screen that lists how many shares various market makers are offering to sell, and at what price. The broker picks the best price and sends an electronic message to the market maker. The market maker must sell the shares to the broker, who purchases the shares on your behalf as a client.

In contrast, buying stocks on an ECN involves the broker sending a buy order to the ECN. The computer looks for matching sell orders on the ECN. If the computer finds enough sellers to complete the trade the transaction is executed, otherwise the order is not executed.

### *Inside Spreads*

A market maker represents an institution, for example, Merrill Lynch, Prudential Securities, Lehman Brothers, etc., that wants to make a market in a particular NASDAQ stock. They are specialists on an exchange or dealers in the over-the-counter market, who create an inventory of stocks for temporary holding. Market makers provide liquidity for a stock by buying and selling any time at the published "bid" and "offered" price.

For the market maker, the downside is that they are obligated to purchase stocks when no one wants them. The upside is they make profit from the "spread".

The spread is the difference between the "bid" and "ask" price. For example, if a stock has a bid price of $10.00 and an asked price of $10.25. By selling shares at the asked price, the market maker profits $0.25 per share. Spreads are most often just a few cents, however, huge volume can equate to substantial profit. According to industry reports, in 2004, market makers earned approximately $2 billion, and more than $2.5 billion in 2005 from spreads alone.

# MUTUAL FUNDS DE-MYSTIFIED

YOU MAY HAVE heard, or already know, that diversification is a good strategy to adapt in investing. However, unless you are a high roller with substantial capital, it is not cost effective to diversify when you have very limited capital. This is one of the main reasons why mutual funds were established. Mutual funds offer you the opportunity to diversify your portfolio through investment in funds.

Mutual funds are priced per share and prices are based on the net asset value (NAV) of the fund. NAV is calculated by adding up the total market value of the securities in the fund and dividing it by the number of outstanding shares in the fund. Thus, NAV value fluctuates with the market value of the securities held in the fund. The SEC requires the publication of the NAVs of every mutual fund at the end of each trading day. The following are two examples of web sites that provide NAV information of mutual funds:

> Lipper: (http://www.lipperweb.com). Lipper tracks 125,000 mutual funds worldwide.
>
> CNN/Money: (http://www.money.cnn.com). This web site tracks just about everything in markets and exchanges worldwide.

With the huge number of mutual funds available in the market, selecting the right one for your personal portfolio can prove to be a formidable task. Like all the other elements of your personal investment plan, you need to take into consideration several issues.

How long do you want to own the mutual fund? How much risk to your principal can you tolerate? Which mutual fund category meets your personal financial objectives? Which mutual fund's investment philosophy closely resembles your personal investment philosophy? The answers to these questions will greatly determine your choice of fund.

### *How Much Do Mutual Funds Cost?*

Mutual fund fees are called "loads". However, not all funds have "loads", but the majority of funds available in the market have "loads". You need to be aware of this fee because this cost will be deducted from your profits, or added to your losses.

Front-end load: This is the most common type of mutual fund fee. Investors pay a fee up-front when buying shares of a fund. No other fees are charged for redeeming or selling shares of the fund. By law, front-end loads cannot exceed 8.5%, and the current average is 5% for stock funds, and 4% for bond funds.

Back-end load: Much less common, these fees are charged when selling or redeeming shares of a mutual fund. Back-end fees are usually based upon time, starting at 5% during the first year and declining a percentage point each succeeding year, until the fee dwindles to nil after year five. However, they often have what are called 12b-1 fees charged to investors for promoting the mutual fund. 12b-1 fees range from 0.25% to 0.30%, but can be legally as high as 1.25%.

Classes of shares: Shares of mutual funds can likewise be categorized into different classes. "A" shares have front-end loads and "B" shares have back-end loads. "Y" shares are designed for institutional investors, and do not have a front-end load. "Z" shares are intended for employees of the mutual fund.

No loads: There are funds that charge neither front-end nor back-end loads. These kind of funds do not have a sales force. This means that you must contact the Investment Company directly to buy or sell shares of the fund. However, it does not mean that it is free of any other kind of fees. These funds typically charge annual service fees for their management services.

### *Types of Equity Funds*

Aggressive growth funds: These funds tend to invest in small capitalized and young companies. They typically make use of options and futures instruments to enhance performance. In a bullish market, these funds can provide a high rate of return. However, they tend to drop the most in a bearish market.

Growth and income funds: Aim for a steady return with capital growth potential. They often invest in companies that are growing, as well as in companies that are paying high or expanding dividends. These funds are more diverse than growth funds because they generally include some bonds. Investments in bonds lower the overall risk profile of the fund. In short, they reap less reward in a bullish market and lose less in a bearish market.

Value funds: Include stocks that have low price-to-earnings (P/E) ratios (*refer to Fundamental Analysis*). Value stocks are stocks that are under priced or are currently popular with Wall Street pundits. They may be mature companies that have not much growth left in them, or companies with poor recent earnings, troubles, or companies that use their earnings to pay dividends.

International funds: Invest in a mix of stocks and bonds from other countries or governments. These funds have inherent risks that are not found in domestic investments; specific examples of these are, political risks (nationalization of resources) and currency risks.

Balance funds: These funds are a mix of stocks, bonds, and Treasury bills. Every fund has its own unique strategy for the allocation of its investments across these asset classes.

Dividend funds: Offer investments in common and preferred stocks of companies that generate a large and steady stream of dividend income.

Fund of funds: Invest in other funds within the same fund family. A fund of funds is an inexpensive way of diversifying a portfolio. Investment in this kind of fund allows you to diversify in several funds on a single account. Furthermore, you only pay for the fee of a single fund instead of several funds.

### *Other Funds to Be Aware Of*

Index funds: These funds are passively managed and track the index of the market they invest in. For example, the Standard and Poor's 500 (S&P 500) index fund tracks and exactly mirrors the S&P 500 index in terms of portfolio holdings and performance.

The operating costs for passively managed index funds are often low, as low as 0.20%. Aside from low cost, index funds are popular for two reasons. First, the index fund's performance will match the returns of the index it tracks. If the market is up, so is the index and the index fund. Second, some index funds better reflect the investor's investment objectives. The downside of index funds is that investors will never have the opportunity to significantly outperform the market. The following are some web sites that provide more information on index funds:

> IndexFunds.com: (http://www.indexfunds.com). A very useful all-purpose source of index fund information. A beginner's message center is available on this site. It also includes a list of ten favorite index funds, useful articles, and links to web sites of index funds.
>
> The Index Investor: (http://www.indexinvestor.com). This web site is useful for investors looking for better index fund performance through asset allocation. Access to the site is divided into two sections, a free section and a subscription section for a fee of $25 per year.
>
> Vanguard: (http://flagship2.vanguard.com/VGApp/hnw/FundsStocksOverview). This site features the Vanguard 500-index fund, which has been in existence for over twenty-five years.

Exchange-traded funds (ETFs): These are passively managed funds that are traded on stock exchanges. A share of an exchange-traded fund is a share in a Unit Investment Trust (UIT). These investment trusts are investment companies established for the sole purpose of acquiring portfolios of shares to be passively managed over a fixed period.

There are different types of ETFs based on the market sector index, or international index they track. ETFs are inexpensive, with fees usually at 0.4%, however, you do have to pay broker's fees to trade them. The following are a few examples of ETFs:

> Spiders: Track the Standard & Poor's Deposit Receipts. The ticker symbol is SPDR.
>
> Cubes: Track the NASDAQ 100 of big non-financial stocks. The ticker symbol is QQQ.
>
> Diamonds: Track the Dow Industrial Average. The ticker symbol is DIA.
>
> Vipers: The Vanguard Group launched these ETFs. Each Viper has a new class of share of one of the company's well-known index funds. The underlying portfolios are the same, though fees and other features are different from that of the normal Vanguard index funds.

Several companies provide comprehensive information on exchange-traded-funds on their web sites, such as the following:

> Ishares: (http://www.ishares.com). This web site offers useful online tools, such as a portfolio allocator that allows you to create and allocate your own portfolio. It also follows the Russell 2000 index.
>
> Investment Company Institute: (http://www.ici.org/funds/abt/index.html). This is the web site of the National Association of Mutual Fund Companies. It provides answers to frequently asked questions about exchange-traded funds. It also contains useful industry statistics, investor education and industry news.

American Stock Exchange: (http://www.amex.com). A summary of all ETFs, product information on specific ETFs, new listings of ETFs, a return calculator, and investor education are available on this web site.

### Mutual Fund Information Online

To assist you in your research on mutual funds, the following is a list of web sites with extensive information on mutual funds:

MAXfunds.com: (http://www.maxfunds.com). Features quotes, top mutual fund performers, and lists of mutual funds by name, category, and ticker symbol.

Brill's Mutual Funds Interactive: (http://www.brill.com). This web site offers tutorials for a beginner mutual fund investor, descriptions of fund strategies, interviews with top mutual fund managers, analysis of the mutual fund market, and links to web sites of funds.

Standard & Poor's Fund Services: (http://www.funds-sp.com). Provides worldwide news about funds, up-to-date fund management ratings, and access to a database showing the latest performance figures of funds.

TheStreet.com: (http://tools.thestreet.com/tsc/research_land.html). This web site provides information on mutual funds as part of its research service. The annual report section offers access to annual reports of mutual funds.

### The Fine Print

You should not invest in a fund based solely on the information that you find on its web site. In fact, it is crucial that you obtain the "prospectus" of the fund that you are interested in, and take the time to read it thoroughly.

To locate the prospectus of a fund, here are a few of the web sites to search: EDGAR Mutual Funds Report (http://www.sec.gov/edgar/searchedgar/prospectus.htm) provides prospectuses for thousands of different types of funds. If you know the name of the fund, you will find the prospectus of the fund on this web site.

If you do not know the name of the fund, refer to another web site called Morningstar (http://www.morningstar.com). This site offers a mutual fund search engine. All you need to do is enter what you know of the fund's name, and the site will try to find the fund.

After you have located the prospectus of a fund, it is best to download it to your computer, so you can read it at your leisure, offline. When reviewing a fund's prospectus, pay special attention to the following information:

Investment objectives: Usually the first paragraph of a prospectus, it defines the investment objectives and lists the types of securities in the fund. If the fund does not meet your personal investment objectives or personal investment philosophy, you can stop reading the prospectus at this point.

Fees: The SEC requires that all mutual funds list all fees, costs, and expenses on a table at the front of the prospectus.

Additional expenses: Some funds charge for extra services such as printed shareholder materials, toll-free telephone numbers with 24-hour service, accumulation plans that reinvest your distributions and related support services.

Performance: Year-to-year data for the last ten years, usually condensed into a financial statement, shows the fund's performance. Many funds show a chart of the performance of a $1000 investment compounded annually.

Statement of additional information: This is where the details are found. It may include complex items, such as the biographies of the fund's directors, the fund's objectives and contracts for professional services.

# ANALYZING MUTUAL FUNDS

MOST OF A mutual fund's information material highlights the performance of the fund. Although this is an important selling point for the fund, it is by no means representative of the potential return that will accrue to investors. When analyzing mutual funds, it is best to scrutinize the relationship between its performance figure and its expense figure. Be mindful of the fact that a return on a mutual fund investment can be radically reduced by hidden costs. It is also prudent practice to compare a fund's expense ratio with that of a similar fund. In evaluating a mutual fund's investment merit, consider the following points:

Returns: Remember the power of compounding. It you are considering two similar funds, one with a return of 8% and one with a return of 10%. Two percent may not seem to be a lot of difference, however, over your lifetime that two percent can mean the difference between living in luxury or in fear that you will outlive your retirement fund.

Costs: Predicting cost is a lot easier than predicting performance. Nevertheless, do not forget that funds charge management fees, transaction fees, and taxes. Shareholders are charged taxes on their distributions or income from the fund. Experienced mutual fund investors typically avoid funds with expense ratios great than 1.25%.

### Mutual Fund Risks

Smart investors select funds based on their risk/return ratio; different investments have different risks. You can find information on mutual funds' risk/return ratios online at RiskGrades (http://www.riskgrades.com). This web site measures the risk grade of a mutual fund based on statistical analysis of the historical price fluctuations of the stocks and bonds in the fund's portfolio. Large fluctuations usually indicate high risk.

You can find more information on a fund's risk/return profile at Morningstar.com (http://www.morningstar.com). This web site calculates all kinds of variables in funds including standard deviation. Standard deviation is a statistical figure that shows how much a fund deviates from its average return over a given period. It is a good indicator of the consistency of a fund's performance. The higher the standard deviation, the higher the risk inherent in the fund.

### Mutual Fund Check List

As you progress towards investing in your first mutual fund, the following is a checklist of factors to review before making the final decision:

Fund manager: A fund is only as good as its management. If a fund's manager has a long history of good management, chances are he or she will continue to manage the fund well. However, historical track record would be irrelevant if a fund manager is new to the helm of the fund.

Stability of funds' philosophy: If a fund is unclear about its financial goals, and is switching investment methodology regularly, it may indicate bigger problems in the fund's management. It is best to avoid this kind of fund.

The size of the fund: Good funds have at least $50 million under management, and should be large enough to accommodate institutional investors. Often funds with more than $20 billion under management tend to have problems with being too large.

Fund's objectives: Some funds focus on certain sectors and special situations. They often offer higher returns at higher risk. These are not necessarily sensible investments for investors who invest in only one fund, or investors with very limited investment capital.

Fees: There is an on-going debate on which is a better mutual fund option, no-load or load funds? All studies and common logic dictate that paying a commission does not ensure a greater return. Nevertheless, investing in a fund with high fees and high returns is better than investing in a fund with low fees and poor performance.

Tax liabilities and returns: Mutual funds' performance figures are shown pre-tax. Therefore, you should take into consideration your tax position when formulating an investment decision in a mutual fund.

Fund ranking: Search for funds that perform well. A good barometer is to invest only in funds that are in the top 20% to 50% of its fund type. Just make sure you are comparing like-to-like funds and not comparing a growth fund to a balance fund.

Price/Earnings (P/E) ratio: Is a measure of the market's expectation of a fund's future performance. The market price of a fund reflects expected future performance, since funds normally report past and current performance. Hence, the more future performance is anticipated to outperform current performance, the higher the P/E figure. Ratios above 30 tend to be high risk. Look for funds in the 15 to 25 P/E ratio range.

Standard deviation: A funds standard deviation should be 17 or less.

Numerous web sites provide scores and ratings for mutual funds. The following web sites provide the most comprehensive information on fund ratings:

> The Wall Street Journal (http://public.wsj.com/home.html) and CBS MarketWatch (http://www.cbs.marketwatch.com) use the Lipper Leaders system (http://www.lipperweb.com), which classifies funds into five categories. Funds are ranked from one to five. One being the best, and five being the worst.

Morningstar: (http://www.morningstar.com) rates mutual funds from one star to five stars, with five stars ranking for the top performers.

Value Line: (http://www.valueline.com) scores mutual funds from one to five; with one being the best.

# DE-MYSTIFYING STOCKS AND SECURITIES

INVESTMENT IN STOCKS and securities begins with the acquisition of shares or stocks of a company. As a rule, you want to acquire stocks at a good or fair price. The primary objective is investment return, accruing by means of a capital gain on the share price. Moreover, you anticipate to earn more from your investment, if you buy a stock that pays dividends. Hence, it is critical that you need to be able to ascertain the fair value of a stock to maximize your return on investment. There are numerous methods employed by investors to make this analysis, however, we will look at the three most popular methods: fundamental analysis; technical analysis, and market timing.

## *Fundamental Analysis*

Fundamental analysis focuses on the underlying economics of the company behind the stock. Analysts try to estimate future sales, earnings, and expenses of a company. This information is in turn used to forecast the price of the company's stock. Most, if not all, U.S. business schools support fundamental analysis because it seeks to paint a whole economic picture of the company.

Fundamental analysis relies on forecasts of the economy, the industry, and the company's commercial prospects. This analysis determines the intrinsic value or fair value of a stock. Comparing fair value to market value determines whether the stock is priced fairly, or if it is under-valued or over-valued. Since the rule is to buy low, fundamental analysis aims to identify under-valued stocks.

In fundamental analysis, the relationships between company figures are used to reveal trends through time. Numbers in a company's accounts do not offer any meaningful information. However, ratio analysis of the figures, when applied cautiously, can provide powerful insights into the operation and performance of a company. They can help identify problems and enable comparisons between companies. There are numerous ratio analyses applied in fundamental analysis, but we will focus on the most commonly used ratios in the stock market.

To have a better understanding of fundamental analysis, it is useful to classify the financial ratios used in this analysis into three categories, to reflect the different aspects of a company's business operation:

| **Profitability Ratios** | **Financial Ratios** | **Shareholder Returns** |
|---|---|---|
| Return on Assets | Debt to Equity | Return on Equity % |
| Profit Margin % | Interest Cover | Earnings per Share |
| Asset Turnover | Current Ratio | Cash Flow per share |
| Inventory Turnover | S&P Rating | Dividend Yield % |
| | | Price/Earnings Ratio |
| | | Price/Book Ratio |
| | | Price/Cash Flow |

Profitability ratios are indicators of how well a company is being managed. These include the following ratios:

Return on Assets is the main measure of a company's operational performance. It shows how well a company uses its assets to produce income. It is calculated as:

Return on Assets: Net Income
Average Total Assets = Beginning Total Assets plus Ending Assets divided by 2

Profit Margin shows how much of a company's sales are retained as earnings or profits. It is a very good indicator of profitability, since sales are assessed along with costs. Profit margins are higher when a company can improve sales, and at the same time reduce cost. Presented as a percentage, it is calculated as:

Profit Margin %: Net Income / Sales

Asset Turnover indicates a company's efficiency in utilizing its assets to generate sales revenue. For example, a ratio of 3.0 will mean that is the number of times the total asset is being turned-over in sales revenue in a given time. Calculated as follows:

Asset Turnover: Sales / Average Total Assets = Beginning Total Assets plus Ending Total Assets divided by 2

Inventory Turnover shows how often a company's inventory is turned-over during a period. A high figure is generally good, since inventory is the least liquid asset of a company. However, an excessively high turnover may also suggest a risk of shortages. This figure must be compared with the figures of other companies in the same sector. Following is the formula for inventory turnover:

Inventory Turnover: Cost of Goods Sold / Average Inventory = Beginning Inventories plus Ending Inventories divided by 2

Financial ratios reflect a company's financial position. They indicate a company's long-term and short-term capability to meet its financial obligations. Financial ratios include the following:

Debt to Equity ratio also known as "Gearing" ratio, measures the solvency of a company. It also shows how much a company is leveraged, or shows the extent a company is using debt to fund its operation. A high debt-to-equity ratio is normally riskier particularly in rising interest rates environment, due to the additional interest to be paid on debts. This ratio relates to the following equation:

$$\text{Debt to Equity Ratio: } \frac{\text{Total Debt}}{\text{Total Equity}}$$

Interest Cover ratio demonstrates the relative security of a company's loan interest payment capabilities. It is calculated as:

$$\text{Interest Cover: } \frac{\text{Income Before Interest and Income Tax Expense}}{\text{Interest Expense}}$$

Current Ratio refers to the short-term assets and liabilities of a company. It shows to what extent short-term assets can cover short-term liabilities. For example, if a company's current ratio is less than 1.0, it means that the company's short-term assets can not fully fulfill its short-term obligations. Short-term lenders favor a high current ratio number. On the other hand, stockholders prefer a low current ratio figure, so that more of the company's assets can be put to use to grow the business. Current ratio is calculated as:

$$\text{Current Ratio: } \frac{\text{Current Assets}}{\text{Current Liabilities}}$$

S & P Rating is an assessment of a company's relative safety as an investment vehicle. S & P, a financial services company that evaluates stocks and bonds according to risk profile, or ability to meet loan and interest payments, issue this rating. Companies are rated from AAA or Aaa, which are the highest ratings, to D, which means that the company has defaulted on its loans and interests payments in the past.

Shareholder return ratios focus on the returns to the common stockholders of a company, instead of the performance and financial position of the company as a whole. The following are examples of shareholder return ratios:

Return on Equity shows how much profit a company generated from the funds the stockholders invested in the company. It is another measure of how well a company uses stockholders money to create profits. Calculated as :

Return on Equity: Net Income / Average Stockholders Equity = Beginning Shareholders Equity plus Ending Shareholders Equity divided by 2

Earnings per Share figure is the most widely used measurement of how much a company earned for the shareholder. It is the amount of the company's profit allocated to each common shareholder.

Earnings per Share: Net Income / Number of Common Shares Outstanding

Cash flow per Share measures how much cash profit a company generated for the shareholder. It is generally more favored by professional investors than the earnings per share ratio. This is mainly because the cash flow figure of a company is not as easy to manipulate as the earnings figure. A company either has cash or it does not.

Cash Flow per Share: Cash Flow = Cash Receipts minus Cash Payments / Number of Common Stocks Outstanding

Dividend Yield shows what portion of a company's share price is paid as dividend. Thus, it only forms part of a shareholders possible return, since it does not take into account the possible capital gain on the share price. Expressed as a percentage of the current stock price, it is computed as:

Dividend Yield %: Annual Dividend per Common Share / Market Price of Common Stock

Price/Earnings (P/E) Ratio is the current market price of a company's stock compared to its earnings per share. Earnings per share can be from the past year's figure or estimates for the current year. When calculated with estimated earnings it indicates what the market expects of the company's future performance. Also referred to as "earnings multiple", it reflects how many years of current earnings must be earned to purchase one share of stock.

Price/Earnings Ratio: $\dfrac{\text{Market Price of Common Stock}}{\text{Earnings per Share}}$

Price to Book ratio compares a stock's market price to its book value. It is a good indicator of a stock's relative value. It is also a useful tool in determining whether you are paying too much for what would remain of a company in the event of liquidation.

Price to Book Ratio: $\dfrac{\text{Market Price of Common Stock}}{\text{Book Value of Equity per Common Share}}$

Price to Cash flow is another useful measure of a company's relative value. Unlike earnings per share, it only takes into account the cash flow of the company. Thus, the effects of depreciation and non-cash activities are eliminated from the equation. Price to Cash flow ratio is computed as:

Price to Cash Flow Ratio: $\dfrac{\text{Market Price of Common Stock}}{\text{Cash flow per Share}}$

There are material limitations to fundamental analysis, the most significant of which being the assumption that stocks are held until the termination of the company. If a company's fundamental analysis shows excellent projected returns, and you hold the stock of the company for only a short time, you will not likely realize the anticipated returns. Another material limitation is human error. Company accountants, auditors, investors, and analysts can make errors in their estimates and projections, or may ignore relevant external factors, which can result in an erroneous valuation of a stock. Thus, it is best to exercise caution when interpreting fundamental analysis.

Several web sites provide stock valuation figures on a number of companies. The following is a list of the web sites that provide comprehensive stock valuations:

Global Value Investing with Stock Valuation: (http://www.numeraire.com/index.html.). This web site offers valuable articles and an online discount cash flow valuator. The valuator uses the discounted cash flow method for establishing the fair market value of a stock.

Stockworm: (http://www.stockworm.com). Developed by academics, it offers stock analysis, customizable technical charts, stock screeners, and portfolio management strategies. There are three types of memberships, ranging from $7.95 to $29.95 per month, depending on the amount and depth of research and analysis you require.

ValueEngine.com: (http://www.valuengine.com). Dr. Shiwu Chen of Yale and a team of experts developed this site. Services include stock valuation models, stock forecast models, and portfolio forecast models. Stock valuations are free. With a premium membership for $24.95 per month, you get delayed quotes, portfolio tools, advanced screening, detailed stock analysis, multi-stock comparisons, research by analysts and benchmark portfolios.

ValuePro: (http://www.valuepro.net). This web site was developed by finance professors to evaluate stocks using the discounted cash flow method. A software package that costs $44.95, allows you to download information from the site. You can also use the site free.

Value Point Analysis Stock Forum: (http://www.eduvest.com). This site uses a computer model to evaluate a stock's worth in terms of its fundamental economic factors, financial factors, and the general condition of the money market. It is a free site.

For beginners, I recommend the Value Point system because it provides the most extensive valuation information on a company. The model uses the following data:

Corporate name, ticker symbol, and exchange of stock. This is how the stock is identified in the stock exchange.

Number of shares outstanding. This shows how many common shareholders of the company there are in the market.

Long-term debt. Long-term debt is the amount of any loans or outstanding bonds that mature in five years or more. Debt with a term of less than five years is considered a short or mid-term liability.

Current dividend payout per share. This is an annualized dividend figure.

Book value or net worth per share. Another way to calculate net worth per share is, total assets less total liabilities, divided by the number of common shares outstanding.

Projected earnings per share. You can use the analysts' projections or your own.

Projected average growth in sales expressed as a percentage. Without sales, there will be no earnings and therefore no profits.

Current earnings per share. The net after-tax income divided by the number of common shares outstanding.

Current price per share. This means the current market price of the company's stock.

Number of years the earnings growth rate is expected to be sustained. Some companies have variable growth rates and others have steady growth rates. You need to decide if the company in question will continue to grow or not. This is a judgement call that investors have to make.

Current yield of AAA Bonds expressed in a percent. The model provides this number for you.

Projected change of AAA Bonds expressed in percentage, 100 basis points or 1%. The model enters a default figure in this section. Should you disagree with it, you can amend the figure.

### *Fundamental Analyzing for Value Shopping*

Astute investing is essentially bargain hunting. However, identifying the good value investment from the multitude of investments in the market can be a challenging task. The following table outlines some parameters you can adapt to help you identify good value stocks in the market:

| FACTOR | ANALYSIS |
|---|---|
| Price/book value * | Never over 2.0 |
| Price/earnings ratio ** | Use 5 yr. avg. earnings, never over 12 |
| Ratio of cash per share to price per share *** | At least 10% |
| Dividend yield **** | Never below 3% |
| Price to cash flow | 80% or less of the S & P 500 cash flow ratio |
| Ratio of long-term debt plus unfunded pensions to total capital | Should be under 50% |
| Financial strength | Credit worthiness should be at least equal to the industry average. The S & P rating should be at least B- |

* Price/book value (P/BV) expresses the current selling price divided by book value. If the current selling price of the stock is below this amount then the stock is underpriced.

** Price/earnings ratio reflects how many years of current earnings must be earned to purchase one share of stock.

*** Cash flow per share expresses the firm's net income plus depreciation and amortization expenses, divided by the number of outstanding shares.

**** The annual dividend divided by the market price.

## *Technical Analysis*

Technical analysis in a nutshell, is the study of the factors relating to the supply and demand of stocks. Technical analysis relies on the Dow theory. This theory maintains that three major market movements exist. The first is the daily fluctuations that represent normal trading activity. The second is the intermediate or secondary movement, which lasts about two weeks to a month, and shows the long-term trend of the market. The third is the long primary trend that indicates either a bull or a bear market.

The principal objective of the technical analysis method is the identification of trends based on mathematical calculations, computer programs, charts and graphs, trading volume, and stock price movements. It is not concerned with the profitability or earnings prospects of the underlying company, and does not take into account the company's fair market value or intrinsic value. Technical analysis is based on the following assumptions:

- The market value of a stock is determined entirely by the interaction of supply and demand.
- Stock market prices are likely to move in trends that persist for a long period, with possible minor fluctuations.
- Reversals of trends are caused by shifts in supply and demand.
- Demand and supply shifts can be detected sooner or later in charts and graphs.
- Chart patterns often repeat themselves.
- Support and resistance levels are identifiable. A support level is where historically the price of a stock shows reluctance to drop below a certain price level. A resistance level is where historically the price of a stock shows reluctance to rise above a certain price level.

Evidently, technical analysis focuses on stock data analyses and stock market statistics. Analysts generally use a series of mathematical methods and calculations designed to monitor market activity. Trading decisions are activated on signals generated by manual mathematical calculations, computer programs, or a combination of both.

If you want to use technical analysis in your research for investment opportunities, the following web sites provide efficient technical analysis service:

ClearStation: (http://clearstation.etrade.com). This web site offers customizable charting tools to illustrate the basics of technical analysis. Color-coded trend indicators and standard charts of numerous companies are available. If you are a beginner, you can get technical analysis methods illustrated with real-time stock price examples.

Investtech.com: (http://www.investtech.com). Daily updated analyses and recommendations on more than 15,000 stocks, in the European and the U.S. markets, are obtainable on this web site.

ProphetNet: (http://www.prophet.net). A free basic membership is available on this web site. This entitles you to 40 years of interactive charting, 20 days of intra-day trading and the ability to save two chart styles. This membership also includes 24 technical studies, five custom sets, draw/save trend lines, access to watch lists, flip charts, two portfolios with 100 transactions per portfolio, risk/reward analysis, delayed market data, and 30 results for your chart toppers market scans. In addition, for $14.95 per month, you can avail of real-time prices, java/charts, snap charts, watch lists, portfolios, and delayed streaming intra-day charts. There are two other kinds of memberships available, one for $24.95 per month and one for $39.95 per month. With these advance memberships, you get all of the previous services with a few more bells and whistles.

Technical analysis involves a large amount of information, which requires a substantial computer memory. Hence, you will need special software to assist you in your analysis. Some programs are designed for beginners, and some are designed for advance investors. Here is a short list of some of the technical analysis software available in the market:

Equis MetaStock: (http://www.equis.com). MetaStock is a proprietary software that is often referred to by some analysts as, the grand daddy of technical analysis programs. It sells for $1,695. It has the ability to screen stocks using various chart patterns.

Inside TA: (http://www.stockblocks.com). This web site uses a box charting style to highlight each trading period's volume, and the high and low of a stock price. The standard version costs $129, and the professional version costs $229 .

VectorVest: (http://www.vectorvest.com). Uses fundamental valuations and technical analysis to rank more than 8,000 stocks each trading day. Stocks are ranked for value, safety, and timing. VectorVest also provides a buy, sell, or hold recommendation. There is a trial offer that costs only $9.95 for five weeks, and various subscription programs that are priced according to the level of service you require.

### Market Timing

The underlying theory of market timing is that you purchase stocks when prices are low and sell when prices are high. The market timing strategy is based on historical data used to discover patterns and relationships that affect market conditions. Market timing analysis requires software. Market timers attempt to time the purchase and sale of their securities, to coincide with ideal market conditions based on their predicted market cycles. For more information on market timing, refer to First Capital Corporation's web site at http://www.firstcap.com.

### Check Out Analyst Evaluations

Often a stock price fluctuates dramatically in view of an analyst's recommendation or criticism. Although you should consider an analyst's opinion as that of an informed and learned professional, it does not necessarily mean that it is infallible. You should always exercise your own judgment. Remember some analysts have vested interest in the financing of the companies they analyze. You should always verify an analyst's report on several web sites, such as the following:

MSN Money: (http://wwwmoneycentral.msn.com/investor/home.asp). This web site offers ratings of analysts, strategy labs, articles and more.

BusinessWeek Personal Investing: (http://www.businessweek.com/investor). Provides coverage of analysts' recommendations. It costs $45.97 per year.

Zacks Investment Research: (http://www.zacks.com). Provides estimated earnings based upon analysts' reports. It lists current earnings surprises, recommendations, and the company's annual balance sheet and income statement.

Briefing.com: (http://www.briefing.com). Offers three levels of subscription service. The free subscription, Silver level, provides upgrades and downgrades information. It also includes several investment calendars including, economic, stock-splits, IPOs, stock quotes, stock tracking, and long-term overviews. The Gold and Platinum subscriptions offer even more information.

# STOCK SCREENING ON THE INTERNET

STOCK SCREENING IS basically searching for the best stock to invest in at the moment. In order to ascertain which stock provides the best value for money, you require a huge amount of information and an extensive computer database. Most, if not all, discount-trading firms, offer you the ability to build your own unique stock screen on their web site.

Discount etrading stock screening programs allow investors to distinguish and filter useful information, from a larger set of market information. The goal when screening for stocks is to identify which stocks are worth your research and analysis time.

### *Criteria for Your First Stock Screen*

Earnings growth: This is the percentage change between current earnings and earnings for the last quarter or last year.

Recent earnings surprises: The difference between estimated and actual earnings.

Price/earnings (P/E) ratio: The current price of the stock divided by the earnings per share – which is net income divided by the total number of common shares outstanding. For example, value stocks have P/E ratios below 12, and growth stocks have P/E ratios above 20.

Dividends: The annual cash dividend paid by the company

Market capitalization: The number of outstanding shares multiplied by the current stock price. Market capitalization is sometimes abbreviated as "cap" or "mkt. cap". This value is a measurement of the company's size.

After you have established your stock-screening parameters, you will generate an initial list of stocks. This list may contain several to hundreds of stocks, which is excessive for effective research. Hence, you may need to fine-tune your screening process with more variables.

If you have special knowledge about a particular industry, that information can be valuable in your research for stocks in that industry. You may want to exclude companies that belong to an industry that you have no knowledge of, or companies in industries that do not correspond to your personal investment philosophy; such as, tobacco, alcohol, and pharmaceutical companies.

If you have done your fine tuning diligently, your second stock screen should have a list of 20 or so companies. It is perfectly fine to have less than 20 on your list. Start a file for each company that you want to pursue, and begin to gather your data for analysis. If at this point, you find companies that do not fit your plan and goals, or even your personal investment philosophy, exclude them.

### *Important Stock Screening Ratios*

Stock screening involves the same financial analysis ratios and measurements used in fundamental analysis (*refer to Fundamental Analysis*). The following is a summary of the most commonly used ratios in stock screening programs, most of which have been explained in fundamental analysis:

Beta: This is the measurement of an investment's market risk. The beta is the relationship between investment returns and market returns. Risk-free Treasury securities have a beta of 0.0. If the beta is negative, the company is inversely correlated to the market. This means that if the market goes up, this company's stock tends to go down. A beta of 1.0 means the stock's volatility is equal to the market as a whole. Betas greater than 1.0 indicate that the company is more volatile than the market.

Book value: As I have alluded to in fundamental analysis, book value is the original cost, less depreciation of the company's assets and outstanding liabilities. Depreciation is the means by which an asset's value is expensed over its useful life for federal income tax purposes.

Cash flow to share price: Another way of calculating the ratio of cash flow to share price is the company's net income plus depreciation (expenses not paid in cash) divided by the number of shares outstanding. For new companies that are building their infrastructure, this ratio will be a better measure of value than earnings per share. This is because a company's earnings figure may not be very informative at this early stage of their business operation.

Current ratio: This is the current assets divided by current liabilities. When the current ratio is 1.0 or more, it means that the company can pay all current obligations without using future earnings.

Debt to equity ratio: Debt to equity is determined by dividing the company's total amount of long-term debt, by the total amount of equity. Equity is defined as the residual claim by stockholders on company assets, after claims from creditors and preferred stockholders.

Dividends: A dividend is a portion of the company's net income paid to stockholders as a return on their investment. Dividends may not be paid out to shareholders on a regular basis, since company Directors decide on the distribution of dividends.

Dividend yield: This is the amount of the dividend divided by the current stock price. You can use dividend yield as a valuation indicator by comparing it with the dividend yield of other companies in the same sector or industry. What if the company does not pay a dividend? Then its dividend yield is zero.

Earnings per share (EPS): This is one of the most important features of a stock.

Price to book value ratio: Book value is tangible assets less liabilities, and price to book value is the current price of the stock divided by the book value. If the company has old assets, this ratio may be high. If it is a start-up company, with fixed assets that have not been depreciated, this ratio may be very low. You need to compare this ratio to industry standards and other information about the company.

Return on equity (ROE): This is equity earnings expressed as a proportion of net worth. You divide the most recent year's net income by shareholders' equity (shareholders' equity is assets minus liabilities) to calculate ROE.

Shares outstanding: This simply means the total number of shares issued by a company.

## *Using Quick Online Stock Screens*

Most discount trading sites offer "quick" stock screens. Quick stock screens can require from two to eighty variables. A stock screen database can include anywhere from 1,000 to more than 13,000 stocks. The best stock screen to use is one that contains the investment criteria in your personal investment plan.

Some stock screens are very complicated and difficult to use; while others are very comprehensive and offer good results. However, as a beginner you want basic but effective stock screens. The following web sites offer good results for as little effort as possible on your part:

> NASDAQ SharpScreen: (http://www.nasdaq.sharpscreen.com). This web site offers a quick printable tutorial for its stock screening service. It screens more than 6,000 stocks. Ten additional criteria are available to refine your stock screen further.
>
> Yahoo! Finance: (http://screen.yahoo.com/stocks.html). Provides a stock screen service that is easy to use. You can choose from preprogrammed screens for high volume stocks, stocks with the greatest sales revenue, largest market cap, strong forecast growth and more.

A few web sites offer pre-programmed screens that you can use, provided their criteria match or closely resemble your personal investment criteria. Some of these web sites are:

BusinessWeekOnline: (http://www.prosearch.businessweeek.com/businessweek/ general_free_search.html?mode-advanced). This web site offers a quick search screener and a more advanced stock screener.

MSN Money: (http://www.moneycentral.msn.com/investor/finder/welcome.asp) Offers the "Power Search Finder" service that helps identify stocks that best match your investment strategy. It has a selection of thirty pre-programmed screening systems.

Zacks: (http://www.zacks.com). Provides several types of stock-screening tools. You can save up to thirteen stock screens and it has an excellent help section.

### Building Stock Screens to Benefit Your Information Search

There are numerous ways to build successful strategies for stock screening. You can design a stock screen for a particular type of stock that matches your investment plan.

The following illustrates some useful parameters to adapt in screening for three types of stocks:

### Screening for Growth Stocks

Growth stocks expand at rates faster than their counterparts. They have different degrees of risk. It is a way to speculate on the business prospects of a company. Stock screen for growth stocks should include the following parameters:

Basic growth: Any stocks that have an earnings growth rate of 15% or greater per annum, for the past three years.

Long-term growth: Any stocks that grew 15% or more per annum over the past five years.

Price/Earnings to Growth (PEG) ratio: Stocks that have P/E ratios equal to or less than the earnings growth rate.

Aggressive growth companies with low P/E ratios: Stocks with annual earnings growth of more than 24% and P/E ratios of less than 15 are preferable, but very rare in the current market.

### Screening for Income Stocks

Income stocks tend to be stocks of stodgy, boring, slow-growth companies, but are steady income producers. You would likely include dividend yield in your stock screen strategy for income stocks. While growth stocks are ruled out, that is all right because if you want income stocks you have eschewed capital appreciation for monthly income.

In times when interest rates on savings instruments are low, dividends can, for just a little more risk, provide a higher return. One way to screen for an income stock is to screen for a stock with a dividend yield that is at least twice the yield of the S & P 500 Index, and with a dividend yield that never falls below 4%.

### Screening for Value Stocks

Value stocks are stocks of companies that have strong financial statements and good earnings, but trading at prices less than their industry peers' stocks. The following are parameters that you can adapt in your stock-screen for value stocks:

Price to Book value: Stocks of companies with price-to-book value ratios below 2.0.

Debt/equity ratio: Companies with debt/equity ratios of 50 or less.

P/E ratio: Stocks of companies with P/E ratios - based on five year average earnings- that are less than or equal to 70% of the average P/E ratio of the S & P 500. Do not include stocks with a P/E ratio greater than twelve.

Under-valued stocks: Small cap stocks with quick ratios -current assets less inventory divided by current liabilities- greater than 1.0 and return on assets (ROA) greater than 15%.

### *Screening for Investment Bargains*

Investors use research to find a competitive edge that will enable them to outperform the market, by identifying stocks that can surpass the performance of the markets. The following are some special situations to search for when screening for investment bargains. However, always take into account your personal investment risk tolerance.

Stocks selling below book value: Purchasing stocks at below book value may sound like a great opportunity; however, you should do more research. One thing to look for is depreciated assets (this means long-term assets). For example, if the company has fully depreciated a 30-year-old building, the market value of the building might be in the millions, but on the balance sheet, it is valued at zero. Always query why a company's stock is selling below book value.

Stocks selling below liquidation value: Liquidation value of a company is defined as the sum that could be realized if the assets were sold independently of the going concern. Sometimes these stocks may appear deceptively cheap because there are priority claims ahead of any common stock you could acquire, should the company go into liquidation. It is important to note that, as a common shareholder you are eighth in line behind: (1) secured creditors; (2) expenses incurred for administration and bankruptcy cost; (3) expenses incurred after filing bankruptcy; (4) salaries and commissions that were earned within three months of filing bankruptcy; (5) federal, state, and local taxes; (6) unsecured creditors; (7) and preferred stock shareholders.

Stocks with low P/E ratios: You are likely to see the term "trailing P/E ratio" in stock screen programs. This means the earnings per share for the last twelve months. To determine if a P/E ratio is low enough, you must first verify what is the standard calculation of P/E ratios in a particular industry. You can verify this information online in two web sites free: http://www.investor.reuters.com and http://www.wsj.com.

Companies reporting deficits: Deficits are operational losses, and in this case, you should look for them in cyclical stocks. You want to find companies with strong support levels, or which are experiencing flat earnings due to the normal cycles in their industry. Garden equipment is a good example, as sales are good during the spring and summer season, but sales start to slow in the fall, and are non-existent in the winter. It is extremely important that you know and understand the company's operations. The trick is, of course, to buy at the bottom of the down-cycle and sell at the peak of the up-cycle.

Prospective turnarounds: The value of finding these stocks is that when they do turnaround they can increase in multiples of as much as three hundred percent or more. They can also turn the other way around, so be very diligent with your research if you included these types of stocks in your investment plan.

# USING COMPANY INFORMATION IN YOUR INVESTMENT DECISIONS

I HAVE ALLUDED to financial statement information in fundamental analysis, and now I am going to show you how to find and use this valuable information in your investment decisions. You will need the following information for your research:

Company information: This means company profiles, management background information, financial statements, reports of trading by insiders, potential mergers or acquisitions and so on and so forth.

Industry information: Market information, and industry standards and trends.

Economic information: National, regional, and local economic information.

Other factors: These could be new legislation, changes in industry regulations, technological breakthroughs and new stock offerings.

The best resource material to use for your initial research on a company is the company's annual report, and quarterly report filings with the SEC. Annual reports are very helpful; however, they do require very cautious reading because you want to be certain that your interpretation of the facts is correct. You may have heard in the media that a company has or is restating their earnings. This usually means that they have made an incorrect entry in their annual report. Unfortunately, restating earnings generally mean that the first reported profit was erroneous and it tends to disappear with the restatement.

There are various ways to obtain annual reports. One is to go a company's web site and see if it is available to download, online. Another way is to go to the SEC web site and search for the company's annual report and quarterly reports. Keep in mind that if a company does not submit a report, it can be prevented from doing business.

You can obtain hard copies of annual reports. However, if you become an active investor, you will soon have to build-on to your house to accommodate the paperwork. The best way to access, use, and save annual reports is to do it online. The following web sites provide annual reports of companies:

> Annual Report Gallery: (http://www.reportgallery.com). This web site offers over 3,000 annual reports that cover most of the Fortune 500 (large) companies. Annual reports are available to download in html or pdf formats.
>
> Investor Relations Information Network: (http://www.irin.com). Offers more than 11,000 reports free. Since these are the actual annual reports of companies, these files are available in pdf formats and are easy to download.
>
> Public Register's Annual Report Service: (http://www.prars.com). You can order up to eight annual reports on this web site. It offers hard copies of annuals reports for more than 3,000 companies.
>
> The Wall Street Journal Online: (http://wsjie.ar.wilink.com/asp/wsj3_search_eng.asp).
> This web site provides annual reports from World Investor Link and The Wall Street Journal Interactive. You can obtain reports in hard copy, or as a downloadable file.

If you use the SEC web site to search for company information, you will need to know what type of reports to request for. The following is a list of the most common types of reports filed with the SEC:

<u>10-K reports</u>: Annual reports that include shareholders information covering the firm's fiscal year.

<u>10-Q reports</u>: Quarterly reports that include shareholders information for the firm's last quarter.

<u>8-K reports</u>: Interim reports covering an odd-period due to extraordinary corporate activities such as mergers, acquisitions, and so on and so forth.

<u>S-1 registration</u>: Forms required for businesses that want to offer stocks to the public, often used in IPOs.

<u>S-3 registration</u>: Forms to register a secondary stock offering.

<u>14-A form</u>: This form provides information about voting matters and candidates seeking election to the board of directors, also known as the proxy form.

## UNDERSTANDING THE ANNUAL REPORT

COMPANIES SPEND A lot of time and money to make their annual reports visually appealing. However, they must also contain the facts of the companies' business operations, no matter how unattractive they may be. Sometimes the truth is stretched to hide problems. Hence, always exercise caution when assimilating information in an annual report. The following illustrates how to approach the nine sections of an annual report:

Shareholder letter: Every annual report has one. I recommend that you do not read this section until you have finished analyzing the rest of the report; so that you can judge if the writer of the letter, usually the CEO or Chairman of the Board, is being truthful.

Company overview: This section generally describes the company's products or services and their distribution channels. Watch out for hype in this section. Always check independent industry analysis of the company's market position.

Ten-year financial summaries: These are selected financial data and not all the data you need.

Management discussion: This section often concentrates on operational data, which is of great importance to your research on a company's business operation.

Independent auditor's report: This report begins with a letter called the "opinion letter" from an independent auditor. Keep in mind that while the auditors are independent of the company's management, they are still hired and paid by the company. As such, there does exist a potential for inaccuracies in the auditing of a company's accounts. The essential thing that must be present in this section of an annual report is the auditor's statement of opinion. It is generally stated as follows: "In our opinion, the financial position stated in the annual report has been fairly stated in all material aspects and in conformity with generally accepted accounting principles". The absence of this statement in an annual report may indicate major problems in a company.

What and where: It is important to know details of a company's business operations. For example, what brands do they own, branch offices they may have, where they operate, who their major customers are, and so on and so forth.

List of directors and officers: While most annual reports do not offer any background information on directors and officers of the company, you must check the background and past performance of company directors. Look out for integrity issues such as the granting of too many stock options, excessive remuneration packages, etc. It is important that you feel comfortable with the ability and integrity of the company's management.

Stock price history: Evaluating the historical movement of a company's stock price can help you verify the classification of the stock. Is it a growth, income, or value stock?

### *What to Look for in Financial Statements*

Prudent investing practice dictates that we seek out quality companies with strong balance sheets, solid earnings and positive cash flows.

Rationale behind the numbers
Financials reflect actual events. The numbers and the resultant ratios are easier to understand, if you can visualize the underlying realities

of this essentially quantitative information. Have an understanding of the company's business operation, its products and services, and the overall industry in which the firm operates.

Differences in reporting format

Although financial statements are universal, do not expect the analysis to be similar across industries. The less-experienced investor may not readily understand presentation of accounts of companies that fall outside the mainstream or "normal" companies. Various business activities result in a diversity of financial statement presentations, particularly with the balance sheet. The income and cash flow statements, however, are less susceptible to this occurrence.

Understanding Financial Jargon

The lack of any appreciable standardization of financial reporting terminology, complicates the understanding of many financial statement account entries. It is very important to have at least some basic knowledge of this complex jargon. Most companies include notes on these in their annual reports.

Accounting is an Art, Not a Science

The presentation of a company's financial position is strongly influenced by its management's best approximation and judgments. Ideally, management should be scrupulously honest and candid, while external auditors should be strict and uncompromising. The risk of inaccurate estimation is inherent in the accounting process; hence, it is best to adopt a skeptical approach when analyzing company accounts.

International Accounting Convention

Generally Accepted Accounting Principles (GAAP) are used in the preparation of financial statements of U.S. companies. A basic understanding of at least two of GAAP's accounting conventions - historical cost and accrual accounting - is particularly important. According to GAAP, assets are valued at their historical cost, which may deviate significantly when compared to their current fair market value. Revenues are recorded when goods or services are delivered and not when cash is received. On the other hand, expenses are posted when incurred. In general, this method does not match with the actual receipt and disbursement of cash, making the cash flow figure of relative importance.

Non-Financial Statement Information

Information on the state of the economy, industry, competition, market forces, technological change, the quality of management and the labor force, is not directly reflected in a company's financial statements. Although financial statement insights are an important component, they are only a part of a larger information puzzle.

Financial Ratios

As discussed in fundamental analysis (*refer to Fundamental Analysis*), in order to make sense of financial statement numbers, these must transform into meaningful relationships to assess a company's overall financial performance and position. The resulting ratios and indicators must be viewed over an extended period of time, to reflect trends. Analytical financial metrics can deviate significantly by industry, size, and development stage of a company.

Notes to the Financial Statements

A thorough understanding of the notes to financial statements is essential in order to assess properly a company's performance. These notes also give effect to disclosures that are required by the regulators.

Consolidated Financial Statements

Consolidation of a parent company and its majority-owned subsidiaries means that the combined activities of separate legal entities are expressed as one economic unit. Consolidation presents numbers that are more meaningful, rather than separate statements for different companies in the same family. Financial statements would then be presented as " Consolidated Statement of Income".

Discerning financial statements

When you study the financial statements of a company, you should take note of the following information:

Growth in sales: Are they increasing, decreasing or cyclical? Sales trend is an important indicator of a company's efficiency in managing its performance. This is particularly true during slack demand. Growth in sales must also be analyzed along with increasing costs. Increasing sales is a good indicator, but it is better to exceed growth in costs.

Growth in profits: Sales do not necessarily translate to profits. Thus, sales should be adjudged in tandem with costs. Margins are better when management can improve sales, while at the same time reduce costs. Pay relative importance to margin analysis, as this indicates management's efficiency towards the proper use of resources. A reduction in direct costs translates to improve margins.

Profits: Did earnings per share increase every year? If not, why not? Did the company rely on operating income to sustain profits? Did it rely on other income boosters to generate profit growth? These are important issues to consider when analyzing a company's profit figures.

R&D (Research & Development) spending: How does the spending in this area compare with competitors? Is the company really planning growth? If so, it will show in this area. Capital expenditure on product improvement normally will translate into profits in the long-term. Immediate results may not be felt. On the other hand, beefing up resources for R&D will support the company's competitiveness. As a rule, spending on R&D should be relatively in line with the company's sales program.

Inventory: If there are changes are they due to changes in accounting procedures or changes in the business?

Debt: Is the company's debt increasing or decreasing? Look at this in conjunction with return on capital. In particular, is the return on capital higher than the cost of debt? Is it sustainable if interest rates rise? Leverage is of particular importance if the company is embarking on a huge capital expenditure, which seeks to improve profitability in the future. However, caution is suggested when using this approach in periods of rising interest rates, making this funding option more costly for the company. On the other hand, if a company has no debt, then taking on some debt may be beneficial, since it offers the company more opportunity to reinvest resources into its operations. However, too much debt may be a bad thing for companies as well, because it inhibits the firm's ability to create a surplus in cash, and debt requires more earnings.

Assets: One thing to look for is how many assets are leased and how many are actually owned. Are they fully depreciated compared with the assets of their competitors? This is especially true in rental or leasing business, e.g. computers, cars, trucks.

Litigation: Are there any pending lawsuits against the company and its directors? Contingent liabilities on lawsuits and cases can threaten the company's overall performance. Damage to a company's reputation may substantially affect a company's profitability, normally resulting in lower sales and an increase in costs.

Pension plan: What shape is the company's pension fund in? Be wary of the accounting method used with regard to company pension plans. Most pension funds are off-balance sheet financing and not included in the balance sheet. So, check out the funding details of a company's pension scheme.

Changes in procedures: Is the company using accounting changes that inflate its earnings? This is particularly true for changes in inventory methods, and depreciation methods of assets.

Certain web sites can further assist you in learning how to read financial statements, such as the following:

IBM Financial Guide: (http://www.ibm.com/investor/index_investorresources.phtml)

Investopedia: (http://www.investopedia.com/university/fundamentalanalysis)

The National Association of Investors Corporation (NAIC): (http://www.better-investing.org)

The following is the actual 2005 balance sheet and the balance sheets for 2004, 2003, 2002, and 2001 of Intel Corporation. Take a close look at the balance sheet and see if you can see anything of importance to you as an investor.

**Annual Balance Sheet Intel Corporation**
*(In Millions of U.S. Dollars)*

| Period Ended | **12.31.05** | **12.25.04** | **12.27.03** | **12.28.02** | **12.29.01** |
|---|---|---|---|---|---|
| **Assets** | | | | | |
| Cash | 7,324.00 | 8,407.00 | 7,971.00 | 7,404.00 | 7,970.00 |
| Marketable Securities | 5,448.00 | 8,765.00 | 8,193.00 | 5,183.00 | 3,580.00 |
| Receivables | 3,914.00 | 2,999.00 | 2,960.00 | 2,574.00 | 2,607.00 |
| Total Inventories | 3,126.00 | 2,621.00 | 2,519.00 | 2,276.00 | 2,253.00 |
| Raw Materials | 409 | 388 | 333 | 223 | 237 |
| Work In Progress | 1,662.00 | 1,418.00 | 1,490.00 | 1,365.00 | 1,316.00 |
| Finished Goods | 1,055.00 | 815 | 696 | 688 | 700 |
| Notes Receivable | n/a | n/a | n/a | n/a | n/a |
| Other Current Assets | 1,382.00 | 1,266.00 | 1,239.00 | 1,488.00 | 1,223.00 |
| **Total Current Assets** | 21,194.00 | 24,058.00 | 22,882.00 | 18,925.00 | 17,633.00 |
| Net Property/Plant/Equipment | 17,111.00 | 15,768.00 | 16,661.00 | 17,847.00 | 18,121.00 |
| Prop Plant & Equipment | 44,132.00 | 39,833.00 | 38,692.00 | 36,912.00 | 34,356.00 |
| Accumulated Depreciation | 27,021.00 | 24,065.00 | 22,031.00 | 19,065.00 | 16,235.00 |
| Interest&Advance to Subsidiaries | 4,672.00 | 3,219.00 | 2,380.00 | 1,234.00 | 1,474.00 |
| Other Non-Current Assets | n/a | n/a | n/a | n/a | n/a |
| Deferred Charges | 60 | 117 | 222 | 398 | 706 |
| Intangibles | 4,502.00 | 4,279.00 | 4,142.00 | 4,766.00 | 4,638.00 |
| Deposits & Other Assets | 775 | 702 | 856 | 1,054.00 | 1,823.00 |
| **Total Assets** | 48,314.00 | 48,143.00 | 47,143.00 | 44,224.00 | 44,395.00 |
| **Liabilities** | | | | | |
| Notes Payable | 295 | 168 | 143 | 295 | 395 |
| Accounts Payable | 2,249.00 | 1,943.00 | 1,660.00 | 1,543.00 | 1,769.00 |
| Curr. Long-Term Debt | 18 | 33 | 81 | 141 | 14 |
| Curr. Port. Cap Lease | n/a | n/a | n/a | n/a | n/a |
| Accrued Expense | 4,080.00 | 4,107.00 | 3,577.00 | 2,984.00 | 2,986.00 |
| Income Taxes | 1,960.00 | 1,163.00 | 785 | 1,157.00 | 988 |
| Other Current Liabilities | 632 | 592 | 633 | 475 | 418 |
| **Total Current Liabilities** | 9,234.00 | 8,006.00 | 6,879.00 | 6,595.00 | 6,570.00 |
| Mortgages | n/a | n/a | n/a | n/a | n/a |
| Deferred Charges/Inc. | 703 | 855 | 1,482.00 | 1,232.00 | 945 |
| Convertible Debt | 3,170.00 | n/a | n/a | n /a | n/a |
| Long-Term Debt | -1,064.00 | 703 | 936 | 929 | 1,050.00 |
| Non-Curr Capital Leases | n/a | n/a | n/a | n/a | n/a |
| Other Long-Term Liabilities | 89 | n/a | n/a | n/a | n/a |
| **Total Liabilities** | 12,132.00 | 9,564.00 | 9,297.00 | 8,756.00 | 8,565.00 |

At a glance, note that assets increased by 8.8% over the five-year period while liabilities increased by 40.5% in the same period. What does that say? It indicates that this company's expenses and liabilities are increasing faster than its assets. Is this a problem?

Upon closer examination of the figures, the following are some relevant balance sheet points:

1. Cash level – despite increasing operating leverage and sales growth, cash level dwindled in 2005. The company increased investments in property, plant and equipment, hoping to sustain future sales growth.

2. Inventory – level grew 39% since 2001, nearly in tandem with sales growth. The biggest jump in inventory was posted in 2005, largely surpassing sales growth. Although constant sales growth may indicate product maturity, increasing inventory levels may indicate continued sales growth, albeit moderately.

3. Convertible debt – the company has secured financing by way of convertible debt. It usually indicates a cheaper alternative to straight debt. This may be in anticipation of rising interest rates. Increased leverage combined with increasing levels of capital expenditure largely indicates management's desire to expand, or perhaps innovate.

4. Receivables – in 2005 registered a remarkable 30% increase from the previous year. Therefore, it is important to find out if there was a change in the company's strategy regarding loans to customers. Was the company allowing its products to be bought on credit? Will this result in an increase in bad debt risk?

The actual income statement of the same company follows on the next page.

***ANNUAL INCOME STATEMENT INTEL***
*(In Millions of U.S. Dollars)*

| Period Ended | **12.31.05** | **12.25.04** | **12.27.03** | **12.28.02** | **12.29.01** |
|---|---|---|---|---|---|
| Net Sales | 38.826.00 | 34.209.00 | 30,141.00 | 26.764.00 | 26.539.00 |
| Cost of Goods Sold | 15.777.00 | 14.463.00 | 13.047.00 | 13.446.00 | 13.487.00 |
| **Gross Profit** | 23,049.00 | 19,746.00 | 17,094.00 | 13,318.00 | 13,052.00 |
| R & D Expenditure | 5,145.00 | 4,778.00 | 4,360.00 | 4,034.00 | 3,796.00 |
| SG & A Expense | 5,814.00 | 4,838.00 | 5,201.00 | 4,481.00 | 4,786.00 |
| Depreciation & Amortization | n/a | n/a | n/a | 421 | 2,214.00 |
| Non-Operating Income | 539 | 337 | -29 | -94 | -17 |
| Interest Expense | 19 | 50 | 62 | 84 | 56 |
| **Income Before Taxes** | 12,610.00 | 10,417.00 | 7,442.00 | 4,204.00 | 2,183.00 |
| Provision For Inc. Taxes | 3,946.00 | 2,901.00 | 1,801.00 | 1,087.00 | 892 |
| Minority Interest | n/a | n/a | n/a | n/a | n/a |
| Investment (Gain/Loss) | n/a | n/a | n/a | n/a | n/a |
| Other Income | n/a | n/a | n/a | n/a | n/a |
| Net Income Before Extra Items | 8,664.00 | 7,516.00 | 5,641.00 | 3,117.00 | 1,291.00 |
| Extra Items & Disc. Ops. | n/a | n/a | n/a | n/a | n/a |
| **Net Income** | 8,664.00 | 7,516.00 | 5,641.00 | 3,117.00 | 1,291.00 |

Note that gross profit increased by 76% from 2001, which indicates consistent growth. However, note that 2001 to 2002 sales figure show only a 0.84% increase. Is this an indication of future sales growth? Could it mean that the same thing could happen again, lowering the company's growth rate? Income before taxes shows an increase of 48% in 5 years. Is this good? Yes, it shows growth. However, is it real? Is it sustainable? The only way to know is to do further research on the company's operations including the historical movement of the company's stock price to see the correlation between the stock price and the financial statements.

The following are some more Income Statement points to consider:

1. Sales – growth has been relatively constant at 13% for the past four years. Again, this may indicate product sales maturity.

2. Profitability

   a. Gross margin – gross margin steadily grew since 2001. Given relatively flat sales growth, the company appears to have embarked on cost reduction programs to improve its profitability. As cost reduction programs are typically limited, the company may need to scrutinize its sales strategy, and or product innovation to improve performance further.

b. Earnings before Interest, Taxes, Depreciation and Amortization (EBITDA) – EBITDA margins have doubled since 2001. While R&D expenditures posted relatively flat growth, direct selling expenses registered erratic growth. There is a slight disconnect between sales growth and selling expenses – while sales inched up 13%, selling expenses increased 20% in 2005, with the same trend being posted in 2003.

c. Net Income – Net income demonstrated a robust growth since 2001, skyrocketing by more than 550% up to 2005. The company has actively reduced leverage, and at the same time aided by income from non-operating activities. Continual efforts on cost reduction also largely fortified net profitability.

3. Trends – The scope of future profitability depends on the company's strategy to boost sales and further reduce costs, particularly in aligning selling expenses with sales growth. While cost reduction may be difficult to sustain, the company may need to focus on improving its sales strategy. While we definitely see that growth is a plus factor, the scalability and sustainability of this trend is of equal importance.

### *How to Analyze an Annual Report*

Companies often use their annual reports as a selling tool to attract new investors. Hence, you should always watch out for fluffs and exaggerations. It should take you about an hour to analyze competently a company's business operation and its financial statements.

The following is a checklist to use in analyzing a company's annual report:

Profitability: How much money did the company make last year? Is this profit sustainable in difficult times? Look back to see how they fared in the last recession. Focus on operating margins, seeing through a combination of improving sales and cost reduction schemes. Improving margins resulting from both trends will result in a better performance picture. It is best to look at EBITDA as well, in order to avoid comparing inconsistencies between companies within an industry concerning the use of creative accounting methods.

Survivability: How does the company stack up with its competition? If the company is a technology company, are they spending enough money for research and development (R&D) in anticipation of future trends in their industry? Consider cash and leverage. These are equally important in determining management's intention to move forward with growth.

Growth: Which way is the company's growth curve going, is it up, down or flat? Sustainability of growth is also a key issue. This strongly demonstrates management's efficiency in the use of its resources. How does this compare with the company's stock valuation historically? Enhancement of growth typically leads to enhanced shareholder value.

Stability: Is the company subject to radical changes and shifts. Defensive companies are more often than not averse to external shocks. Cost reduction programs support defensiveness. A clear stream of recurring revenue is also an important defensive factor.

Dividends: If the company pays them, are they consistent with the company's financial strength? Dividends are often used as a way to enhance shareholders' appreciation of the stock. It is also an indicator of the company's performance and efficient use of cash. On the other hand, be wary of non-recurring huge dividend payouts by closely held companies.

Problems: Does the company have any problems with pending lawsuits, regulatory problems or labor problems? These problems pose risk of damage to the company's reputation, and have huge implications on its future operating performance.

Risks: Is the company subject to any environmental, political, or currency risks?

Management: Is the management team experienced? Does the company need additional executive talent or product development talent? Reputation of management is important. A good management team looks after the enhancement of shareholder value.

## INITIAL PUBLIC OFFERINGS: ARE THEY INVESTMENT GOLD?

WE HAVE ALL heard stories of people who bought an IPO stock and made millions. What we do not hear about are the people who bet their house on an IPO and lost it.

Prior to the introduction of the Sarbanes-Oxley- Public Company Accounting Reform- Act of 2002, which have made the standards for IPOs more onerous, the U.S. markets averaged about two hundred and seventy five IPOs annually. These companies sell their shares to underwriters at an agreed price. The underwriters in turn resell the shares to investors. To create a demand underwriters often under-price issues by approximately 5% to 10%. The best possible time to be involved in an IPO is on its initial distribution phase.

Most IPOs are sold-out long before the public learns of its initial distribution, since IPOs are most often divided up amongst a "syndicate" of large investment banks or institutional investors. The syndicate assumes the risk related to the successful completion of the offering. Frankly, these large institutions can afford to absorb the high risk of IPOs as some crash and burn.

You can acquire some stocks of an IPO on the first round of distribution, when brokers, banks, investors, and companies begin to sell. Most IPOs that fail seldom fail in the initial stage of its offering. It takes time. If you judge an IPO to be high risk but with a considerable potential for capital gain, monitor it closely. Nevertheless, keep in mind that the "syndicates" are formed based upon their willingness to hold the stock for a period of time, as well as their willingness to assume the risk should the IPO fail.

Understanding the basics of IPOs, performing fundamental research, and knowing how to acquire shares at the early stage of an offering can increase your chances of success.

The following guidelines may help you select a winner out of the IPO market:

Read the prospectus: Companies planning an IPO are required to file a preliminary registration statement with the SEC. Preliminary prospectuses are referred to as "red herrings". This is mainly because it contains a statement in red that states that "the company does not intend to sell its shares until the SEC approves their registration". Red Herrings are often updated several times before becoming a final prospectus. The prospectus provides information about the companies anticipated growth, the company's current capitalization, plans for the new money, names of officers and members of the company's board of directors, litigation problems, if any, and a description of the business. Examine the prospectus of an IPO, as you would normally analyze a regular annual report.

Perform fundamental analysis: Again, evaluate the company's operational, financial and shareholder returns performance just like you would any other stock.

Check out management: Examine the backgrounds of the company's officers and senior management. Do they have a long track record in the sector? Any integrity issues, or litigation in the past?

Read the mission statement: Investigate the company's business strategy. Is it realistic? How large is the company's market? How competitive is the company's business model? If the company plans on a market share of less than 15%, the firm may not be a long-term success.

Investigate the planned use of funds: Determine why raising a certain amount of capital is so critical to the company's success. If the money is to be used for expansion, that should be considered a good sign.

Compare IPO prices: Compare the price indication during the filing of the red herring, with the final price in the prospectus. If, the price is higher in the later, then the underwriters are enthusiastic about the offering, and this normally indicates a robust demand for the IPO. Conversely, a lower price in the prospectus indicates a lack of interest in the IPO.

Determine if it fits your investment plan: You may not want to buy an IPO because it does not fit with your plan. Do not let the prospect of high profits lure you away from your investment plan.

Estimate your holding period: Decide how long you plan to keep the shares. If you want to bet on the long-term success of the company, plan for it. If you want to make a quick profit, plan for it as well by monitoring the stock carefully. Once in the market, an IPO is subjected to the volatility of the stock market.

There are sites on the Internet that specialize in IPOs. Investors frequently discover that most of the cutting edge IPO information they find fits their unique investment plan. Checking out and subscribing to an IPO site may be in your best interest. The following is a list of web sites that specialize in IPOs:

EDGAR Online's IPO Express: (http://ipoportal.edgar-online.com/ipo/home.asp). This web site charges $58.95 per quarter for their information service.

Edgar Online Pro: (http://www.edgar-online.com/products/edgarpro.aspx). Access to this web site costs $100 per month.

Hoover's IPO Central: (http://www.hoovers.com/global/ipoc/index.xhtml). You must contact this web site to get their subscription prices.

IPOHome: (http://www.ipohome.com) . This web site is free to use, however there is a charge of $60 for every IPO report you order.

IPO Monitor: (http://www.ipomonitor.com). Offers free information on recent IPOs. However, its subscription-based service provides a greater amount of detailed information that is relevant to the IPO market.

IPO news is equally important and the following web sites provide excellent coverage of IPO news:

CNN/Money: (http://www.money.cnn.com/news/deals). This site offers useful information on mergers and acquisitions as well as IPOs.

Yahoo! IPO news: http://biz.yahoo.com/reports/ipo.htm). Covers most IPOs in the market.

IPO Data Systems: (http://www.ipodata.com). Use of this web site costs $15 per month. It offers an IPO calendar, company profiles, listings of top performers, IPOs by underwriter and other pertinent IPO information.

NASDAQ: (http://www.nasdaq.com/reference/IPO.stm). This web site lists recent IPO filings with ticker symbols, pricing, share information and summaries.

123Jump IPO Center: (http://www.123jump.com). Provides company profiles and performance statistics. Subscription costs $99 per year.

IPO Data Systems: (http://www.ipodata.com). This web site offers free daily headlines and a pipeline link to EDGAR. Subscriptions cost $15 per month.

TechWeb News: High-Tech News: (http://www.techweb.com). Offers a free newsletter and tracks IPO news on the technology industry.

# DIRECT PUBLIC OFFERINGS

IN OCTOBER OF 1995, the SEC relaxed prospectus delivery rules to allow for electronic delivery. This new rule revived the Direct Public Offering (DPO) market that had been floundering for almost twenty years. As the name implies, DPOs are stock offerings by companies made directly to investors. Small companies, who would have trouble with the multi-million minimums of traditional IPOs, use this method to sell their stocks to the public, without the expressed benefit of an underwriter.

DPOs can be beneficial for online discount traders. This is primarily because traditional IPOs are more often than not, beyond an average investors reach, until after the initial bump in the offering is over. With DPOs, an investor can be involved in the initial stage of the offering by purchasing stocks directly from the issuing company.

Nevertheless, there are reasons to be very cautious when investing in a DPO. The investor should check out the offering very carefully. There are two major issues of concern:

Blue sky laws: Issuing companies must be registered with the SEC, and in the states in which they offer securities. However, legislation allows companies to use the Internet to present direct public offerings. As the Internet is non-geographic, it therefore offers worldwide distribution opportunities. At present, this issue is still unresolved. Nonetheless, companies generally register their DPOs in all 50 states.

Fraud and abuse: As the Internet is totally unregulated, and will hopefully stay that way, the SEC is kept busy enforcing registration rules. The incidence of fraud is considerably higher with Internet offerings than all other types of offerings.

Buying a DPO is easy. All you need is the prospectus of the DPO and the subscription agreement from the company. Generally, subscription agreements are the last pages of the prospectus. Once you have returned the agreement with a cheque for the amount you wish to subscribe for, the company normally sends a confirmation letter within five days and the stock certificate within thirty days. Do not forget to make a copy of your signed agreement and cheque before you send it to the company.

Information on DPO is available on the Internet. The following web sites provide comprehensive information on the DPO market:

SCOR Report: (http://www.scor-report.com). This site is really for companies anticipating their own offering. It answers all the pertinent questions regarding their particular offering. It can be a very useful tool for an investor as it could provide information on companies. Furthermore, information from this web site can be used to confirm that you have covered all variables in your company research.

Direct Public Offering: (http://www.gopublictoday.com/financing/financing-types-dpo.php)
Sponsored by registered investment advisors, this web site offers a short but informative tutorial about DPOs.

Mellon Investor Services: (http://www.chasemellon.com). This web site allows you to search for information on DPOs. With their "InvestDirect" search service, you can compare DPOs that are currently available in the market.

# DIRECT PURCHASE PLANS

THERE ARE MORE than 3,500 companies that use the direct method to sell stocks to the public, along with the more traditional method that involves the services of a broker. To allow investors to buy their stocks without using the services of a broker, companies established Direct Purchase Plans (DPPs). Since DPP eliminates the need for brokers, transactions are often free of trading commissions. This benefits both the companies and the investors. For the companies, DPP provides a more stable shareholder base, since investors who use DPPs, generally adapt a long-term investment strategy. On the other hand, shareholders benefit from DPP, because the cost of purchasing stocks is drastically reduced with the absence of brokers' commissions. This is the primary reason why DPP stocks are also known as no-load stock.

In addition to DPP, companies also provide Direct Reinvestment Plan or Dividend Reinvestment Plans (DRIPs) for existing shareholders. These plans allow the shareholders to reinvest their dividend payments to purchase more shares of the company. As in the DPP, DRIPs do not require the services of a broker.

There are several web sites on the Internet that provide in-depth information on DPPs and DRIPs of companies:

American Stock Transfer & Trust Company: (http://www.investpower.com/). This site allows you to search over 3,500 DPP plans by entering a ticker symbol or company name. You can also purchase shares and fractional shares to match the amount you want to invest. Fees to buy DPP through this web site begin at $2.60.

MyStockFund: (http://www.mystockfund.com). Integrates dollar-cost averaging and dividend reinvestment programs. Three plans are available starting with the basic plan at $5.98 per month.

NetstockDirect: (http://www.netstockdirect.com) This site allows investors to purchase common stock without a broker. You can research nearly 1,400 companies, buy fractions of stocks, and enroll online.

# CONCLUSION

THIS BOOK IS a good starting point on your journey to discount etrading success. I strongly recommend that you use the web sites I have enumerated in every section, and any others you can find to help you start discount etrading.

While the Internet makes discount trading possible, you still need to keep to the true honored tradition of investing – do your homework and research. Develop your own investment plan. Do not accept advice from others until you have verified, validated and researched the information as thoroughly as possible.

Knowledge is investment power! Not investing in an opportunity is just as important a decision as making an investment. Once you are visible online as a discount trader, be prepared to be inundated with numerous unsolicited investment offers. Be intentional, and discard or ignore unsolicited investment offers or information. Often mass email campaigns supporting a certain penny stock, with OTC or Pink Sheets, are used to push the price of a particular stock. They often sound like great deals – some even predict the immediate future results (invest today and make 300% in two months, etc.). The sole purpose of this kind of hype is to separate you from your money.

If you have an efficient computer, reliable high speed Internet connection, good common sense, and the right attitude, you can become a successful discount etrader; by working on the essential research, which will enable you to make profitable investment decisions. Luck plays only a small part, if ever, in investing. Luck usually affects only things that neither the company, the markets, nor, you have any influence on.

## ABOUT THE AUTHOR

MEG NOLASCO-BREWER HAS extensive international experience in the financial markets. Over her 20-year career, she has worked for various financial institutions in Asia, in the U.S. and in the U.K.; including Prudential Securities and Merrill Lynch in New York, and Nikko Securities Plc. in London.

She has direct experience in institutional stocks, futures and options, trading, sales and funds marketing. An alumna of the London Business School, she has lectured on fund management, portfolio management, commodity futures and stock trading for various organizations in Asia and in the US.

Recently retired at an early age, Meg now enjoys her main passions in life: stock, futures and options trading for her personal portfolio, travelling, and various types of charity work.

In this book, Meg shares her unique insights and experience in stock, futures and options, trading in a single comprehensive resource. All the trading tips, tricks, techniques, and secrets you need to know to play - and win – in the stock market as a discount etrader.

Printed in the United Kingdom
by Lightning Source UK Ltd.
118922UK00001BA/8

9 781425 981259

December 1996.

To dear Jim

Thanks. for the happy
memories we will all
treasure.

All our love

Marion & Dave
xx

# King Tide

*Peter Doyle is a restaurateur, a fisherman, a bon vivant and a man who lives life.*

*Janise Beaumont is a journalist who has worked in television, newspaper and radio in England and Australia.*

# KING TIDE

## PETER DOYLE

*With Janise Beaumont*

William Heinemann Australia

Published 1996 by William Heinemann Australia
a part of Reed Books Australia
22 Salmon Street, Port Melbourne, Victoria 3207
a division of Reed International Books Australia Pty Limited



Typeset in Century Old Style by Eagle Graphics
Printed and bound in Australia by Griffin Paperbacks

National Library of Australia
cataloguing-in-publication data:

Doyle, Peter, 1932, –.
King Tide — my story.

ISBN 0 85561 691 1.

1. Doyle, Peter, 1932 –. 2. Restaurateurs — New South Wales — Sydney — Biography.
I. Title.

647. 95092

*I dedicate this book to my grandchildren.*

*May you be on the beach the first week in November each year when the first nor'-easter hits and swirls the sand (keep your eyes closed). I hope you are well rugged up in June when the sou'-easter slips its moorings in the Blue Mountains and throws itself with its icy blasts towards the bay, turning the lovely blue waters white. I just hope you are not ten miles out to sea when it hits, in a small boat with a leaky bucket.*

*I am sure if you pray, your prayers will be answered.*

# Contents

# ACKNOWLEDGEMENTS

The stories I have told are to the best of my memory. Many have been handed down through the family from generation to generation. Wherever possible I have asked some of the old-timers for verification. But, like us all, their memories may have faded. For example, when I tried to verify how many baskets of mullet my grandfather had penned up in Dark Corner, Old Bill Sweeney the spotter swears it was five hundred baskets. Dark Corner is on the northern end of Watsons Bay beach. The net was tied to the rocks and anchored out into the bay. It was eventually torn loose during the Maitland gale. Eddie Brooks wasn't sure how many baskets but he said it was a lot of fish and that it took two trucks to carry them away. Five hundred baskets of mullet was not uncommon in those days; Uncle Reggie said the family did well out of it because he got a new pair of shoes.

When I suffered a stroke in 1995, Jean never missed a daily visit to me in hospital. Since my return from hospital, semi-paralysed on one side and unable to eat solid foods, she has washed me every morning and cooked me special meals. She has not had a moment's break. Without her love and devotion I would not be out of hospital. We have been together for forty-five wonderful years. To you, Jean, my love forever.

My eldest son Peter has consequently taken over running the business. He does that very professionally and with a lot of devotion. My three daughters, Robyn, Gayle and Sharon, have rallied around their mother and have been wonderful. Robyn and Gayle both work in the family business and do a marvellous job. Sharon has become a lawyer and I could not be more proud of her. My younger son Shaun is a first-class judge of fish and has taken on the added responsibility of making sure the restaurants buy only the best from the fish markets. He is fastidious when handling fish and has become one of the best filleters (a skill in itself) in the market. My nephew David Doyle, who has taken over as fish buyer during my illness, is also a first-class judge of fish and is almost equal to my brother John in judging seafood — no mean feat, as I believe John is without peer in Australia.

My son-in-law Robert, apart from working in the business, has done an outstanding job in running my farm during our grape harvest. This year has been a record crop for us.

My thanks to my granddaughters Alexandria, Kimberley and Victoria for looking after me during their daily visits and my grandsons Christopher, Matthew and especially Thomas for teaching me how to use a computer.

I am also eternally indebted to Mum and Dad and my brothers John, Michael, Tim and Richard. My old mate Mickey Sergis, a shrewd old-time fish buyer, reminded me the other day that it was John who once bought all the turtles from the market and saved them from becoming soup by releasing them into the harbour. And it was my brother Michael's invaluable financial prudence that has helped keep the business on an even keel over the years. His boys have been a great source of joy too. Tim, despite suffering from bad health himself, has shown wonderful support.

For refreshing my memory, where would I be without Eddie Brooks, Frank Newton and his family, and Jackie Marks? I am also grateful to Billy and Jean Dun, Vince and Tony Marantino, the late John Woodward, Eric and Ruth Love and Russell and Betty Wong. I apologise if I have forgotton anyone.

I am by no means the best hospital patient and could fill a book with thanks for those who looked after me at St Vincent's Hospital — to Sister Jennifer Fahey and Sister Jacinta especially for their help and prayers — and to the Eastern Suburbs Private Hospital and the Royal Prince Alfred. I would like to name them all individually but space does not permit it. However, you and my constant stream of visitors will be in my thoughts forever. Pat Moss deserves special gratitude for looking after me *and* my very good mate Mick Young.

My special thanks to Mickey Sergis and Georgie Gemo, who always arrived with a box of tempting chocolates and promptly ate them. To my good mate Johnny Bollici, who spoke to me in broken English. I have since resolved to learn Italian so that I can confuse him as much as he confuses me. To Ian Tinkler and Phil Ryan, for taking care of my wine. To Nova Linden Smith, a special friend to both myself and Jean. To Brother Dan, who gave me a daily blessing and a horse tip. To Reverend David Luke from St Peter's. To Stan Pine, Billy Robinson, Ray Durham, Dawn Fraser (who wanted me to recover in time for the Olympics), Vince Caribs, Albie George and Jim Saul (who travelled down from up North to see me), to the Godfather from the South Coast, Tory Puglisi, Jan and Geoff Karpin, Bev and Bob Rigby, Lou Moss, Kate, and to my overseas and interstate visitors, Sophie and Michael Kailis and their family from Western Australia, Jiro Shimuzu, Yasu Yamazki, Yuki Tabata and Mike Hambly from Japan, Lady Paula Brown from Monaco and the Angelakis family from Adelaide. To my old film director mate, Jack Lee, who never missed a day. To John Brown, a wonderful former federal minister for tourism, who is also one of the few politicians whose word is his bond.

And last but not least my heartfelt thanks to my ghost writer, Janise Beaumont, whom I must have driven mad. I have certainly learnt one thing while writing this book. I won't do another during the fishing season.

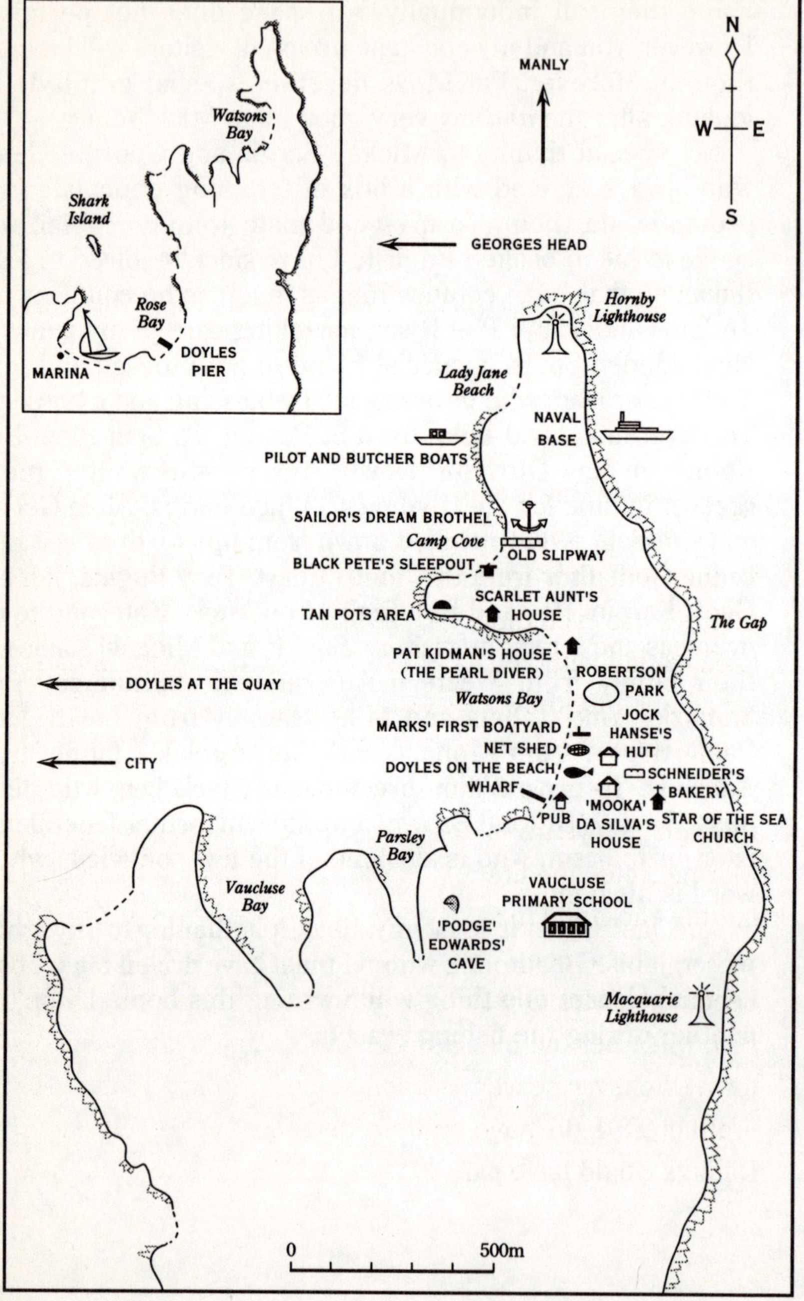
Watsons Bay
Shark Island
Rose Bay
MARINA
DOYLES PIER
MANLY
N
W
E
S
GEORGES HEAD
Hornby Lighthouse
Lady Jane Beach
NAVAL BASE
PILOT AND BUTCHER BOATS
SAILOR'S DREAM BROTHEL
Camp Cove
OLD SLIPWAY
BLACK PETE'S SLEEPOUT
SCARLET AUNT'S HOUSE
TAN POTS AREA
The Gap
PAT KIDMAN'S HOUSE (THE PEARL DIVER)
ROBERTSON PARK
DOYLES AT THE QUAY
Watsons Bay
MARKS' FIRST BOATYARD
JOCK HANSE'S HUT
NET SHED
CITY
DOYLES ON THE BEACH
SCHNEIDER'S BAKERY
WHARF
'MOOKA' DA SILVA'S HOUSE
PUB
STAR OF THE SEA CHURCH
Parsley Bay
Vaucluse Bay
VAUCLUSE PRIMARY SCHOOL
'PODGE' EDWARDS' CAVE
Macquarie Lighthouse
0
500m

# Watsons Bay

Watsons Bay is rich in colourful history, astounding really, that so much has happened in such a tiny pocket of Sydney. I'm now referring to the days, way, way back, long before I was even thought of. I want to share some of the Bay's background with you, because I'm a big fan of the notion that we all need to know where we came from in order to make a decent go of the present.

One of the most interesting, albeit bizarre, legends to last through the years is of Mr and Mrs Billings, who had the Marine Hotel, the first in the Bay. They established a small zoo out the back, and in their crazy menagerie was a zebra, which, so the story goes, was used to pull the Billings's sulky. Seemingly, Mrs B was quite a sight driving around Watsons Bay, while her old man would take the zebra-drawn sulky into town whenever he went. Of course I'm convinced this is all true – although I do have trouble deciding where on earth Mr Billings would have parked the zebra in the city while he went off to do business! Presumably a large crowd would have gathered by the time he got back.

Now for some more reliable information, and I've learnt much of this from the hard-working Woollahra History and Heritage Society.

On Monday, 21 January 1788, Governor Phillip set out from Botany Bay with a small party to search for a better site and entered Port Jackson (Sydney Harbour) – he liked what he saw. It is believed that he landed at Camp Cove before exploring the upper harbour and a few days later established a settlement at Sydney Cove.

In order that ships following the First Fleet did not miss the settlement, a lookout was established and a flagship erected on the clifftop in January 1790, and whitewashed cottages for the lookout party were later built near the beach. An early resident, and possibly signal man, was Robert Watson, after whom the Bay was named. The name Watsons Bay came into general use in 1811. Previously, the area was generally referred to as South Head or Camp Cove.

With the struggling colony desperately trying to feed itself, a fishery was established at South Head in May 1792, under the supervision of one Barton, who was also appointed the Pilot. The first land grant around here was Roddam Farm, established by Edward Laing in 1793. The grant extended from the present Laings Point (Green Point) up to Robertson Park. However, not being farm country, grants were not extensively worked.

Robertson Park is adjacent to our pub, which opened in 1939, on the site of the Palace Hotel, which had been built in the 1880s by the distinguished architect, James Kirkpatrick.

# 3

## Watsons Bay

From earliest times, it was found necessary to pilot vessels entering the harbour, in view of the dangerous nature of the reef known as Sow and Pigs, which divided the two shipping channels. As the volume of shipping increased, pilotage developed into a competitive but income-sharing operation, based at Watsons Bay.

Using whale boats, it was a hazardous business requiring exemplary courage and expert boatmanship. Portuguese seamen from visiting whalers filled this role well, and many settled in the Bay.

In 1811, Governor Macquarie, along with a party of notables of the time, took a boat trip from Sydney Town, picnicking under a particularly fine fig tree on the Watsons Bay beachfront, thus setting a pattern which became highly popular and for which the Bay was eminently suited. The following years saw several hotels established.

A pier was also constructed, inviting excursion boats, which also allowed visitors to enjoy the small zoo and pleasure ground that were set up. The Bay became very popular for weekend trips, until supplanted in popularity by Manly.

Further along on South Head, the Army established fortifications. A surprise visit by American vessels in 1839, fears of Russians in the 1850s, and the French in the 1870s, pointed to the need for a coastal defence system, which was put in place there in 1873, with the guns staying in place into the 1960s. From World War II on, Royal Australian Navy installations developed, becoming HMAS *Watson*, which together with the Sydney Harbour National Park, comprise most of South Head.

Watsons Bay developed through involvement in fishing, pilotage, signalling, defence and recreational pursuits, into a tightly-knit and relatively isolated village. Transportation improvements in the early 1900s, and the spread of urban development, terminated this isolation. Nevertheless, the area retains its uniqueness: natural features, architecture, historical associations and, most of all, community spirit.

# PROLOGUE

I was born a thousand years ago in a small private hospital on the hill overlooking Watsons Bay, on 26 July. There was a slight wind blowing from the west and a chill in the air. It was one of those grey days when you wish you were sitting around the old fuel stove with your hands wrapped around a mug of soup.

The fishermen did not go to sea that day. Instead, they did what they always did in such weather – they gathered in front of the net shed and lit the great tan pots, heated with crackling driftwood that the wind and the sea had brought onto the beach from around the globe. Bits of softwood from the cargo holds of the old rusty tramp steamers and offcuts of hardwood from the small north and south coast trading steamers – all mixed up with coke and seawood. The net shed had a lean to it, and the ancient iron roof was full of holes. The walls, made of stone and weathered timber, had fought off countless gales.

Non-believers might describe the inside as messy and smelly, but for anyone passionate about the sea, this was without doubt a five-star establishment. Close your eyes for an instant and try to imagine the aromas of fish, tan bark, pipe smoke and oil, all tossed in together. It's the most intoxicating mixture on earth.

Piled high inside were the cotton and linen nets, along with coconut fibre ropes slowly turning white as the tan bark lost its rich honey colour. Those old nets held a million stories. In a dark corner was my Uncle Walter's net, which had trapped eight hundred boxes of sea mullet; next to it was the Smith brothers' net, which had been responsible for taking one hundred tuna on Rose Bay flat in a single haul. And there was one net that had become folklore in the Bay – it had captured ninety-nine schnapper after a big sea and a hard easterly blow, and the fishermen nearly lost the boat when it was swamped while rowing back from Quarantine Bay. Do men get any braver or more interesting than this rough bunch I came to love as a child? I think not.

They stood facing away from the fire, with their hands behind their backs, to warm their gnarled and split palms. They'd shift a bit when the heat got too much for their threadbare serge pants, then they'd shuffle a few inches away and look up at the sky, mumbling about the weather. I can see them now in their identical outfits: the trousers, with one leg rolled higher than the other, a collarless flannel shirt and a waistcoat that had seen better days, plus a hat – always a hat. And bare feet, hardened by salt and sand; these characters could walk through hell on hot coals and not even blink, and I wanted more than anything to be like them.

Their faces were carved from a soft stone that had withstood the strongest winds God could lay on. Their eyes watered from too much salt spray; they spoke through cracked lips, with a touch of a smile. These were the last of the hunters. These were the men who would shape my life, the fishermen of the Bay.

# CHAPTER 1

# Fishing with Headache and Aspro, and Other Stories

It was a Saturday morning in 1937 when we shifted to Watsons Bay, into our family's then-vacant restaurant on Marine Parade, wedged in between the hotel and Graham's Boat Shed. Even though I was only five, I noted that the sun was shining – prophetically perhaps, given the happiness and success that has been bestowed on the Doyles in the years since. I was given my pillow to carry, a contribution to the moving effort, and as soon as we got there, I ran out onto the beach, this wonderful beach that was to become my playground, my backyard. It was there I was to play pirates and reenact the Battle of Iwo Jima. I felt I owned that beach.

We have always referred to our business at Watsons Bay as 'the shop', and to prepare for our arrival, my grandfather, a painter by trade, covered over the front shop window with white paint, and that front room became a bedroom. Partitions went up to create other rooms. My grandparents lived upstairs and I moved in with them. My grandmother was one of the world's greatest cooks, always wore a black dress with a white collar; I don't think I ever saw her in anything else. She was a Newton, and therefore a descendant of one of the families that first settled the area.

In an old cottage behind the shop lived Aunty Maggie and Uncle Victor, and further back was the original dwelling. It sounds like the property was enormous, but it was really quite compact. In another part lived Jack Hanse, a family retainer who kept the yard clean, and in the flat alongside were two Greek fishermen, only ever referred to as Axle and Grease. Next door again and still in the compound resided Black Peter, who also helped my grandfather in the yard.

Jack Hanse was assigned to look after my grandfather, which he did very well, beginning first thing in the morning by bringing him a cup of tea. Jack had no teeth, but that didn't stop him making short work of a decent-sized slice of Mum's plum pudding every Christmas Day. Mum would always make sure Jack got a piece with a threepenny bit in it. That was pretty gracious of her, considering that years earlier, Jack Hanse had warned my Dad, 'Be careful of her; she tells her mother everything.'

Jack Hanse aside, nobody much went by their real name. Some of my favourite fishermen were Sooty Jack, the Lion Tamer, Mick the Liar, Protex – a popular brand of soap which he was dubbed because he never washed, Marble Kennedy, who had lost an eye after being hit by a marble from a slingshot as a kid, Bull Fighter – and of course my pals and teachers, Headache and Aspro.

I wish you could have known Headache and Aspro – and better still, come out on one of our hilarious fishing expeditions to Rosa Gully, under the lighthouse. We went in a skiff and took along a demijohn of water, and it was my job beforehand to go up to Nip Schneider the baker, opposite the Catholic church, and get a loaf of bread. The smell of fresh bread was worth the walk up the hill.

I'd say, 'Mr Schneider, can I have a loaf of bread for Headache and Aspro? We're goin' fishin', and he'd say, 'No, you can't; they haven't paid me for the last ten loaves. They only ever pay me with fish.' We'd go through this ritual every time, then I'd say, 'Well, I'll tell 'em.' He'd give me a loaf – usually a burnt one he couldn't sell – and I'd break it open and eat the centre out of it on my way down the hill. I've always thought the best part of bread was the centre.

Headache and Aspro would be waiting for me and when they saw the bread, they'd say, 'Look, he's robbed us again!' I wouldn't say a word. By the way, lunch, if you could call it that, was water and a slice of onion, chopped up with a fishing knife and stuck between two slabs of unbuttered bread. Off we'd go, after flathead. Headache and Aspro measured all catches in pints and quarts of beer, according to what they thought they could buy with the haul.

From that first day at Watsons Bay, I was at one with the sea; it was all I knew. Mum would put hats on us boys and strap us into harnesses and hitch us to an upturned boat. Sometimes, as a joke, the fishermen next door would come down and pretend to move the boat and I'd scream out, 'Mum, Mum, they're trying to kidnap us.'

I marvelled at fishermen coming up out of their boats onto the beach with loads of fish, with the wind blowing in the winter from the west, howling at one hundred miles an hour, and the old building shaking, and sand drifting in, and Mum cooking on the fuel stove.

Each day the fishermen of the Bay gathered in front of Graham's Boat Shed to tell stories; when they weren't at sea they'd be talking about the weather, or discussing goldmines they knew were a million miles away, or mountains they'd been to as boys, or perhaps just dreamt about. Dick Palmer stood out as being very learned, because he helped the paper man, so he got to read the paper. They taught me that there was another world out there. Even though many of them had never been out of Watsons Bay, they fostered in me a sense of adventure. That's what it was all about.

They'd sit back and watch the ships coming into the harbour. There were old tramp steamers from around the world, belching black coal smoke into the atmosphere, and big ocean liners arriving from England and America. The fishermen watched them glide by in the distance and each would try to guess its name.

As they strained their eyes to read the lettering on the side, Uncle Wilkie would say authoritively, 'It's the SS *Ocean Pearl*, out of Hong Kong', or 'That's the *San Chow*, out of Singapore'. He was always right, the bugger, because he helped in the paper shop, too, and had read the shipping news, so he knew about all the arrivals and departures. No one could beat Uncle Wilkie.

I had always wanted to hunt; to fish and hunt. There was this longing inside me, a kind of basic instinct, to not buy food but to let the land provide. And that's how it was at Watsons Bay; the sea provided food and a wonderful style of life. You'd get up in the morning, and if it was inclement, you just didn't go to sea; instead, you'd potter down and talk to your mates. There was no pension, no dole, no handouts, so you had to hope the weather allowed you to go to sea and hopefully make a few bob – although there were no guarantees. And if the fishermen couldn't go out, well, they lived simply and had few needs. The uncertainty of the sea could be a torment, but it was it also part of the lure.

When I got a bit older, we'd go down to the beach and pick up wood and coke for the fuel stove, the coke having been washed up from the coal-fired ships; when they threw the ash out, it would turn to coke. This process of combing the beach became very territorial, with each person having their own section.

Most of the incoming ships had no refrigeration, and by law they had to dump all fruit and vegetables, which were kept on the afterdeck in wire cages. So if you were from overseas, you cleaned out your cages and threw the leftovers into the ocean, where they sank and broke up – except for the onions, which eventually washed up on the beach. The fishermen and locals, myself included, picked up the onions, and although I know they'd deny it now, it was most popular. We'd then plant them in our gardens and they'd sprout after a couple of weeks. We ate onions from all over the world.

So the harbour and the sea provided us with fuel and fish and lobsters (which were easy to catch) and the rocks supplied plenty of mussels in the summer time.

After heavy rain which eroded the sand, we always searched along the beach for money, looking for halfpennies that had fallen out of people's pockets; it was unusual to be lucky enough to find a threepence or a sixpence. But you had to be quick on that, because everyone'd be down there. We'd also look under the wharf. To this day, I check my section of the beach each morning.

From as young as eight, I often sold the coke I collected. Even then I wanted to contribute to the household. Bringing in the fuel for the stove made me feel useful, and by nine or ten, I was helping the man put up posters at the local picture theatre. I carried the paste, and he'd give me sixpence and a free ticket. With the first sixpence I earned, I bought a loaf of bread for the family.

I don't believe I ever squandered money; I was business-oriented from the word go. I get this, in part, from my mother, Alice, who's a very clever businesswoman. Everyone's had a marvellous mother, but mine is exceptional. A million people would say the same thing about theirs, and they'd be dead right, too.

Mother was a stunning blonde when I was a child; beautiful, and athletic, a grade-A tennis player and champion swimmer. From the outset, I saw she had strength, which gave her a certain power; Alice is the foundation of what we've achieved as a family. Dad was the steam engine and Mum drove it. Alice Doyle has always stuck to the same important priorities: love, loyalty, the church on the hill, her country and the Queen.

She seemed gorgeous to me, and my father, Jack, looked nine foot tall. He was very handsome, too, with a moustache. He and Alice met on a blind date, in 1928, upstairs in the old restaurant. The story goes that a chap who was also keen on Alice threatened to commit suicide with a bow and arrow. Thank God for blind dates.

Alice was known for her shapely legs, hence the nickname Shanks. She had a reputation as a Charleston whizz and I believe she was doing a step called The Honey at the moment Dad first laid eyes on her. There was no one else for either of them from then on, and they were married at St Peter's on the hill at Watsons Bay.

With her encouragement, when I was about ten I opened a school account with the Commonwealth Bank in Rose Bay. (I still have those yellowing bank books at home.) I saved £22 and bought myself a boat when I was twelve. The boat was built by Fisher's at La Perouse. They were the best, and thinking back, it may have been second-hand because it came from Manly. My Dad caught the ferry over and rowed it back for me; it nearly killed him, but that's the kind of father he is.

There was not much money around during the Depression, which didn't leave Watsons Bay until after the war. However, we never went to bed hungry; Mum saw to that. Even though there was no money to spare, we didn't feel poor; we just all stuck together. Alice says she knitted us jumpers during those tough years. Maybe she did, but all I remember is that every time she started to knit anything, it ended up as a tea cosy.

Alice's open heart knew no bounds. She raised four boys, along with her nephew, Richard Everitt, whose mother had died in childbirth. Richard repaid us richly by being an invaluable help in the early days of the restaurant. Christmas always overflowed with extended family and friends, and Alice would go out onto the parade at Watsons Bay looking for people who had nowhere to go.

Somehow, there was no shortage of treats when we were small; for instance, each afternoon when we got home from school, my grandmother had hot cocoa and a freshly-baked cake waiting. As I've said, there wasn't a better cook alive. And when Jack Hanse went to the markets and brought back a whole lot of apples, she'd whip up toffee apples, making the sticks by splitting packing cases with a knife, then she'd give them away to local kids. She was quite something.

Watsons Bay was a true village. Our little shopping centre consisted of a post office, Mrs Priestly the chemist, Billy Dawson the barber, Doc Clayton the other barber, plus a fruit shop-cum-milk bar, a grocery shop and a drapery shop. There was the picture theatre, a couple of shops which used to chop and change all the time under the old flats, the paper shop on the wharf and two restaurants – one owned by the Marinato family, which is ours today on the wharf, and another called the Gap Cafe. The Council Chambers were in the park.

There were a few who lived well in our community, such as the Foys, of the prominent retailers, Mark Foys, Professor Stead, father of novelist Christina Stead, the Carrs, the well-known jewellers, and the artist Pixie Harris, but for me, the real Watsons Bay centred on the beach, with the folks who made their living by fishing. Sunday was dress-up day for them, and they'd sit on the wharf swapping stories, led mainly by Dick Palmer. Especially for those who couldn't afford to go to the pictures, this was free entertainment – to get all dolled up and just sit and yarn and watch the movement of people. In those days, the pubs weren't open on Sundays.

The main fishermen were the ones who netted the harbour, and I loved going with them on Saturday mornings when they went for what they called 'the pub shot', when they caught just enough fish to sell up at the pub in exchange for a beer, and raffle what was left. We'd take the big boat and row out. I was eight or nine and I'd be in the back of the boat; I loved lying among the nets. We'd go over to the Low Waterworks at Clifton Gardens, and also to Camp Cove and perhaps Tailor Bay, and have what was known as a blind shot: shooting the net without actually knowing if there were any fish. We'd get bream, whiting and flathead and we'd always have to be back by ten for when the pub opened.

The main net crews working out of Watsons Bay were the Smith brothers, the Newtons, and Connie Voight. Over at

Georges Beach, the Smiths had a lookout man, Bill Sweeney. Different fish throw off different shades as they hug the cliffs going out to sea, and in those days, there'd be lookout men on various points watching for them. Bill was a fisherman who had gone to live at Redfern with his sister, Biddy, who always cooked him a bit of fruitcake to take with him. October was an important month, and Bill would catch the tram across the Harbour Bridge and walk down through the scrub to Georges Beach, where he'd climb a pole the fishermen had erected so he could watch the travelling fish in the bream season. The bream were invisible as they swam around from Clifton Gardens; their shadow would show up on the white sand beneath them.

The lookout men would light a fire to create smoke and then send a signal. The word got around, 'There's smoke at Georges Head', which meant Billy had seen fish. So next day the fishermen went to Georges Head. The idea was to see who could get there first, entitling you to the beach for twenty-four hours, although if you left before the twenty-four hours were up, you automatically forfeited your rights. All of this had long been recognised between fishermen, and has since become written law.

The race would be on to beat the others across the harbour and there was many an act of sabotage. Once you got there, if you didn't think the school was big enough, you could let the second boat in (some blokes might shoot the net within half an hour and be gone). They'd all go ashore and boil the billy and tell terrible lies, mostly about catches of the past. I was in heaven being with them; they were the men I wanted to grow up to be. They were my heroes. And after the talking was done, I'd wander up through the bush to the lookout, from where it felt I could survey the whole world. I can honestly say as I stood on that pinnacle that I had no fear of the sea whatsoever.

By the age of ten, I had built my first tin boat. My mate Jimmy Chapman and me sneaked into the nearby Army Barracks and nicked sheets off the corrugated iron roof of the observation post to make the boat. Every kid had a canoe and I wasn't going to be the only one out. As we were dragging our loot down the hill, a local copper caught us and gave us a kick in the bum, that being the standard sentence for smart-arsed boys. Luckily we were allowed to keep the tin, because Jimmy threw in some story about his mother's roof leaking. Next we scraped some tar off the road for sealant and took nails out of a fruit box; we had all we needed. It was a fine boat, and to our great relief, it didn't leak.

Next door to the net shed was Marks's Boat Shed, where they built magnificent boats that fished the ocean. Mrs Marks helped old Mr Marks, and she was a good worker, too. It was a great celebration when one of their seagoing vessels was to be launched. Measuring anything between eighteen and twenty-five feet, they were always launched on a Saturday, and the locals gathered and there would be a mile of willing workers because they knew there'd be a keg on. It was a great occasion, with a picnic atmosphere, however if there had been no keg, I doubt anyone would have turned up.

Everything was improvised, even the brass bulks. Mr and Mrs Marks would make a washer, or a nut for the end of it, using a penny. Many a boat was launched with pennies and halfpennies.

The harbour produced a marvellous amount of fish; the men brought in tuna and big schools of mullet, salmon, bream and garfish. They'd catch the blue fin tuna on the Rose Bay flat; as the tuna came in from the ocean, they'd shoot them into the nets – sixty to eighty at a time. Tuna is such a wild fish, and as the nets were made of only cotton or linen, you'd have to bring them in very slowly and let them die in the shallow water, otherwise the tuna punched holes in the net.

It was the same with the kingfish, which is also a very strong species. Unlike others, which would follow the rock coast along, the kingfish swam straight across the headland. To entice them to the beach, you'd throw a bit of wood or a rock into the water, and by this time, the net boat, which was about one hundred yards away, would shoot them in. You'd have to be careful though, because they were big, tough fish, weighing around twenty to thirty pounds, and if seagulls swooped down and scared them, they'd punch holes in the net. If you shot twenty kingfish in, you'd have twenty holes.

You could tell from the smell in the air when mullet were running. They would start over Easter, and we would smell them because they travel close to the surface, jumping and flicking all the time as they move out to sea to spawn. They create a lovely fishy sea smell. When the fishermen brought them into Watsons Bay they'd store them under the wharf, with wet bags over them for shade, as there was no ice. They'd wait for the buyers from the markets to come and take them away in trucks. None of the fishermen took their own catches in, as no one had a car.

A hard worker was Sugar Bag Cossey, who fished for flathead for us when we eventually re-opened the shop. He'd have the catch hanging over the side of his boat in sugar bags. A wet sugar bag weighs about two pounds, and as soon as he'd hit the beach he'd run up to the shop and along the side passage yelling, 'Get the scales! Get the scales!' As soon as I'd see him coming, I'd say to my brother John, 'Here comes Cossey', and John would wind the scales back three pounds.

We were only kids and we'd watch Sugar Bag Cossey put the fish on, then we'd say, 'What about the wet sugar bag, Mr Cossey?' He'd frown. 'Your father never takes anything off for the sugar bag.' We'd catch him for a pound every time, but he'd be catching us for two. His other nickname was the Lizard King, because flathead was also called lizard. Despite our battle of wits with Cossey, we regarded him as good and decent. He lived across the park with his family and we'd often see him looking after Benji Abrahams. Benji had lost his legs in World War I and Cossey would push him around the Bay in a wheelchair.

The theatrics of life by the sea meant as much to me as the joy of fishing, and Sugar Bag Cossey and our slapstick routine with him was but one treasure in this colourful circus. Another beauty was the double act of my Uncle Walter, the dandy of the family, and Black Peter, as we called him. Black Peter, was an American negro who had jumped ship off the Great White Fleet that visited Australia and the Pacific in 1908, to show off the might of the American Navy. He was a fifteen-year-old mess boy, and when his ship sailed, he stayed and ended up at Watsons Bay where he worked with my uncles in the fishing industry. (He and Uncle Walter had a particularly entertaining friendship which saw them often having arguments.)

Peter's best mate was Mooka da Silva, who was part-Portuguese and lived and worked at Graham's Boat Shed. He taught me to splice ropes. Peter lived up the back in our old shed and stayed for close to fifty years, until the day he found religion and rowed over to Manly to save the heathens there. Unfortunately he didn't give up the grog at the same time, so his career as a missionary was short-lived and he ended up living out of an old wooden piano box.

What must they have made of him at Manly, this six-foot black Adonis who hadn't worn shoes for half a century?

The visit from the Great White Fleet is worth mentioning for another reason. Even though it was only in Sydney for three weeks, the prospect was seen as such an event – similiar to the advent of the Olympics – that the old restaurant on the beach, then merely a little timber shop, was pulled down, and the building that survives today was built. You might say that the Yanks started us on the road to a fortune.

# CHAPTER 2

# GROWING UP IN HEAVEN

As a child growing up in Watsons Bay, I didn't know a single truly awful person. Even the ratbags and the eccentrics had a charm or a humanity that made them enormous fun to be with. Uncle Walter might be dismissed as peculiar, but that would be selling him short, and totally missing the point. He'd get all done up in his tuxedo and row over, and tie up at the Waterman's Wharf (now called The Man o' War Steps), right where the Opera House is today, then he'd go off to grand balls at the Sydney Town Hall.

And when he and Black Peter went out fishing, invariably a yarn came out of it that would do the rounds for ages. For example, one Saturday morning they wanted money for beer, so they arrived at about half past ten and were selling their catch on the beach, when Uncle Walter called me over and said sharply, 'Go up and ask Aunty Eva [my grandmother] to make us some sandwiches.'

She hastily put together corned beef and pickle sandwiches – she was a great picklemaker, my grandmother. I took them down to the beach, wrapped in a tea towel. By this time, they had sold enough fish to buy a quart of beer, which they were drinking straight from the bottle, swig for swig. I put the sandwiches down, and Black Peter opened the tea towel, picked one up and gave it to Uncle Walter, who knocked it out of his hand, screaming, 'You black bastard! How dare you touch my food!'. Yet it was fine to be drinking out of the same bottle. The stupid thing was that they really thought the world of each other.

To the best of my knowledge there was only one member of our vast clan who was persona non grata, and that was Aunty Em, who lived up the end of the beach in a little old house, before I was born. The family didn't talk to her; I think it was because she drank and had boyfriends. I could have tried to find out more, but there was an unspoken rule about raising such a dangerous topic. Instead, I preferred to have her exist in my imagination as a woman of mystery. Aunty Em, the Scarlet Lady of Watsons Bay.

I loved Sunday lunch, when we all got together. In preparation for that, Mum sent me to Bowden's Butcher Shop every Saturday morning, and I was instructed to say, 'Mr Bowden, give me a leg of lamb; no more than four shillings.' For us kids, the big treat to go with the lunch was a bottle of Zips or Marchant's lemonade, which costs fivepence, plus a penny deposit. Those were the days of collecting bottles to earn pocket money. We got twopence a dozen on beer bottles, and if we were really lucky, we found a quart one, for which they gave us threepence.

There was no such thing as being allowed to get lunch at the school tuck shop. Mum would give us a jam or Vegemite sandwich and a piece of homemade cake, and after school I'd find scones or cupcakes or toffee apples waiting. I couldn't wait to get out of school each afternoon, toffee apples or no toffee apples. I was a terrible scholar at Vaucluse Public; school didn't impress me very much at all. I was always dreaming about being on the harbour.

I was a real dunce; the only thing I excelled at, and I don't know why, was history. My favourite teacher was Mr Nancarrow, who lived behind us. He, at least, treated me well. Later, like my Dad, he joined the Army when the war came.

I really feared the headmaster, old Pop Martin; every time he looked at me, I'd tremble. I'm sure I was singled out, just so he could give me the cuts. There was plenty of caning in those days. Pop Martin was a fat man, only five foot six. His demeanour and threatening manner reminded me of a German officer. In fairness, I should point out that my family wasn't unanimous in denouncing the principal; he was in the Masons with my grandfather, Charlie Everitt, who was the Grand Master of the Vaucluse chapter.

I must say that the journey to and from school was much more enjoyable than actually being there. In the mornings, I'd go along the parade and up through the little glen behind Gibsons Beach. There was a big lagoon into which boats were launched. At the top of the lagoon, two fishermen, the Edwards brothers, lived in the caves; they had cooking pots and everything. I'd stop to have a chat with them and then continue on up the hill, past the quarry on the left and the bootmaker's shop, and just as I turned into school, there was Smith's wood, coal and iceyard. Mr Smith delivered all around the district, and the ice, for iceboxes, was from Rose Bay, a couple of kilometres away.

As I'd pass the pub on my way home each day, I'd see the men drinking lager and the ladies in their finery having afternoon tea in the pretty garden. Mr Thompson was the publican and I remember him quite distinctly, because he had three daughters and one of them was my age and I used to talk to her over the fence.

Dad never went into the pub; he wasn't a drinker, although my Uncle Walter was a great supporter. One particularly significant event sticks in my mind, and it features an appearance by Mr Thompson. When Dad joined the Army in World War II, we were all so proud of him. He was home for his last leave before being sent somewhere, and we were walking him to the tram. He had his kit bag and rifle, and it must have been a winter's day, because we all had heavy coats on. As we walked past the pub, brother Johnny and I were fighting over who was going to carry the rifle; brother Mick was with us and Timmy must have been a baby in Mum's arms. As we got level with the hotel, Bill Thompson was standing out the front. He was a typical publican: not very tall and rather fat, and he wore a magnificent watch across his chest, like in the John Bull ads. He got hold of this big watch and chain and said to my father, 'You're off, Jack?' and Dad nodded, 'Yes, I've been posted.' He said, 'Well, we'll all be here when you get back, and I'll keep an eye on the family for you.'

Dad smiled and thanked him, then when we got on a bit further he stopped, with me and Johnny still fighting over the rifle. He finally spoke, 'I want to tell you boys something. One day we'll buy this pub, but the only way we'll do that is if you never go in it. That way we'll save enough money.' These were words of wisdom which stuck in my mind. It took fifty years before we bought it outright and I reminded Dad of his words spoken all those years earlier, and he laughed, 'But you *did* go in there and that's why it took us so long to buy it.'

The pub of my childhood was an engaging mixture of gentility (as with the ladies and their afternoon teas in the garden) and serving as a meeting place for the rough-and-ready locals, such as Bow Wong. Bow Wong was a Chinese who blew into town, a real drifter. Word was to reach my ears some time after the event that he had been barred from the Watsons Bay Hotel, although none of the grown-ups would tell me why. Eventually the horrible truth was revealed. Bow Wong had caught a pelican, plucked it and raffled the bird off as a turkey, down at the pub. The chap who won excitedly took his prize home for his wife to cook, but they couldn't get their teeth through it.

That was almost the last anyone saw of Bow Wong. When word reached him he had been sprung on the pelican scam, he rowed off to Manly for a drink (why else?) and his boat capsized off the point known as The Old Man's Hat, off North Head. They found his boat and his body a couple of days later.

Around this time, a great many people were evacuated from Darwin, and as Watsons Bay had largely emptied out due to men going to war, a lot of Darwin evacuees were moved down to Watsons Bay. How could I know that this exodus from up north would change my life?

I must come clean and admit I was a rather agressive child; as the oldest, you tend to be. I always thought I was a pretty good fighter; my Dad used to say, 'If someone's beltin' you and you're not winnin', take a paling off the fence and belt 'em back.' I'll never forget Johnny coming home one day, all bashed and bleeding, and Dad saying, 'Why didn't you grab a paling off the fence like I told you?' Johnny told him, 'I tried to, but it wouldn't come off!'

That's what I was like, and if any girls walked along 'my' beach, I'd terrorise them. So this particular morning, I was most intrigued because coming towards me along the parade was a black girl, with a younger girl about my age. I noticed that the younger one had plaits, although I was more fascinated with her companion, as she was the first Aborigine I had ever seen. As they got closer I let go with a rotten orange that had been washed up on the sand.

Next morning I lay in wait, but they didn't show up; it turned out they had taken the top road. In the meantime, I discovered they were part of the new Army people from Darwin who had moved into the big house on the point at Camp Cove, just around from us; the older girl was in fact their maid. The girl with the plaits was called Jean and it wasn't long before I became pals with her brothers, Harry and George. I often visited their house, where I always took the opportunity to pull their sister's plaits. At this stage, she didn't think very much of me at all.

We swam together at Camp Cove and fished off the rocks, and I treated her like one of the boys. Her Mum and Dad were very strict. When it was time for her and her brothers to go home, their mother would hang a towel out the window, and as soon as they saw the signal, they were off at one hundred miles an hour.

When I turned twelve, I went to Bondi Tech, which meant travelling for part of the journey with Jean, who by then was attending a girls' high school at the bottom of William Street, in the city. We'd both catch the tram as far as the cemetery and then I'd get off and catch a bus the rest of the way. One morning I told her that I had decided I was going to marry her.

She looked at me, quite horrified. 'Never! I'm not going to marry you. You're terrible.'

# CHAPTER 3
## THE WAR

The war arrived before my adolescence. I'll never forget the moment we first heard about it. Uncle Harry had bought Mum a wireless, which he put up on the wall in the kitchen. He made this shelf for it above the old pine table Dad used to scrub every Saturday, until it was white. Uncle Harry was a terrible carpenter; he'd use an axe if he could to shape anything, and a house brick to knock a nail in. He was a rough old feller, but also the loveliest person, who had spent his seventeenth birthday at Gallipoli. He had no children of his own and he did so much for Mum and us boys.

So, Uncle Harry brought a wireless over and we all gathered around. Marvellous. We listened in awe, and after a few minutes, a voice announced that Singapore had fallen. That was 1942. Everyone in the family was very solemn, although I must confess I couldn't fully comprehend what it was all about.

Shortly after, Dad applied to join the Air Force, but they knocked him back because he's deaf in one ear, so they put him in the Army, and we were most proud of him. When he came home with his uniform on, the war was won as far as we were concerned. 'If Dad's goin' to war, it'll be over in a week,' we reckoned. 'They had better watch out.' Dad was a helluva tough bugger and we thought those Japs were in for a bloody big shock.

On the night of 31 May 1942 the Japanese raided Sydney Harbour. Dad was on the guns at Cape Banks and he'd come home on short leave. We were sitting around having dinner when the sirens went off. Dad got a sofa out of the lounge room and put it in the side hall, turned it over and made me and my brothers get under it and sit there with pegs in our mouths, in case there was an explosion and we got concussed and swallowed our tongues. Plus we had earmuffs on, made out of powder puffs. We must have been quite a sight, but we weren't the only ones; this was the official kit – albeit makeshift. It's a wonder we didn't win the war by making the Japs laugh themselves to death.

There was a blackout and Dad peered through the window of the pub next door and saw they had a light on, so he yelled out for them to turn it off, quick smart. My aunties and uncles were upstairs, groping around, and as Dad had to go back to the Army post, I was left in charge. I was just ten, and I felt rather important.

Suddenly Mum yelled, 'Where's Nanna?' I nicked upstairs and there she was, sitting on the edge of the bed, wearing a new black dress. We had been instructed to pack an essentials-only bag, in case we needed to be evacuated. Nanna was sitting there in her new frock, clutching a Globite suitcase, all packed. As I came up to her she said, 'Have they come to get us?' I wasn't sure who she meant. 'I'm ready; everything's packed,' she told me, sounding prepared for the worst the Japs could hit us with. I insisted, 'Mum wants you downstairs; you have to hide under the table.'

Eventually she agreed and headed down, while I lingered upstairs gazing out the window, which, like all the others, had been secured with sticky tape, as the big guns going off made the windows rattle and the glass break. I stood there, not yet a man, but suddenly no longer a boy, watching the fireworks. It was a fantastic light-and-sound show; there were searchlights and tracer bullets hurtling through the sky, as well as explosions. Finally I was dragged downstairs, but I went kicking and fighting, because after all, I was in charge.

It wasn't much of a night for sleeping. The next morning we got up early, and me and my brothers ran out onto the beach to see how many ships had been sunk, only to find that the water was full of dead and stunned fish. Big jewfish, schnapper, red morwong, whiting and bream were all floating, or washed up, or turning over, stunned. It was one of the strangest sights I've ever laid eyes on.

I wish we'd had the fish shop open then – we'd have made a fortune, although some people were saying, 'Don't eat them; they're poisonous.' It was a bonanza. I collected a few myself and took them up to Nan, and then I got ready for school. When I got there, I was very disappointed, because I'd had high hopes of the joint being torpedoed so that we could go home. As it was, Vaucluse Public was untouched and I thought that there's no way those bloody Japs could win the war if they couldn't even destroy the biggest building in the district. What bloody hope did they have of winning the war?

Shortly after that, we were packed off to the country. Mum decided we should play it safe and move out for a while, so we went to live at a tiny dot on the map in rural New South Wales:

Crookwell, outside Goulburn. As happened to so many other Sydney families, we didn't even know the people we were to stay with, a Mr and Mrs Wong. The Wongs were a fine family; their eldest son was away at the war and Mr Wong and his daughters were working a big sheep station. We loved it there so much that from then on, we went to stay with them every year when the shearing or crutching was on. It became a ritual. Today my brother Michael owns that property and it is still a great treat to visit. Mum and us boys travelled for what seemed like all day on the train (Nanna and Pop stayed behind at Watsons Bay), then we got a branch line train to Crookwell. It was winter and freezing. From Crookwell Station, we drove without lights through the night to the property; it was very dark.

I woke up next morning and looked out onto the fields which were all white. It was frost and we boys had never seen it before, so in our excitement, we ran out in bare feet (we hardly ever wore shoes at home), and within ten minutes, they were icy and hurting like anything. We raced inside and put our feet practically in the fire to warm them, and next day Mrs Wong took us to a shop to get boots. I scored a pair of ladies' lace-ups – my first boots.

We soon settled into the life there and attending school in the hamlet of Hadley. There were twenty of us in the composite classroom, and I would walk through the paddocks to get there, chasing rabbits along the way. I became quite good as a rabbiter and I'd often go out with the professionals. The whole thing was a remarkable experience, all fourteen months of it, although it was just another adventure as far as I was concerned. Mr Wong even let me have my own garden, and I loved helping bring in the cows at night. I also became a wonderful horse rider and liked nothing more than to help with mustering and herding cattle. I wasn't ever thrown off a horse until I was forty. I was some wild bugger on a horse.

My favourite oddball was Vance Hogan, whom I presumed to be religious because his favourite word was 'Bejesus'. He drove a bullock team and had names for all the beasts, giving them orders in a most colourful way, 'Come on Red, you bastard.' He had a whip that was over six foot long, and he spoke very slowly. His chores were helping to keep rabbits down and acting as a general hand about the place. He rode a horse called Swagman. Vance lived in an old shed, and would bring a whole tree up to the door and put one end on the fire inside and just keep moving it further in as it burned. I'd watch the tree slowly getting shorter and shorter as I chewed the fat with Vance.

Dad came to see us just once in Crookwell during the war, when he was home on leave. We got word that he was on his way, and us kids walked down to the main gate to wait for him to arrive on the mail cart, which came out twice a week, bringing mail and supplies. I can see me and my brothers sitting there, waiting, as though it was yesterday, and every time I drive along that dusty road I think of it. And there came Dad who'd travelled all night in his uniform. We then walked back to the house with him, showing him everything of interest in the bush. What a day that was.

When we returned to live in Watsons Bay in 1945, I pestered old Pop Jackson at the paper shop on the wharf for a job selling papers. First off, I did a morning run around the Bay. I got myself a leather strap and a money bag and away I went. Then, a short time later, I scored the big one: the Barracks run, which meant papers of a morning and again of an afternoon.

South Head was a bustling place: there was Army, Navy, the Australian Women's Armed Services (AWAS), the Yanks; everyone was there. Plus they had a tent city. The big guns on the coast were manned constantly and there were also anti-aircraft batteries.

I'd start each morning by getting up early and helping Pop Jackson roll the *Herald*s in the tram shed, which is where they were dropped off, and then we'd do the run in a Buick open tourer; after that I'd head for the Barracks.

The morning sales weren't that brisk, but the afternoon sales were very busy. The first place I'd go was the married quarters at the gate, and then onto the officers' mess, then down to the AWAS. I did an extra bit of business on the side, taking notes to the women who were isolated from the men's camp. I was very mercenary – I'd charge a penny a letter. Next was the sergeants' mess, where I'd buy Coca-Cola and chewing gum, which were impossible to get in the outside world. I'd go to the main mess and have dinner, and then go back to the sergeants' mess for a second feed. It was easy to get away with because I could eat while they all had a free read of the papers.

I would finish up at the Navy and get home about half past six, pushing my pram all the way. (My grandfather had pulled an old cane pram out of its frame and replaced it with a box, so I could sell papers.) It was one of the biggest runs in Sydney and I was earning about one pound a week. If I got back into the Bay before the pub closed at six, I'd make extra sales there, but I was stretching it to make that. Some of that quid I made each week was tips – although there weren't too many of 'em would sling a penny. With the soldiers, they'd order their papers from me and I'd leave them in their letterboxes at the sleeping quarters. And you know what? No one ever robbed me – not even those who were transferred suddenly; they'd always leave the money for me.

I suppose I was a bit of an entrepreneur; for instance, the Coca-Cola and chewing gum I received at the Barracks I'd swap or sell at school, or use it to bribe the teacher. And then there was the matter of my lucrative undercover work for a certain brothel.

I delivered to a lady who lived on the beach at Camp Cove, and she always seemed to have a lot of different men and women coming in and going out – men and women I had never seen before. This lady said to me that if I gave out her card ('Only to officers, no blacks'), she would pay me in American cigarettes. That was the deal and it was a very good one, because the whole world was on the barter system, and if I gave a packet to the milkman, he'd exchange it for a jar of cream, which he was only supposed to give to invalids who had special permits. He'd slip me a jar and when he got back after his run, he'd tell them he had dropped and smashed one.

I did very nicely during World War II. The lady at Camp Cove was true to her word and I regularly collected my American cigarettes as arranged, from the glovebox of her car, parked outside her pleasure palace, which traded under the name of The Sailor's Dream. It was easy to offload her business cards, because when I delivered papers up at the Barracks, the first thing the Yanks'd say to me was, 'You haven't got a sister at home, have you?' Can't imagine why they picked on me, because I wasn't exactly an oil painting! If they were officers, I'd tell them, 'No, but here's a card from a nice lady who lives down on the beach.'

Mum would have been shocked as hell if she knew what I was up to, but as far as I know, she never found out, and I kept the paper run going until the end of the war.

# CHAPTER 4
## GROWN UP AT THIRTEEN

My secondary school education was stunningly brief, and perhaps that's partly why I later became an overachiever; I wanted to prove that a man without much of an education could still take on the world and win. I was training to be a carpenter at Bondi Tech, and it became clear I wasn't going to pass any exams, so I left when I was thirteen. The carpentry training has come in handy, and I enjoyed the work; I was very good with my hands and could build anything.

Academically, I wasn't too smart, but finance-wise, I was very cluey. I would go out in the boat I bought, rowing around the harbour fishing, sometimes on my own and often with my three younger brothers, Michael, John and Tim. We'd use a hessian bag as a sail. It was nothing for me to row up to the Harbour Bridge on my own. I was a very good rower, even though I was small for my age. From fourteen, I grew rather quickly.

By this time, Mum and Dad had re-opened the Ozone Cafe on the beach. They decided to base it on the original restaurant, which sold seafood, bacon and eggs, and steak and chips. The meals were cooked in our kitchen, with Nanna baking scones upstairs and sending them down in a dumb waiter.

It was at the end of the war, and there was no cutlery or crockery, and we were still on rationing. All restaurants were price-controlled so you couldn't charge any more than 2/6d for a meal. There were only sixteen chairs and we'd bought some second-hand bone-handled knives and forks at an auction, along with an odd assortment of plates – some floral and some plain, and a pile of chipped cups and saucers.

John was a scream. Because we had so few knives and forks, when things got busy, he'd walked through the restaurant, and if patrons who had nearly finished their meals put their cutlery down to talk to their companions, he'd swoop – knocking off their knives and forks. He was so good at it that they often didn't realise what had happened.

The first customer came in and ordered a steak, and Dad cooked it and then watched, through a peephole we had put in, to see how the customer was faring with it. (You should know that Dad had spent half an hour sharpening the knives; these knives were so sharp you could have shaved with them!) Anyhow, Dad watched this bloke trying to cut his steak and it was like watching someone saw through concrete. Dad stared in total horror as the customer chased his meat off the plate and around the restaurant. He would have done better chopping it with Uncle Harry's axe.

That was the turning point. Dad said to my grandmother, 'That's it. I'm never going to sell another bit of meat as long as I live.' And my grandmother cried, 'You'll go broke. We always had a mixed meal in the old place.' Then Uncle Harry was sent for to try to talk Dad out of his reckless decision. The next day,

Mr Marks came in with some schnapper and flathead, and I got a ten shilling note from Mum to buy a schnapper. Ten bob was a lot of money, but it was a big fish. I took it home and from then on John, Dad and I did all the cleaning of the fish in the back yard.

Jack Doyle, my Dad, should be held up as a role model to all. He is the hardest-working man I've ever seen. He would work in the kitchen of a day, cooking the lunches and evening meals; he'd clean the restaurant and the fish, then catch the last tram, at 11.30 pm, to go off to his other job as a printer at John Fairfax & Sons. After working the night shift, he'd come home, have a bit of a sleep and get into it again.

We weren't exactly making a killing with the restaurant, because apart from price controlling, there were very few people around. In fact Nanna always sat upstairs, looking along the parade for any sign of life. Then she'd yell at us down the dumb waiter, 'There's two walking along now.' We nearly went out and lassooed them! And to make matters worse, the pub closed at six and there was never anyone around after that. Customers never brought wine with them; it was only ever beer, and even that was done furtively. If you turned up with wine in the 1950s, you'd become known as a plonko.

As to the menu, we had one thing going for us: there was plenty of fish, because the fisheries had had a good rest for five years, due to the war. The main fish we served were from Watsons Bay: traglin and flathead, and sometimes we'd have jewfish and a bit of schnapper. Each fish was cooked the same way: deep-fried on a gas ring in a shallow pan. And, unlike today, we made all our chips on the premises.

When no fish came in locally, we'd get the tram down to the bottom of William Street and walk along to Woolloomooloo where we bought fish from the Italian boats, which were large and could therefore work the bigger seas. We put the fish in bags and slung them over our backs and walked up to catch the tram home.

Nanna's scones were a weekend-only specialty, introduced because no fresh bread was allowed to be baked between Friday and Monday. There would be inspectors raiding bakeries; it was bloody ridiculous. Men actually went to jail for baking bread on weekends. Just as outrageous was the shutting of pubs at six o'clock of an evening.

Despite helping out in the family business, I was in no way committed to the restaurant game; in fact, I'm sure the family saw me as a no-hoper at this stage. I tried a bit of everything, including cleaning boats, fishing, a stint as a telegram boy, then as a shop assistant at Malley's hardware store, at the back of Broadway. I also worked in their foundry for a while, where they made taps.

Dad's outlook was entirely different to mine. If we told him we'd be at the shop to start work at 6 am, he'd be there at 5 am and would have had the job done already. He could not pause for a second, whereas all I wanted to do was muck about with my mates at the beach, swimming and romancing. I wasn't the least bit focused, but I was never short of money and I never asked my parents for money.

I was offered a place as a trainee bricklayer with Alex Spears & Sons. It was the building game that I loved, and I didn't mind getting up at 5 am, due to all those years doing the morning paper run. The first project I was involved with was building Housing Commission cottages all through Rydalmere, then putting up a building down the bottom of Wylde Street, Kings

Cross, and later we added three storeys to Rupert Murdoch's News Ltd's headquarters in Surry Hills.

I stayed with Alex Spears for three years, and in the periods when there were no building jobs, I'd go fishing. I'd even fish when I got home from work at night. That's really what I wanted to be – a fisherman. The bricklaying came in handy at the restaurant though, as I was able to make the iceboxes for the fish, as well as several brick sheds and the cleaning room.

When I turned twenty, a position came up as an inspector of fisheries. I applied and, to my surprise, got the job, although my spelling and writing were atrocious and I didn't even have the Intermediate Certificate. I was appointed as a junior, to work in the Sydney Fish Markets, Sydney Harbour and surrounds. The markets were administered by the Chief Secretary's Department, which was also responsible for Aboriginal Affairs, weights and measures, greyhound racing and a few other odds and ends.

This was my first taste of bureaucratic life, to which I was not suited at all. In fact I thought it was pure bullshit, the writing of reports and so on. I just wanted to be out of there! Instead, I had to fill in thirty forms before I blew my nose, and after I blew my nose, there were ten more forms. And I had to make sure they were filled out in duplicate.

# CHAPTER 5

## SEASONS BY THE SEA

I was still living at home, enjoying the summers by the sea and somewhat dreading the winters, which were always bleak at Watsons Bay, where the westerlies come rolling down, reaching across the harbour, blowing white water everywhere, and sending a shiver through your bones.

I had this big old bed with a wonderful, ancient feather mattress, and on those cold nights I'd sink down into it and listen to the wind shrieking up the side of the house, and to the heavy rain pelting onto the tin roof. In the dead of winter, I never seemed to have enough blankets, so I would put a worse-for-wear Army overcoat on top of me and snuggle in. When it was really icy, I'd scrounge every coat I could find.

Sleeping in of a morning was something I never did; my battered alarm clock still went off before dawn, just as it had in the paper run days, and if I overslept by a few minutes, Dad would rouse me. He never needed an alarm clock – he'd just set his mind, wake up and away he'd go.

Down in the kitchen, there was always a billy of cocoa

waiting to be heated up, which Mum prepared before she went to bed. The billy would be there on top of the fuel stove, which was the heart of our home. The person (probably a woman) was right who said, 'Important things happen in kitchens.' It's where problems tend to get solved, bellies get filled and families talk over the day's doings. In our case, this was where we all gravitated. The Doyles would have frozen to death without that stove, as it was the only heating we had. Its comforting warmth wafted into most nooks and crannies.

The big challenge was to keep up adequate supplies of fuel, and one day I thought I was doing Mum a good turn by paying a visit to the nearby nut factory in Watsons Bay, where Australian bush nuts were processed. By fair means or foul – I can't recall which – I obtained a sackful and lugged them back. I was thrilled with myself as I emptied them into the stove, but the ensuing blaze was so fierce that the chimney caught alight. My grandfather roused on me something terrible and I was forbidden to go to the nut factory again.

It was bleak going out into a galey morning, but as the days brightened up, I'd feel better. Despite my reservations about the big chill of winter, I was occasionally drawn to the high cliffs, even on turbulent days. I'd walk along the cliffs and gaze at the big rollers come thumping up and down; they'd shake the cliff face and spray would go up in the air for hundreds of feet and then drench me. I realised the power of the sea very early in life; for mysterious reasons I don't understand, and believe are best left unfathomed, it would suck me to its shore as I watched flotsam and jetsam wash up against the cliffs and the birds battle the wind.

As a child, there was a stage when we went through a mad pigeon craze, started by Teddy Kavanagh. We'd climb down old ladders and cuts in the rocks, put there in the past by fishermen. Other times, the climb would be to get cungi, so we could fish for drummer and bream, or to just marvel at the waves rolling in.

As I talk to you now about this tempestuous love affair of mine, I am aware of conflicting thoughts about the ocean. I can't explain that, either; all I can tell you is that the sea often feels like my best friend one day and my enemy the next. Those same cliffs that appeared so welcoming and benign on occasions have also reached out to me like a wickedly alluring woman, and I have found myself trying hard to stay away. The ocean perturbs me and makes me have wild thoughts; it doesn't automatically offer me the peace of mind that others speak of. The closest I ever get to that is strolling along the harbour's edge or a lake foreshore very early in the day.

When you're out in a boat, the sea is at its worst at dawn; it's always at its roughest. It's the breeze that comes in with the dawn that causes waves to lift higher and to feather cap. This is the most frightening time, when everything seems magnified. I hate it. Then as the sun lifts and the breeze dies down, so does the sea; it's as though she has been given a new life and her cruelty and vigour have been taken away. A smoothness prevails.

And speaking of calm, there surely can't be anyone alive who hasn't enjoyed the bliss of walking barefoot along the water's edge; it's magical, in a way that nothing else can compare with. Your feet sink, as though you're about to disappear into quicksand, and sometimes the capricious sea swells up and you think it will only brush up against your ankles, but next minute it's risen past your knees, up to your waist, then almost knocked you over. This mystical substance has a power – it takes over a person's body and tries to pull you back in; it doesn't wash you up. When the sea surges around you, it's like it wants to draw you into its womb. You could almost say that. Then when it's finished, the sea will cast you up, unless you're a living, breathing thing, still capable of letting the sand run through your fingers.

All I can say for certain on this strange yet lovely subject is that I need the sea as surely as I need oxygen.

One day, when I was under Hornby Lighthouse fishing with a bunch of boys and girls, the unthinkable happened. My brother John got swept out, along with Maggie Lewis. My heart stopped. What on earth would I tell Mum when I got home? I ran to the edge of the rockface and saw them come around the reef, much to my relief. Shortly after that, there was a tragedy down at The Gap, involving brother Tim's best friend, John Rollinson. For those who don't know, The Gap is a notorious spot, infamous in Australia and beyond, as a place where the hapless both fall and jump to certain death. It demands respect. Without warning, a wave burst over John Rollinson and took him away. It was so sad – especially as he was a local boy – a member of the Graham family. I can remember when the body was brought in by the fishermen, because there weren't too many water police then. The pilot vessel, *Captain Cook*, would lower a boat if anyone was swept off The Gap and bring the bodies in, and there were quite a few, I can tell you – especially during the Depression, when suicide seemed like the only way out of a bleak existence.

My interest in the idea of the sea as a creature with a mercurial personality and an awesome might goes way back, although my first encounter with the open sea, at the age of six or seven, was not one of terror. It was my very first trip in a power boat, with Dick at the helm. Because Dick was given to seasickness, we had thankfully ventured out on a calm day.

Even with the sea at her most ladylike, the swell takes you by surprise; the waves come from nowhere and lift your boat up in the air, and next minute you're down in the froth, meeting another wave.

In my teens, I had started going outside the Heads with a fisherman by the name of Phil Wagner, in his little boat. Unlike Dick, Phil always went out, no matter what the weather. He'd risk rougher conditions, and one day we copped a helluva hiding going around Coogee in a howling southerly blow. It shook me up and made a temporary dent in my confidence as far as the sea was concerned.

There were no two-way radios; just you, your boat and the elements. One night, it was black and very rough, with a fierce wind trying hard to do us in. Again, Phil was the skipper, and also on board was his son, Ernie, who was my best friend. (Tragically, Ernie was burnt to death when he was sixteen.)

As we tried to take a turn to come around North Head, we felt as though we had run into a solid wall of water. Crash, she went, and we stopped. The boat shuddered and suddenly a whale came up alongside. It hit the water, sending spray everywhere. To our horror, we realised the boat had sprung a leak up forward.

We must have been a desperate sight, limping into the Bay, bailing like mad. It was either that, or we would have drowned, and no one would have found us in such a black, ferocious night.

I was only ever washed overboard twice, the first time was

when I was just a kid. It was a silly thing: I was fishing for tailor with Doc Kenny and Jimmy Chapman on a bad night, over at the Sow and Pigs. As usual, we'd rowed over; no lights, no nothing. This particular evening, there was a vicious, dark sea running outside, which was causing a big sea to come down the harbour, so we moored for shelter in the lee of the Pigs, on the southern side. We'd only just done that when the next minute a wave broke and kept going, swamping the skiff.

I remember falling over and being washed out, and then washed back in again, all in a matter of seconds. The skiff lay there, nearly submerged, and we bailed like crazy to get back in. We eventually emptied it and just kept fishing. I don't think anything stops you when you're fishing.

On the second occasion, my brother John once wanted to join us, so Max let him come along one weekend, on one of those beautiful oily swell days, with the sun sparkling off the ocean and the sea as calm as it gets. The plan was to fish at Long Reef for a big shark, after we had harpooned a porpoise off Manly for burley and bait. We trolled for a few mackerel for bait as well, and eventually dropped a pick off Long Reef wide, and set a dan buoy on the anchor line, ready to throw it overboard if we caught a shark or marlin, so we could play the fish.

The porpoise was cut and scraped and this formed a blood oil-line slick; the current was slowly carrying this south, and within half an hour, we had a couple of whaler sharks and a hammerhead hanging around the back of the boat.

Although they were large, they were not considered big enough. Very shortly a tiger shark attacked the porpoise carcass, and Max decided that that was the one we'd catch. Meanwhile, John's sitting up watching from the wheelhouse and being violently seasick; he's vomiting over the starboard companionway.

We rigged up a slab of porpoise for the tiger shark, but as there were other sharks milling around, we had to wait until it came in close. At the right moment, I tossed the bait into its mouth. Straightaway I ran up forward to let the dan buoy go, so we could fight the shark away from the anchor line; coming back I slipped on Johnny's vomit, flying into the air and over the side.

As I became airborne, I could hear my brother's sickly whimper, 'Peter's fallen overboard.' As I hit the water, I looked at the side of the boat and it seemed like a ten-storey building – I literally climbed up with my fingernails and fell into the cockpit. Lawson, by this time, was in earnest battle with a tiger shark, and he spared me a glance as he grumbled, 'I didn't bring you out here to go bloody swimming.'

Winter was about survival. Then summer would come and we could let our defences down and have fun. It seemed that the sun shone every day, and it was so hot walking on the footpath that it scorched your feet.

The water was bright blue, and crabs bit your toes as you waded out. Our main swimming hole was Camp Cove, where the pristine sand screeched as we bounded across it. There weren't too many people there, just my mates engaging in the usual banter about girls, as we eyed off the good sorts. We were heavily into acts of bravado – trying to see who could swim out the farthest, who dared jump off the old military wharf and who was the best swimmer. Sometimes the gang wandered along the cliff to Ladies Haul Beach; we'd take a few bits of bread and cook periwinkles. Often we'd catch a lobster and eat that too. Mutton-fish were plentiful – it was as simple as picking them up – but we wouldn't eat them there. I'd take mine home to my Aunty.

It was from the military wharf that the butcher boats went out to meet sailing ships coming in from overseas; the men rowed out for the meat and grocery orders, as the ships might have to wait for a favourable wind to come into port, and needed supplies in the meantime.

When I think of the sea, invariably Uncle Nugget Newton looms in my mind. He had a great boat and I occasionally went out porpoise catching with him. We would set sail from the flat rock, just in from Green Point. I didn't query it as a boy, but after the porpoises had been harpooned, their heads were sold to the Burns Philp Trading Company; a pound a head they paid Uncle Nugget, and the teeth were used as currency to pay the natives in the New Guinea highlands. You were also allowed by law to take porpoise for bait.

Once you got out to sea, it wasn't long before the porpoises started jumping around the bow. The men would sink the harpoons into them and a morning might yield as many as ten; then they'd bring them back in and cut the snouts off. The carcasses lay alongside Nugget's boats, and there wouldn't be much left the next morning. Sharks would clean them up, because if there's anything that's icecream to a shark, it's porpoise flesh.

Of a weekend, while I was bricklaying, I had a job on a big game fishing boat owned by Max Lawson of the well-known auctioneering firm. Connie Voight and Phil Wagner were the boatmen, and we three were employed, because Max regularly took a team of celebrities out chasing marlin and shark. It was nothing to hook three or four marlin in a day – and the sharks were there for the taking. The guest list often included the legendary quizmaster, Bob Dyer. He came out with us, way back before he got his own boat, which was when he developed a reputation as a formidable fisherman himself.

Soon after my second mishap, I was out with a wonderful fisherman called Billy Love, who was one of the finest I ever saw. He was also a part-time boatman for Tony Hordern of the Hordern retailing dynasty. Such was his reputation that before the War, when American writer and angler Zane Grey came to Australia, he asked Billy to be his boatman.

A defining moment for me occurred when I was out once with Billy. I harpooned a porpoise as several of them flashed past the bow of the boat. This was when there was little compassion for these magnificent creatures; they were simply a means of making a living, and were harvested like the whale.

This time it was a female. We hauled her in and tied her alongside the boat and moored up on a ground wide of Manly called The Masons. Twenty minutes later I heard a baby's cry; we looked around and, there sucking up to the dead porpoise was its calf. It came so close, I patted it. The calf kept up this pitiful cry, and it affected me so deeply that I never again killed a porpoise.

## CHAPTER 6

# FALLING IN LOVE

When Jean was fourteen, her family moved from the Bay to Fairfield in Sydney's west, coinciding with her father leaving the Army and entering civilian life. We didn't see each other for a couple of years after that, although her brothers regularly came back to visit. Then one day, she rang up and asked me to join her and some friends on a picnic to Burning Palms, in the National Park. She said it was a wild sort of spot and that you could only get there by train and a long walk through the scrub; she also mentioned the fishing was good, so I was in straightaway.

Not only did I take my fishing rod on that first date, but I also dragged along a rabbit trap. I was a real suave devil. We met up at Central Railway Station and set off. After the train trip, we walked along a sandy track, down this bloody mountain. It was delightful when we got there, but I couldn't find anywhere to set my trap and I didn't catch any fish, so I wasn't very impressed.

I can't imagine why she wanted to see me again, this petite, pretty brunette, but she did, and after that we often went with a group on outings to Narrabeen on the northern peninsula. We'd either go by bus or catch the ferry to Manly and then the bus. (Jean was working as a dressmaker in a building next to the famous Tivoli theatre). Although she was seeing another boy, things led to this and that, and I eventually took her out to dinner and the pictures in the city

I used to go out to Fairfield and stay the weekend, at the invitation of her parents, who were wonderful people. It was a happy home, filled with seven children and lots of laughter. Fairfield was semi-rural then, and Jean's dad had a vegetable garden and a cow out the back. Life was simple, and one of our favourite things to do was get on our bikes and go swimming at Liverpool.

The romance blossomed, and one day, after a big catch of fish, I bought an engagement ring. She was nineteen, I was twenty. Mind you, the diamond was terribly small, and it nearly didn't fit. My mate, Jimmy Chapman, knew a wholesaler and that's how I got it. Whatever I paid, it seemed like a fortune, given that I was out of work; my years as a builder had ended, due to a slump in the building trade.

Like most Aussie blokes, I suppose, I can get tongue-tied when it comes to talking about feelings, so I was both excited and apprehensive on the night I planned to ask Jean to marry me. We went to the pictures. I wish I could remember the name of the film, but in the state I was in, I noticed very little of what was happening on the screen. It could have been my pin-up girl, June Allyson up there, and it still wouldn't have caught my attention.

In what I thought was a romantic gesture, halfway through the show I handed Jean the ring, without saying a word. She promptly passed it back. Afterwards, we got the train to her place and I formally proposed, and to my great relief, she said, 'Yes.'

It was also to the delight of her parents, whom I suspect had just about had me as their regular weekend guest by then. Not that they could have possibly seen me as the catch of the century; I wasn't much more than a kid, with no job and no future. I was basically just bumming around.

The next hurdle was to tell my own parents the news. I started with Dad, seizing the opportunity the next Saturday morning when we were driving home from the fish markets. I took a deep breath and announced I had proposed to Jean. We were coming up Rushcutters Bay hill into Edgecliff and Dad almost crashed the Austin truck. We got home and told Mum and I don't think she has ever got over the shock. I could see their point – there I was with no prospects. Luckily, just about then, the Fisheries Department position came up, and I thought: if I'm going to marry her, I'd better get a decent job.

We married when I was twenty-one and Jean was twenty. The decision was made to have the wedding at Smithfield, near her family's home, partly because Watsons Bay didn't have a reception place. It's a heck of a way from the Bay and the locals just about fainted when they realised how far they'd have to go, as only a few had cars to make the forty-odd kilometre journey. It was a real expedition. The lead-up was busy. Jean's parents bought cockerel chickens and fattened them up, because they were doing the catering for the party, which was to be held in the hall next to the church.

The day finally arrived: 14 November 1953. My brother John was best man, and I couldn't tell you how many guests we had, but it was plenty. Jean's side included members of her clan from the Northern Territory, who were bush people. I particularly remember her Aunt Kath, who came down with her husband, Joe Yates, driving all the way in their ex-Army staff car, a 1942 Chev. Talk about tough! They put a roll of chicken wire on top of the car, looked at the map and set off. There were no highways, so Joe took the stock route, driving through the corners of Queensland, South Australia and New South Wales. When they got into sandy spots, Kath and Joe lay the chicken wire down and that became the track, and they finally got through to Sydney. I was madly impressed with them.

It was a glorious day – and a long one, beginning with the groom catching public transport to the wedding, along with the rest of the Watsons Bay contingent. We took a tram, a train and a bus. It was even further to come for my other Uncle Harry, who lived at Port Hacking. He certainly made the most of it once he got there, getting quite tipsy and trying to race off all the single women.

I made a fine speech, even if I do say so myself. I said how lucky I was to be marrying Jean, who looked so beautiful in a long dress she had made herself; next, I mentioned how thrilled I was to be marrying into her family; then I apologised to everyone from Watsons Bay for having been such a cheeky kid when I was growing up.

My Uncle Russ stood up and spoke; he was terrific too. He was the fancy fellow of the family, Uncle Russ, and always wore a bow tie. He was the first of us to get a car – although he'd get Aunty Doris to drive, and when that was about to happen, us kids would run for cover.

Jean and I began our honeymoon at the Morris Hotel, next door to the People's Palace, down near Sydney's Central Railway. It had this big white horse on it and the sign read,

'The Morris Hotel: 100 rooms'. Ours was absolutely miserable, but I suppose it seemed a five-star job to us, never having stayed in a hotel before. Next morning we caught the north coast mail train to the town of Forster, where I had rented part of a house for a week. Forster is a fishing port, and after two or three romantic days alone with Jean, I went for a tour around the lake with the local fishing inspector. Everywhere we went, he'd introduce me: 'This is Peter Doyle; he's a junior inspector about to start at Newcastle and he's here on his honeymoon', and they'd give me a feed of oysters to take back to Jean. That night we got stuck into the oysters and had a real feast. I don't think Jean had ever eaten them before and during the night she shook me hard. 'Wake up, wake up. Were those oysters live?' I mumbled, 'Course they were', and she said, 'I thought so, because they're swimming around in my stomach.'

After our honeymoon, I was left with only a couple of quid to my name. We got the bus back to Newcastle where we'd rented half a house at Mayfield, ready for me to begin my new job. We had this terrible old landlady, and it was the worst few weeks of our lives. Thankfully we soon found better accommodation – a pleasant cottage – at Lake Macquarie. After our long courtship, I was very happy to be getting on with making a life with Jean.

Peter Doyle, married man. It sounded good.

# CHAPTER 7

## INSPECTOR DOYLE TO THE RESCUE

I was in charge of the shark meshing operation off Newcastle, which meant going to sea twenty-one days a month, netting sharks. Throughout summer, netting is put in place, parrallel to the beach, about a quarter of a mile out. It is checked every twenty-four hours. I was stationed there with a fine officer, Albie George, who guided me through my early days in the Department. We set the nets in two distinct areas – from Stockton to Mereweather and the beaches in between, and from Red Head to Catherine Hill Bay, and we went out in all weathers and there were some nasty times, but I was proud to be following in a family tradition: an uncle on Mum's side, one of the Newtons, had been an inspector, as had his father.

As well as shark meshing, I had general duties that kept me busy, as Newcastle was a boom fishing area in 1953 and '54. It was the beginning of ocean prawning off Stockton beach, and fishermen would come from everywhere to work on the boats.

Many of these boats were old river tugs, but just about anything that could float and pull a net arrived in Newcastle for the prawn industry. And what prawns they were – so plump and juicy, and plenty of them, so that the nets would sometimes close after only a twenty-minute trawl. The fishermen were at their finest (and noisiest) at the regular prawn nights held in a local boatshed. I think I'm right in saying that this was the first prawn night anywhere in Australia; you could eat as many prawns as you wanted and drink any amount of beer – all for ten bob – while everyone sang sea shanties.

When I turned twenty-two, I became the youngest fishing inspector ever appointed in New South Wales – with the whole of Lake Macquarie to patrol. This was a great step forward, and with it came a house, a ute and a boat with an outboard. Mind you, the Holden ute was rusting to bits, but I was on my way. Lake Macquarie is gigantic and beautiful, and I was there to see that the law was upheld. Half the lake was closed to netting – professionals were allowed in but with restrictions on where they could go.

It wasn't long before I got a bigger boat, which I needed, as there was a lot of work checking the amateur catches during the day, and chasing fishermen around the foreshores at night. Quite often, I put in eighty-hour weeks. The wages were not out of the box at all, and I wasn't paid any overtime, so if it wasn't for my vegetable garden and the few chooks in the backyard, Jean and I wouldn't have managed.

At one point I had just three quid in the bank when Alfie Clark, whom I had known since I was a kid, pulled up to see me one day. His truck had broken down and he asked me for a loan to get it fixed. I withdrew the three quid and gave it to him, and to this day he's never paid me back. That's life, I suppose, although helping Alfie out meant that things were pretty tight and we got very close to the breadline, but I was able to catch a few fish, and we survived.

I might have been poor and overworked, but I was never bored, not with such crazy goings on. I had barely arrived at work when one morning I got a report that illegal netting was going on in Fern Bay, which is a backwater in the Hunter River on the way to Port Stephens. It's a bay of mud, and I crept down through the mangroves, watching a boat that was pulling a net come along past me. I appeared from the mangroves and, rolling up my pants, proceeded to wade out to the boat yelling, 'I'm the fisheries inspector. Stop!'

I waded for only about twenty feet before I sank up to my waist in pure mud. This was my first pinch, as you might say, and there I was waving my badge, screaming at the top of my lungs, 'Stop! You're breaking the law. Stop – or I'm going to charge you!' And of course the fishermen just kept going. I was a sorry sight when I got back to shore, covered in stinking Fern Bay mud – I needed a hose down. And to make matters worse, I didn't even have a prisoner.

This was at the same time as the new ruling came in about prawn sizes, and it was our job to measure them, which kept Albie and me busy, considering how many roadside stalls were selling undersized product. What made it frustrating was that the offenders had a cockatoo system so that when we approached one stall, they would signal ahead, and the signs would quickly come down and the prawns would be hidden.

The front of the Travellers' Rest Hotel at Hexham was a popular spot for selling prawns, so I was often called in, in my official capacity. It was the great meeting place for locals in the industry. One day, we were travelling along the back channel from the steel works, onto Hexham Straight, and up past Ash Island, when we came upon six trawlers working illegally. They went for their lives and we didn't know which boat to try to catch. We decided to pursue one offender by the name of Carl.

We chased him in our old tub, which blew out more smoke than speed, and Carl ran his boat high and dry up onto the island, beaching it. He was screaming at us as we took off next after one of the Dean boys. We couldn't gain much on him, and each time we'd go around the island, which is in front of the pub, all the locals stood there yelling and clapping encouragement for young Mr Dean. It was like a Derby race in a country town – cars were pulling up and people getting out to watch us do laps around the island.

Very slowly but surely, we were gaining on him, with me up forward pumping the boat out, as it was taking on water, while it's blowing out all this smoke. Meanwhile young Dean is throwing boxes of prawns and nets overboard, trying to get rid of the evidence. On the last circuit, our boat blew up, gave a sigh and stopped, much to the delight of the crowd. The hotel did a roaring trade and the boat we were pursuing disappeared.

Don't imagine that we never had any successes, because we did – although some of them felt like hollow victories, especially when we'd travel to outlying areas, raid fish shops and persecute every poor bugger, as we upheld the Fisheries law. I was heavily abused from all quarters. One time for example was when Albie George and I pulled up at a fisherman's house near a railway crossing. We said to this lady, 'We have to inform you that these prawns you're selling are undersized, and we're taking them.'

She wailed, 'You're not taking poor Alex's prawns?' (Alex being her son), and Albie said, 'I'm afraid we are', and with that she let out a torrent of expletives. We grabbed the prawns and as we were backing off the verandah she said, 'What a bastard of a thing you've done.' I might add that all this was being watched with interest by motorists at the railway crossing, waiting for a coal train to go through. She saved her most savage criticism for Albie; her parting shot to him was, 'And you call yourself a bloody Mason!'

Albie and I often took our lives in our hands, like the time we descended on a pub in Mayfield when we had information that a bloke was selling undersized prawns from the back of a truck. When we arrived, the perpetrator turned out to be a dwarf. His name was Billy Lindstrom and he drove a truck in which the brake and clutch pedals had been extended. He couldn't have been more than three foot tall and there he was selling prawns to burly steel workers who had come off their shift.

As we approached, Albie had to squat down to eyeball him. We measured the prawns and found them to be undersized. It was pretty embarrassing pinching prawns off this midget, in front of all these irate patrons, who were yelling as one, 'Let the bloke have a go, you bastards.' We had our day in court with him, and when the name Billy Lindstrom was called, in came Billy, all three foot of him. The magistrate couldn't see him over the bench; he could only hear his voice.

As for the mountains of prawns we regularly confiscated in the line of duty, we had to take them to government institutions, which usually meant the Watt Street Mental Hospital. The inmates had to clean the prawns themselves, and they hated that, so they'd yell at us like mad. A lot of the poor buggers would eat the prawns, shells and all.

In some ways my heart wasn't in investigative work, but I fancied a bit of intrigue now and then ... take the dark, stormy night (I'm exaggerating about the weather) I was out with a relieving inspector, Ralph Clark. We pulled up at this house on a raid, having been there the previous evening to seize some gear, and as we left, a neighbour ran out and whispered, 'I've got some information for you. Last night I was sitting on the toilet in the backyard, and through a crack in the door, I seen a truck arrive next door and they took away two baskets of prawns and some nets. I wrote the number plate down on the back of the dunny door.'

AJF436. That number will stick in my mind forever. I said to Ralph Clark, 'I know that number; I've seen it on a truck somewhere.' So we proceeded back to the office and knocked off. Next morning I went along to the Motor Registry office to run a check. Just as the bloke was asking me what I wanted, it hit me right between the eyes. It was *my* truck!

It was a fairly isolated life for Jean, living on the lake, with me working such long hours. I was only too aware of that, so it was a relief when some kind soul gave her a cocker spaniel, which Jean named Penny. One day I took Penny out for her first trip on the lake, but unfortunately her pleasure cruise around the foreshore turned to drama.

It all began gently enough at the southern end of the lake, with the sun dancing on the still waters, back when little of that section had been mauled by man. The tall gums with their wind-twisted branches dropped leaves onto the green native grass, and wild boronia scent drifted across the waters on one of those days you wish could go on forever. My launch was twenty-two foot long, and it had steering inside the small cabin and a wheel outside, it was painted grey, and had a canvas hung over the glass windows so they wouldn't reflect the sunlight. This was most important, as boats can be spotted miles away when the sun acts as a mirror on the glass.

On this golden afternoon, the only noise was the purr of the engine at half throttle and the soft fall of the bow wave. A few gulls swooped over us. Rin Tin, my cattle dog, who would lay down his life for me, had taken up his spot in the cabin, where he acted as my other pair of eyes. Often, in the evening blackness, a fisherman hiding in his boat in closed waters, thinking he's invisible, has cursed the bark of the inspector's dog.

Penny, meanwhile, was curled up on my lap, shaking in terror. After half an hour, I eased her onto the cockpit floor, from where she eventually gained enough confidence to go exploring around the boat. Around the point, the bay opened up, and I saw a lone trawler, with the fisherman hunched over his catch as he sorted the prawns from the seaweed, crabs and catfish. Straightaway I recognised it as a Swansea boat that I know is faster than mine. Slowly I came up on him, and I noticed that Rin Tin had stood up. I opened the throttle, closed the cabin door and moved up forward, having learnt long ago that I can get an extra knot out of it if it's balanced. The gap was only a hundred yards when the fisherman, quick to smell danger, looked up and in two quick movements, cut his trawl ropes and gunned his motor. The chase was on, with me yelling 'Stop!' – which of course was a waste of breath.

He frantically threw the seaweed, crabs and small fish overboard (anything linking him to trawling), although he hung onto his prawns, knowing there was not much chance he'd be caught – unless his boat blew up. All I could do was throw over a marker where I thought his net was, planning to come back and grapple it up, with a bit of luck. The gulls were having the time of their lives swooping on the bounty that suddenly appeared; Rin Tin was barking, adding to the commotion.

The chase had been going for ten minutes, and I knew this bloke was headed for his truck, parked at the head of the valley. I was betting he'd run the boat up onto the shore, grab his prawns, hop in the truck and take off like the hammers of hell. Then a few minutes before he made it to safety, a yelp echoed across the lake, followed by a whimper. I worked my way to the cockpit and there was blood everywhere – the propeller shaft had taken Penny's ear clean off.

I wrapped her in my cardigan and cut the engine; both boats were drifting in a sea of shock. 'You have to live,' I told her, knowing that in *my* boat, the nearest vet was an hour away. I was holding her tightly when I heard a voice call out, 'Are you all right?' The escapee had come back to help. I told him what had happened and he said, 'Why don't you leave your boat here? Mine's faster, and we can get her to the vet in Belmont.'

Despite the urgency, I couldn't help but consider how on earth I could write this up in my report and still have a job. So I declined the generous offer, and made a rush trip home in my own launch. As I started up the engine, I heard the fisherman say, 'Might see you up this way tomorrow.' His name was Noel Mitchell and several months later he was killed in a truck accident, so we didn't cross paths again.

Penny, on the other hand, got better, although she was a bit lopsided, and definitely phobic about boats. She never did come on patrol with me a second time.

# CHAPTER 8

# INSPECTOR DOYLE RIDES AGAIN

In less than a year, I got my big chance – I was made inspector in charge of Swansea, so we moved there, to a house in Wattle Street. I remember my first pinch; a fisherman, Bern Baxter. He couldn't go anywhere because he had his nets in the water, and as we approached him, we called out, 'Stop!'

Bern did as we instructed, but he picked up his oar, and when we boarded the boat, he said, 'You do and you'll cop this.' We told him, 'Don't be silly; put it down', which he did, thank God. Then we took him back to where he kept his nets; we were supposed to take them all, but only confiscated half. I never believed in depriving a man of his livelihood, especially when you're living side by side in a small community.

There was very little social life in my line of work. I had few friends, save for the local policeman, George Godfrey, and Tudor Evans, who lived on the lake with his sister, Biddy, in their wonderful 1920s family home built from their coal mining fortune. Tudor loved a drink, and would ring me up and say in his husky voice, 'That you, Peter? Next time you're coming down the lake, bring me a bottle of brandy and some port wine.' I'd pretend to be concerned. 'Have you got diarrhoea again, Tudor?' (Brandy and port wine are supposedly an ancient remedy, and he rather enjoyed imagining that he was fooling me.) He'd sigh, 'Yes, I can't seem to get rid of it.'

The lake is about 365 miles around, if you count every nook and cranny, and Tudor was one of the more pleasant of the waterfront inhabitants – but there was no shortage of ratbags. Thomas Alfred Bruce Smith (TABS for short) was a real doozey, in fact he was a deadset nutcase. We pursued and caught him one day, and took his gear. He was furious and giving us plenty of language. Then, later, as we went past his house, his father waved at us from the jetty, so we went ashore and he said, 'My son's terrible upset at what you've done and he's gone for his gun. He's got a bloody rifle and he wants to kill you and I thought you should know.'

I said, 'Why did you bring us in here to tell us that!' He shrugged. 'Don't worry, I've hidden the bullets.' That didn't comfort me and I asked if there was any chance TABS might find them. 'Yeah, come to think of it, I didn't hide 'em that good,' he grinned. We took off very quickly, I can tell you.

A few weeks on, there was a loud knock on my front door at 5 am, and standing there was TABS. He said, 'Christ, can you help me? I've run over me mate. He was asleep and I got in the ute and took off and I felt a bump. I looked back and there he is lyin' in the park.'

We went down to the park in Swansea and there was this bloke, spreadeagled, with an empty wine bottle beside him. I shook him and couldn't see any damage. All he was doing was snoring. I inspected the damage, and sure enough TABS had run over him – there were tyre marks across his legs, and he hadn't even woken up. I said, 'He's all right', and TABS roared, 'The bastard; he's only doing that to get me upset', and gave him a terrible kick.

I loved the unconscious wit and occasional wisdom of these lakeside eccentrics. There's more to life than making money and sewing up deals; there's having a yak on the lake on a starlit night, with the like of Arthur Nelson, who lived in a horrible shed on the Swansea Flats.

Arthur had a romance with someone else's wife up the road and her husband poisoned him with thalium, and all Arthur's hair fell out. His shack consisted of two rooms: a bedroom and a kitchen, with a curtain between them. It had a bare floor and fuel stove. Out the back was a battered truck used to transport greyhounds, and Arthur's sons, George and Arthur, slept in the truck, rather than in the big bed with all the others.

Whenever I caught up with Arthur, he would expound the theories of the world. One night I met him on the lake, and it was just when the first Russian sputnik was going over. We sat there watching it float across the stars, and Arthur said, 'There's a bloke in it.' I looked at him. 'How could there be a bloke in it?' And he replied, 'Yeah, you keep an eye on it. He won't hit one bloody star; there's someone up there drivin' it.'

'Don't be stupid; the stars are a million miles away', to which Arthur replied, 'Yeah? That's what they're telling you – but I know better. I've been readin' up on it.'

Often Uncle Harry Newton accompanied me on my watery rounds. You may remember him, Mum's cousin who chatted up all the single birds at our wedding. That was the first time Jean had ever met him and, understandably, he didn't make a favourable impression. One day, after we had been at Swansea for a while, he turned up unannounced, telling Jean, 'I've come to stop with you.'

He stayed with us on and off for almost twenty years and met his end when he fell out of bed at the Repatriation Hospital. In a grand gesture, he left huge amounts of money to various people in his will; the joke was that he didn't have two bob. He loved coming out with me on Lake Macquarie, and was always going on about astrology (both of us being Leos).

Once he told me most authoritatively that we were in for a terrific day. Next morning we go out, and the boat catches on fire, blowing the bloody windows out. After I rescued him from the water, I reminded Harry of his wildly inaccurate prediction, but he just smiled, 'I told you it would be lucky. We're still alive!'

My wages weren't good, so Jean and I continued to be strapped for cash. It was a permanent state for us. By now, Jean was pregnant with Robyn, the first of our five children, and I worried that my frequent night work meant she might be alone when labour began. So I came up with a great idea – although it initially backfired on me.

My boat was originally stationed in the channel, but the fishermen were always letting go of the ropes, so I moved it to Marks Point, to a wharf owned by Charlie Hollis, who worked for the CSIRO in fisheries research. He and his family were lovely and we had arranged that if Jean felt her time had come, she'd ring Charlie and he would switch on the powerful floodlight, which I could see from most places on the lake.

This particular evening, at 2 am, the floodlight came on and I was right down the other side of the lake, past Toronto. I swung into action, and opened the boat flat out and, at a one hundred miles an hour, headed for the wharf, almost driving the boat ashore on the way. I jumped off and drove home as fast as I could, only to find Jean sleeping peacefully.

In the morning I found out from Charlie that his son had come home from a party and switched on the light. Fortunately, when I was *really* needed a few weeks later, I was at home, and Robyn was born in the Mater Hospital in Newcastle. It was a difficult birth, and Jean spent three days in labour.

We were now a family, which meant someone new to love, but it also meant a greater strain on our limited finances. We never starved, but one day it got dangerously close, and I vowed then to make sure it never happened again. It was a Wednesday, just before pay day, and there was no money whatsoever. All there was in the house were a few slices of bread, one egg and a small tin of tomato soup. It was winter and a miserable cold night to boot.

I said to Jean, 'I'll go and catch a fish for tea', and I took the boat out in a howling westerly gale. There wasn't much shelter on the lake in a westerly and I fished and fished and nearly froze to death. I came home empty-handed and very depressed. Jean gave Robyn the egg for tea, and she and I shared the soup. It was a turning point in my life. For all the hardship I've faced, I've never been short of food – except for that once. I decided that somewhere along the line I'd become a rich man and my family would never want for anything.

A year after we had Robyn, her sister Gayle was born. As I drove Jean to hospital, there was a strong southerly blowing; trees were being blown down, so we called her after the gale. I should explain that we didn't jinx her with the name; she's a wonderfully calm person.

I was so happy with my family, and they and the job were pretty well all there was. Being an inspector meant you didn't socialise much, because of the nature of the job; you were regarded as the enemy. Regular as clockwork, there would be a lookout sent to check if I was home (and therefore not out on the lake). They'd ring at all hours, and then hang up if I answered. To get the jump on them, I'd often drive to the lake, leave my car where it could be seen, double home the back way and then walk to the lake, or go to the pictures with Jean and slip out at half-time to head out on patrol.

Once a year the prickly pear people came through the district, killing off this pest, along with lantana and blackberry, and they'd use my boatshed to store the poison over the weekend. One day an old fellow had jumped off the wharf into Swansea Channel, leaving a suicide note, and as I possessed the only official boat in the area, I was asked to watch out for the body. I finally found him up on the Swansea sand flat after about five days.

There he was, lying half-submerged, and as I approached, a chap fishing about fifty yards further up asked what I was doing. 'Just moving this', I said, without saying what 'this' was. 'I'll give you a hand', he said, thinking it was a bloody great log. So he rode his punt over onto the flat, got out, and saw it was a body. 'Oh, my God!' he cried. 'Oh, oh, I'm going to die. I'm recuperating from a heart attack. I can't help you.'

He was in such a state that I had to tow him home across the flat. Then I reported to the local policeman, George Godfrey, that I'd found the body and was going to put it in my boatshed after towing it back in a dinghy. So I did that, and asked George around to identify the body. 'Yeah, that's him. I'll notify the morgue.'

In the meantime, a prickly pear official had come to stash the poison for the weekend. He'd opened up the boatshed and started unloading. It was quite dark as there were no windows, and suddenly he felt something wet and clammy against his bare leg – he only had shorts on. He turned around and struck a match and there was this bloated body.

He took off to the police station, where he burst in on George, just getting ready for lunch. He screamed out, 'There's a body in the fish inspector's boatshed!', and George replied with a straight face, 'I've got him! I've got him at last! I knew I'd catch him sooner or later. I've had a suspicion about him getting rid of bodies.'

With that, the bloke bolted, never to be heard from again. This was a bit of a godsend, because he left behind all his poisons. I had been having trouble with blackberries in my backyard, so I was able to eradicate them over the next twelve months.

As I've already mentioned, Rin Tin was my partner in fighting crime, whatever the hour, and many a fisherman appeared in court because of him. He also saved my life on several occasions, such as the dark twilight when I was attacked by three men in Swansea Channel and Rin Tin went for them. This was followed by a similiar drama over the back of Swansea flat. Mind you, there was no shortage of not-too-clever blokes who were easy to spot and easy to pinch – even without Rin Tin's able assistance. Dirty Dick Henderson won through to the finals in this category with an inventive act of lunacy.

Dirty Dick was a wanderer, who fished between Tuggerah Lakes and Lake Macquarie, the Hunter and up around the Myall Lakes. Most of the time he lived in the back of an ex-ambulance, but at the stage of which I speak, he had decided to take up residence at Lake Macquarie. Much to my horror.

He desperately needed a boat, and the house he was renting

had a big pine table in it, so he took the table and built a punt, using Masonite for the bottom. His first night with it on the water, I caught him, and in Dick's excitement to beat me, he threw his net out and jumped onto the punt, which promptly sank. (I heard that his old lady was going to kill him because henceforth they had to eat all their meals off the kitchen sink).

I suspect that everyone in life, sooner or later, has some sort of rort going, and in the mid-50s, I was especially impressed with a harmless little con thought up by Jimmy Harkness, the Pilot Master at Swansea Head. Originally from the Shetland Islands, Jimmy spent most of his time fishing, when he wasn't attending to pilot duties. His rort involved me – but I was a willing participant. Once a year, Maritime Services officials came through, visiting the outstation, and Jimmy would get dressed up, resplendent in his uniform, for this one day.

Jimmy was paid £1 a week for supplying his own boat, and as his tug was merely an open fishing boat, it would not do to take the Maritime Services people on a tour of the lake. He'd borrow mine and pretend it was his. Invariably our times clashed and Jimmy'd come in, with me waiting on the wharf. In front of the officials he'd say to me rather grandly, 'Give the boat a good wash', as though I worked for him, and I'd doff my hat and reply, 'Certainly, sir.'

# CHAPTER 9
# Inspector Doyle Heads North

After three years in Swansea, I was appointed to beautiful Nambucca Heads on the north coast, halfway between Kempsey and Coffs Harbour. It was one of the most exquisite places I had ever seen. I felt like Adam in the Garden of Eden. It was the opposite of the life we had just left; here we were in a house with a big yard, where we grew bananas and other tropical fruit.

I was content here and socialised a bit more than in my previous postings. The wonderful thing about the job was that my time was my own, and this was something I never abused; I rarely took sick days. For a man who loved the water, this work was a dream come true and I explored every creek and river. You name it, I explored it. And everywhere I went, I'd throw a line in. I felt I was really on a long, paid fishing holiday.

As inspector, my district took in a huge area, and the job differed from Swansea in that there was much more ocean fishing – both off the beaches and from boats. I brought in a different style of fisheries management and policing wherever

I went; I was more severe than my colleagues. It wasn't long before I had a reputation, and various locals, beginning with the Foley clan, decided to test me out over the size of some fish.

The Foleys were well known up and down the coast, and the mum and dad, a lovely couple, had retired to Nambucca Heads. The Foley boys occasionally gave a bit of trouble; whenever a boxing tent show came to town, you could bet there'd be a Foley fighting. Word had got around that Steve Foley, a real tough guy, was arriving from Minni Waters to take me on. It got back to me that he had said, 'I'm not going to put up with this bloody new inspector. I'll straighten him out.'

It was like *High Noon*. It was midday, on the Saturday, and I was rather apprehensive as I drove down the track to Shelly Beach. Steve Foley arrived shortly after. A large group had gathered to watch the shootout. I said to him, 'G'day, I'm the new fishing inspector', and produced my warrant card. With that, he picked up a knife and shouted, 'If you touch any of my fuckin' fish, I'll carve you up.'

Suddenly there was silence, which should have sent a chill up my spine, but I remained calm as I had Rin Tin with me. I thought I'd better make the first move, because if I waited for him to lunge, my only defence would be to throw sand in his face. So I said to him, 'If you don't put that fucking knife down, I'll take it off you and shove it up your arse; now, let me look at these fish.' To my great surprise, Steve Foley backed down and said, 'All right', and *High Noon* kind of melted away. The climax had passed. And do you know what? From then on, he always called me 'Mr Doyle'.

This posting was for three years as well, and they were golden years – partly because our next two children, Peter and Sharon, were born here. Similiar to Gayle's birth, when Sharon was due, there was a cyclone in full swing, and we had to drive through it as I raced Jean from Nambucca to the hospital in Macksville. There were trees down across the road and it was a real howler.

As I was driving out of the hospital after dropping Jean off, she was actually giving birth – it all happened so quickly. Unbeknown to me, the Sister on that night, the only one on duty, had come out chasing me to give her a hand – but unfortunately (or fortunately), I had already left.

The years went by very fast, years that were important for my development. It was there I got my start in life, when I paid £100 for a little holiday house, which was part of a cluster being sold off. They had operated as McClung's Cottages, and were rented out in the school holidays. I saved up to buy it and I also won some land in a ballot and so I moved the house there. My bricklaying skills came to the fore and I added extensions, so we were able to rent it out.

I also made some friends up there who have stayed true to this day. One way or another, Nambucca was very kind to me. I still own a block of land there, and I don't think I'll ever sell it.

I was constantly on the move in my job and it often involved long drives, such as one particular trip to Coffs Harbour. On the way back I was bringing a parcel of prawns for a policeman at Nambucca Heads. It was rainy and misty as I drove along, and at the Bellingen turn-off, a young bloke with a leather coat over his arm waved me over. I slowed down and noticed an overturned bike beside him. He asked, 'Can you give me a lift? I have to get to Sydney urgently. I've got an aunty there who's dying and my bike's broken. Someone's coming out from town to pick it up.' I told him I could at least take him down the road a bit.

I couldn't figure out why he had the coat over his arm, instead of wearing it – given it was such a bleak day, and as soon as he settled into the car, I felt a wave of uneasiness come over me. He instantly looked at the petrol gauge and said, 'Looks like you need some petrol.'

I asked exactly where he was going in Sydney and he enquired if I'd ever been there. 'No, never,' I lied. He replied, 'I'm going to Wagga Wagga, it's a suburb of Sydney.' I was getting really nervous by this stage, especially as he seemed to be edging closer towards me. Then when we got to the shopping centre in Nambucca, I turned into the police yard, to drop the prawns off. With that, my passenger burst the door of the ute open, screaming, 'You bastard!'

Thankfully, Ray Yells, one of the officers, was outside hosing mud off his vehicle, and I called to him, 'I think this chap's got a gun.' Ray shouted to his sergeant to come out, and they chased the bloke down the street and caught him.

As the local Justice of the Peace (one of the youngest ever appointed) I was called later to deal with the prisoner, who had been armed, as I suspected. You should have seen the look he gave me and heard what he said; 'You bastard. I was going to kill you.' He'd killed a jeweller on the Gold Coast and had taken his revolver. As JP I remanded him into custody and he was sent to Macksville. When the case came up, Ray Yells, the constable, was given a commendation, and the bloke was extradited back to Queensland on a murder charge. I should have been the one to get the bloody commendation! My consolation prize was an increased awareness of picking up hitchhikers.

As hairy as my half hour with the killer was, it didn't cause me too much heartache; in fact only one event stands out as truly painful from those three years in the sun. It had to do with Rin Tin, my companion, who took the loneliness out of patrolling and who had become part of the family. The legend of Rin Tin continued to grow and nervous fishermen were heard telling their mates, 'You want to be careful of the inspector's dog because he's trained to identify undersized fish. Doyle sends him in first and he barks if they're too small.'

I owed that remarkable cattle dog so much – both in terms of affection and for the many times he defended me against baddies (except for that day I came close to being murdered by the hitchhiker, when I had left Rin Tin at home). And if I left him with Jean and the children, I knew they'd be safe.

Towards the end of our stay in Nambucca, Rin Tin unfortunately bit an old lady, who had the habit of walking very close to our fence line. She reported the inicident to the police and they said, 'If he does that again, you'll have to get rid of him.' A while later the same thing happened; the police came around, put him in the truck and we drove out to the forest. I placed the gun in my mate's ear and pulled the trigger.

Part of me died that day.

Word came through that I was being transferred, much to my disappointment. One of the tragedies of moving so frequently was that the kids didn't have the chance to form lasting relationships. I would have given it all up had I realised this at the time, but I admire them for the way they've come through, and for how stable they are.

It was 1960, and it was 'Ballina here we come', via a train to Lismore and then a bus into town. Our house was near the pilot station at the heads. I controlled a district from Ballina and Evans Head, following the Richmond River up to Casino and Lismore, through to Lennox Head and almost halfway up to Tweed Heads. Byron Bay consisted of a big prawning fleet and a whaling station. The Ballina station had the first outboards with trailers, which made us very mobile.

When we arrived, I was very sick with the flu and was laid up. About five o'clock the next afternoon, I got a call from the Lismore police, asking if I would take my boat there, as there had been a serious flood, and they needed my assistance. This was the last thing I wanted to do, but I left in the pouring rain, feeling lousy.

When I arrived at the Lismore Base Hospital, the Richmond had broken its banks and was swirling through the adjacent park. It was dark and raining heavily. I was asked to take two senior officers to the police station, which was on a knoll on the edge of the river. We set off and it was most eerie, with the raging water halfway up the trees – the trunks were submerged and only the branches were showing. I followed the path that ran between the street lights. It was an open boat, with an oar resting above my head on top of the windscreen. As we got to the band rotunda, an eddy caught us and knocked me off course. The next minute I was tangled in overhead electrical wires, which were alive. The whole cockpit lit up with sparks, and what saved us was that the oar over my head had run down it and fused it.

We almost died, and were only too aware that just a few years earlier, soldiers had been killed in identical circumstances during the Maitland floods. With God on my side, and a helluva lot of luck, I escaped and went to the police station, where we stayed for the rest of the night. The next day, I was attached to the Civil Defence, and I made my headquarters in the Lismore Rowing Club. My tasks included taking food to outlying areas, and in one case, transporting a pregnant woman to hospital.

When the floodwaters had moved downstream, I was told to proceed to the Broadwater Hotel on the Richmond, to an area where there was no longer any food or power. I was to deliver food, along with some human cargo: the Acting Prime Minister, Doug Anthony, so he could inspect the disaster firsthand.

We arrived at dusk, which is when floods are at their loneliest – there were no lights – and when it's easy to get lost. As we walked in, we were greeted by the publican and the locals; water was lapping at the bar. The publican said, 'You two had better stop the night.' I quickly agreed, as there was no way we could have returned to Lismore that night. Then he gave us the *bad* news. 'I've only got one room left, and it's a double.' So I shared a bed with the Acting PM – fully clothed. It was the only time I've ever slept with a head of state. Next morning the publican gave us breakfast, which consisted of some black ducks he'd shot himself – they'd been swirling around in the flooded backyard (the fact I was also the game warden was put on hold).

As we prepared to leave, we thanked our host and he thanked us for bringing the food in, then presented us with a bill for a quid each. I didn't have two bob. My family had no idea where I was – there had been no contact for days as the phones were out and word of mouth was the only means of communication. There was Jean in this strange town with four kids, not knowing where I am, and this bloke gives me a bill for bringing him supplies. Give me a break!

He wasn't going to get a quid out of me, the miserable bastard, so Doug Anthony said, 'I'll pay for both of us', then added, 'And don't bother voting for me. I don't want support from your type of voter.' With that, I made my way home to my family, to begin my new role in Ballina.

It was here I taught my children to swim, and we surfed on the magnificent Ballina beach. There is no doubt about it: the north coast of New South Wales, with its temperate climate and laidback lifestyle is a wonderful place to bring up kids.

Opposite the main Ballina slipway lived the three Burke brothers: ageing bachelors, they had set up home in a rickety boatshed which fronted onto a back creek. Harry Burke told me he never had rheumatism because he always slept on an empty salt bag. He had a million tall stories, such as how he'd get visions about horse races – especially the night before a Melbourne Cup.

The year Rimfire won he said, 'I had a vision about that, you know.' I said, 'Oh yeah, what was it?' And he told me, 'Well, I dreamt there was a toilet seat on fire; there's this wooden toilet seat burning away. What does that remind you of?' I shook my head, 'I'm not sure Harry; the only thing it makes me think of is that you wouldn't be able to use the toilet.'

Harry was not impressed. 'Nah; it means rim of fire – so I backed Rimfire the next day, and it won.'

Another time I called by, Harry was opening oysters, and swishing around his feet were half a dozen big black eels. 'Those eels are my pets; I don't let anyone catch 'em. They're here now because they can see I'm opening oysters.' I must have looked rather startled. 'Oh yeah,' I said, trying to sound like this wasn't the weirdest thing I had ever heard, 'how many oysters can they eat?' Harry grinned. 'See that fat one? I fed him ninety oysters in a single sitting once, and I only stopped because my arm was just too tired to open any more.' Ninety bloody oysters!

Tragically, one of the Burke brothers died, another shot the third, then set the place on fire – all in the same day. A whole era disappeared with those three old men.

There were many people, like the Burkes, who I enjoyed chatting with, but as usual, I was fairly much a loner, with the exception of being a Rotary member and having a weekly beer at the pub. When you're an official in a small town, you're never loved by everybody, and so you have to become self-reliant. The upside is that you gain a wealth of knowledge about what's going on, by virtue of standing back and observing. I became a sharp observer of human nature and quite adept at deciphering what is true and what is fiction in a wide variety of situations.

I got into something of a rut, drinking once a week with the police and other officials, growing my own vegetables, and working hard. I was a home man at heart, and one of my great delights was taking my kids fishing. As the office was in our home, the kids grew up with me always around.

Was I a simple man then? Oh, absolutely. My biggest dream was to stay in Fisheries, but somehow to move on, hopefully making it to the top job in Maclean, which was the biggest station on the coast. This was my wild fantasy, and I couldn't see beyond that.

I valued the shelter of the public service: my job was assured, as long as I didn't do anything stupid. This was enough for me, knowing that if I played the game and worked hard, I would become a chief inspector, which was all I wanted. This came to pass in 1963, after two-and-a-half years in glorious Ballina. We were off to Maclean, on the Clarence River.

It's true what they say about being careful what you wish for, for fear it will come true. The reality of Maclean did not seem much like a glittering prize: the house was dingy and rundown, there was no town water, and the tank in the yard was rusty. The big plus though was that we could fish off the end of our own jetty. And in professional terms, I felt a certain elation at being responsible for the area of New South Wales that produced the most fish.

Overall, it wasn't a very happy time. Jean didn't like it and it was hard for the children, especially the younger ones, to become enrolled in yet another school. Maclean depressed me and it depressed Jean and me as a couple. During our fourteen months there, I felt an increased sense of isolation. I became all too aware that people often feigned friendship to cover another agenda, and that you often had to sort the chaff from the straw.

And then a phone call – the sort that changes your life. It was my brother John. He and Mick and Mum and Dad had bought the Pier Restaurant in Rose Bay some time before. He said the magic words: 'Why don't you come down and work with us, because business is picking up and we're doing all right.'

## Dishwater Trout

**Ingredients**

200g butter

2 pieces Alfoil

2 rainbow trout

4 slices lemon

1 dishwasher

1 dirty kitchen(optional)

**Method**

Butter one side of the foil. Lay fish on and place two lemon slices on top of each fish. Wrap fish up very, very tightly.

Clean up kitchen and stick the dirty plates in the dishwasher.

Find room for two trout and stick in as well. Put dishwasher on longest and hottest cycle. Wait until finished. Unwrap trout and put on clean plates and enjoy!

# CHAPTER 10
## Coming Home

Giving up a secure job was not that easy. Despite my excitement at rejoining the rest of the Doyles, I had a wife and four kids to support, and all I owned to see me on my way was a battered Holden ute and £150 in the bank. It was risky, but I knew the time had come to start over.

I put Jean and the kids on the train and they went off to stay with her mum and dad in Sydney; the cat and I followed a couple of weeks later in the ute, which was weighed down with personal effects we didn't want to trust on the moving van. As soon as I left Maclean and was driving in the open, the cat jumped out and I haven't seen her since. It's silly, but there's always the thought that she might still be around, waiting for us to come back for her.

The other thing I have reflected on when I drive up north is that if we'd been happy in Maclean we might have stayed – and how different our lives would have been. It's funny the way things work out, isn't it?

My parents, having worked themselves nearly to a standstill

at Watsons Bay, had leased the restaurant out, although they continued living upstairs. It was then that John, Mick, Mum and Dad took over the Pier at Rose Bay. I joined them there, and it was all new to me. I mean, I'd cleaned fish when I was a kid, but there had been an eleven year break.

The famous (some would say infamous) Doyles' queues began about one year after the opening, once word got around that Doyles' Pier served the best fish and chips in town. Another attraction was the dazzling view – our pier jutted over an especially picturesque area of the harbour. As with a lot of old Sydney houses, it originally had small windows, but we renovated and the place took on a different ambience.

I started at the bottom, so I could learn the game, as I was only too mindful of the fact that I had to prove myself. We were living with Jean's parents in Granville, which is a good hour's drive from Rose Bay, so I was leaving home at dawn and not returning until ten or eleven at night. It was a rude awakening, coming into the world of commerce, and no longer being under the shelter of the public service. In those days when you became a public servant, it would take an earthquake to get you out of the job; it was like being on the pension. In fairness, there were some terribly hard workers, but there were plenty of others you wouldn't even feed.

As usual my dad, Jack, was doing a double shift – he was still in the printing industry, as well as cooking of a Saturday and being in charge of the finances – he's always been the book man. Johnny was in charge of fish buying, and I don't think I've ever seen a finer fish filleter. Mick was in the kitchen, my youngest brother, Tim, gave up the butchery business to work in the kitchen, and Mum, of course, did front of house – a role for which she was legendary. We boys never had a punch-up, but there were plenty of disagreements; Mickey and John were the peacemakers.

From somewhere deep inside me came the determination and ambition that had previously lain dormant. I wanted to excel, and I began to realise that the world could be our oyster (pardon the pun) if we pushed our name. I envisaged the exemplary reputation we had from Watsons Bay soaring even higher.

I developed a plan which began with me writing letters to newspaper editors to develop my personal profile. It was helped along when my old mate Cliffie Ryan, who formerly worked at the markets and had become 'The Housewife's Friend' on the Sydney *Sun*, would quote me about various fish threatened with extinction.

I became very outspoken – much to the horror of Mum and Dad; I once took the then Premier to task for declaring his interest in protecting fisheries in some remote country, while not paying the same attention to what was going on at home. Poor Dad would say, 'You shouldn't be saying those things', and Mum would add, 'Someone will sue you.'

The potential of our business was pretty well unlimited – it was all up to us. I should point out that I still had no say, as Mick, John and Mum were the owners, but it was agreed that Tim and I should be given shares.

Simplicity was part of our success, and soon we were seeing high-flyers taking their chances with our 'no bookings' policy, along with everyone else. One night we had Bette Davis, Robin Williams, and William Conrad (of *Jake and the Fat Man*) – all dining at different tables.

We could seat one hundred and fifty, and when we opened the doors, there would invariably be two hundred hopefuls lined up in single file outside. Alice was in her element managing the crowds, and in her generous way, she'd give chips and drinks to the kids to keep them happy. The press had started writing her up as 'Ma Doyle', a tag she has always disliked.

We'd start early in the morning, and the first thing we'd do was sweep and mop the floors. We'd clean the toilets, and then prepare the potatoes for chips, along with various dishes and soups. We were constantly frantic.

Lunch ended, and it was a mad rush to sweep the joint and clean the toilets before gearing up for the night-time trade. And speaking of toilets: I had found a life jacket somewhere once, and just for fun we kept it hanging in the ladies' loo. One afternoon, an irate woman came up to me and said, 'It's disgraceful. You've only got one life jacket in the whole place!' Where did she think she was – on the Queen Mary?

We had a board meeting once a month, for which Mum cooked her special sponge cake. (I think the only reason we kept having board meetings was because of the cake.) When we allocated the jobs, we made Michael treasurer and secretary, because he still has the first penny he ever earned – it's nailed to the floor under his bed with a six-inch nail. Other than the sponge cake board meeting, we weren't really people for having meetings, as we were all too bloody busy to sit down! We used to chuckle when any of us would ring up someone and they were always said to be 'in conference'. How do these guys ever get around to achieving anything?

When Rose Bay first got going, we were mainly serving deep-fried fish, but the public was slowly becoming more health conscious, and we had to include grills. They'd eat any fish, as long as it was fresh. We realised with the expansion that people might copy us, and plenty tried, but the great mistake

'I could never sew, Peter, but then I thought they would grow with you.'
Mum talking about my new overalls when I was sixteen months old.

The Doyle family in 1950 at Watsons Bay.
From left: John, Dad, Tim, Mum, myself and Michael.

*Above* Our wedding day. Doesn't Jean look beautiful?

*Below* Jean and me just after Gayle was born in 1957.

*Above* Down on the farm from left:
me, Robyn, Gayle, Shaun, George (a friend), and Peter in front.

*Below* Jeff Marriott, a banana grower from Nambucca Heads, Uncle Harry Newton, who lived with us, and me, sitting next to the Darling River at Balranald.
When the esky runs dry, we'll go fishin'.

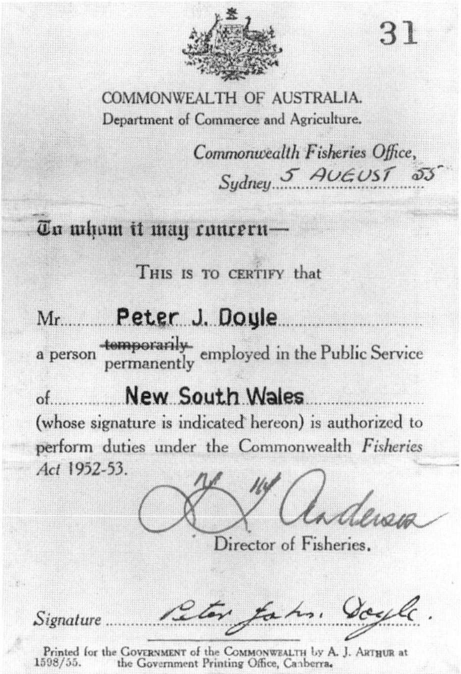

31

COMMONWEALTH OF AUSTRALIA.
Department of Commerce and Agriculture.

*Commonwealth Fisheries Office,*
*Sydney* 5 AUGUST 55

To whom it may concern—

THIS IS TO CERTIFY that

Mr. Peter J. Doyle

a person ~~temporarily~~ permanently employed in the Public Service

of New South Wales

(whose signature is indicated hereon) is authorized to perform duties under the Commonwealth *Fisheries Act* 1952-53.

L. J. Anderson
Director of Fisheries.

*Signature* Peter John. Doyle.

Printed for the GOVERNMENT of the COMMONWEALTH by A. J. ARTHUR at the Government Printing Office, Canberra.
1598/55.

*Left* Peter Doyle's Commonwealth Fisheries' licence.

*Below* In my shiny suit of armour as a council alderman in 1963.

*Above* Original restaurant at Watsons Bay in 1898.

*Right* The family shop was rebuilt four years earlier in readiness for the arrival of the Great Fleet in 1912.

*Left* Mum and Dad taking advantage of the first outside dining room in Sydney in 1967. It was one of the few times they sat down.

*Below* Out the front of Doyles in 1968. Mum, Dad, and the four boys, from left, Tim, Michael, me and John. I worked out the date by the bell bottoms!

*Above* The only photo of Black Peter in existence. Next to Black Peter are Mr Roams and B Kennedy.

*Right* 'Podge' Edwards and his brother Jackie lived in a hut built into the caves at Gibsons Beach. I used to chat to them each morning on my way to school. Alas, there are few characters like them around today.

imitators make is that they think they can do *better* than you, by taking something that is a real hit and putting a different spin on it. It's like the mugs who reckon they can improve on McDonald's.

We had our heads down and our bums up, and Rose Bay was going like a rocket. In 1967, the lease was up on the restaurant at Watsons Bay, then held by Michele Ray, and we decided to buy him out. It was a joint decision, but don't think for a moment we never had rows. Don't think there wasn't any screaming and ranting and raving – because there was. And what a shock when we got down to our new restaurant; settlement was on the Monday and at the end of Saturday trading, he had just walked out of the kitchen and left it as it was. We moved into the most terrible mess and muck. But it was a small price to pay for being back in our beloved Watsons Bay.

We all had our own ideas, but by the same token, what drove us was the hunger to succeed, and the best business in the world is a hungry business. Too many companies start out rich and end up poor because they give the managing director a flash new car and he wants to start having golf days. They are fundamentally not hungry. Never be frightened of anyone opening up alongside you who isn't hungry. It's the hungry ones who'll beat you every time.

My deep longing to make something of myself, and to make my family proud of me, was about to get the opportunity of a lifetime.

# CHAPTER 11

## NOTHING CAN STOP US NOW

As always, the Doyles did not shrink from hard work – we decided to do everything ourselves in order to get the shop ship-shape again. My building skills came in handy. I even made the new grease trap. We mended the pipes and did all the painting, while Uncle Reggie, Mum's brother, did the wall-papering.

Marinato's milk bar and tea rooms on the wharf opposite came on the market, after seventy proud years in the same family. I talked my brothers into buying out the lease, which was a helluva strain as we never seemed to have any money. The old tea rooms were pretty rickety, and we knew that somewhere along the line we'd have to rebuild them, but that was all right; the main thing was that we had established the bridgehead, we had the restaurant on the beach and now one on the wharf. We could keep the competition out.

Acquiring both sites gave me more confidence in what we could achieve as a family. Shortly after, a restaurant opposite the Manly ferry came up for sale, and we decided to expand further, with brother Tim as manager. On reflection, I don't think Manly was ready for us, although we did good business there. At that time, people over that side of the harbour didn't eat out as much as those in the eastern suburbs. Also, Manly didn't have the tourism infrastructure it has now, so there was no flow-on. For the hours we put in, it just wasn't worth it.

Once again, my brothers and I despaired as to when we'd get a return on our money as we always seemed to be paying piles of it out. While all this was going on, Jean and I and the kids had moved from her parents' home at Granville; her mum and dad had been marvellous to us, but it was a strain. I used my long-service money as a deposit on a house at Maroubra – which was only a twenty minute drive from Watsons Bay.

By 1968, Sydneysiders had begun going out more and drinking more. We were surprised by the number of customers who brought along bottles of wine and beer. We had been turning the tables over at least twice a night, but with the advent of the flagon, and later the cask (pre-breathaliser), all that changed. We had couples arriving with a flagon, staying all evening, drinking the lot and ending up legless. Our turnover dropped alarmingly.

Being a bring-your-own establishment, we decided that the best thing we could do was become licensed, which was easier said than done. For some reason, politicians have always kept Australians in check on their drinking habits. Our drinking laws should have been liberalised many years before they were. And there should never have been the notorious six o'clock swill, or the law which stated that you could only buy wine on a Sunday if you purchased a dozen.

Be that as it may, my brothers declared that as I was the one who liked wine so much, I should talk to the guru, Len Evans, whom I first met when he came into the restaurant with the well-known art dealer and bon vivant, Rudy Komon. Rudy would march into the kitchen and say to me, 'What is fresh today?' in his wonderful European accent, and I'd have to show him the fish. If he'd made a sale, he'd select the most expensive item on the menu and he'd order the same thing for his client. If, on the other hand, the sale hadn't gone through, he'd have the lobster himself, adding, 'My guest will have the jewfish.'

One day he brought a podgy-looking chap into the kitchen, saying to me, 'How's the lobster?' By chance, we had just had a delivery from Moon Brothers and they had broken out of the sacks and were crawling all over the bloody floor while we were trying to cook. Rudy pointed imperiously. 'I will have that one, and Mr Evans will have one too.' And that's how I first met Len, who was about to open his landmark wine bar in the city, in Bulletin Place. He and I soon became friends.

We finally got our liquor license in 1974, but only with great difficulty, as the police objected to it. You have to install so many toilets, you'd think everyone had galloping diarrhoea and no kidneys. Our restaurant at Circular Quay has more toilets than a jumbo jet – and we only seat a quarter of the people.

Tim, John, Michael and myself came up with a brainwave: for the next three weeks, we'd count the empty bottles and take note of what were the most popular wines. In those days, Ben Ean was a huge seller, followed by Lindeman's Bin 23. The moselles were way out there in popularity, while reds did not figure hugely. I think we only counted one red: Moyston Claret. We kept an eye on the empties and ordered accordingly. Ben Ean then appeared on our brand new wine list for $1.60.

To strengthen our name internationally, I spoke to a number

of executives on the Tourism Commission, and told them that any overseas visitors – whether they be journalists, authors or travel groups – would be most welcome at Doyles as my guest, and that I'd have lunch with them. This was the beginning of my evolution into a public figure. It wasn't long after this that the press started ringing me for statements, and I worked out early on that it was best never to tell lies, as you'll always be found out. Mind you, although I told the truth, what *they* made of it was sometimes a hash-up. I also made the commitment to be available and reliable when approached by the media. My comments at times meant clashing with governments and various public servants, but I'd had eleven years of the public service so I knew how to play the game.

By the mid-70s, Doyles had developed a name internationally. It was music to my ears whenever I heard of an overseas celebrity raving about one of our restaurants, and how Doyles was their first stop once the plane had landed. David Frost came out in the early seventies and ate at Watsons Bay, then six months later he returned to interview the prime minister. He was stopped by a radio reporter at the airport and he was asked what else he'd be doing. 'Oh,' replied David, 'the first thing I'll do is go straight to Doyles.' Lee Marvin said the same when asked what he did as soon as he got to Australia for his annual fishing holiday. 'Go to Doyles.' And he did, too.

So we were becoming established, and we were also becoming known at the fish market for buying the best product. The market was now switching from only selling traditional lines to incorporating squid, octopus – and more prawns. This change was tallying with what we were seeing: people were becoming more sophisticated. We had sold very few entrées in the early days; our standard meal was fish and chips, a cup of tea, bread (not rolls), and a bit of butter. And boy, were we at the forefront when they brought out little packs of butter in foil!

Part of our credo has been to give customers what they want, and they were certainly demanding more oysters. My brother John decided to put prawn cutlets on the menu, with Dad warning him, 'You'll never sell 'em.' For once my dad was very wrong.

As we moved from one or two lines into secondary lines, we needed to employ more staff in the kitchens. At Watsons Bay especially, we took on several Portuguese, a nationality which has a long affiliation with the Bay. Quite a few of the families, such as the da Silvas and the Portos, go way back.

We were going from strength to strength, but when you're establishing a business, it's hard on those at home. Jean and the kids had gone from being with me all day to having me spend long hours at the restuarant, and it changed the way we lived. I left early in the mornings to go to work, and at night I wouldn't get home until ten or eleven. I'd fall through the door, mentally and physically exhausted, and all I could be bothered having was a sandwich and a glass of beer. I'd flop in front of the television, which always closed with a religious program. I reckon I must have seen more religious programs than anyone else in Australia, with a beer in one hand and a sandwich in the other. I just needed to wind down.

The pressure my job put on Jean was enormous, as by now we had five kids, with the arrival of Shaun, seven years after Sharon. The older ones were in their teens and they needed guidance, and I wasn't always there for them. Jean though, never failed them – she's a wonderful mother and a wonderful sewer and knitter; she made clothes for all of them.

I've been more than blessed in having Jean as my partner; Jean, who took control of the kids more than I did, and they have turned out so wonderfully.

Jean and I didn't get out alone together as much as we would have liked, but on another front, the social scene, I found we were starting to be asked to the kind of functions that get written up in the papers. I felt we should go to a lot of them to be seen. I suspect people tend to look down their noses if you cook fish and chips for a living, and I figured we should position ourselves more upmarket, because we were selling upmarket fish and chips. And that's how and why I edged my way into the jet set – unlikely player though I was. Mind you, I'm referring mainly to fundraisers. Every charity had a guest list, and if they thought they could squeeze a dollar out of you, you got an invitation. Also on their mailing list is the mob who love getting their pictures in the columns, but who have never given a cent away in their lives.

The hard part was reinventing myself as far as my wardrobe went, and in this, I enlisted the aid of Kings Cross outfitter to the stars, Len Kosky. Len put me into superflash pants and sports jackets – and I finally bought a dinner suit. Prior to that it was a hired job, except for the night I borrowed a tuxedo from one of my brothers – the sort with bell bottoms and a red cummerbund. I was off to a $500-a-plate slap-up do for the Liberal Party, and when I got in the cab, the driver looked me over and said, 'Off to work are you, mate?' It was definitely time to get my own dinner suit.

A few months into the new me, I lashed out on my first pair of Italian shoes, which turned out to be somewhat of a disappointment. I had fishermen's feet – much too broad for the Italian loafers I was trying on, but I bought them anyway to spite the snooty salesman. They nearly crippled me after an hour. I was at a lunch and I slipped them off and then couldn't find them under the table – so I had to go to the loo barefooted at this very posh affair. My very first expensive tie was equal in price to a pair of my work trousers – I just couldn't get over it. To be honest, I still preferred Stubbies, a T-shirt and a pair of knockabout joggers.

Jean always looked the part when she accompanied me on social outings, but she found the cocktail set very boring; she didn't like making false conversation, and I have to agree with her that all that 'Darling' rubbish gets annoying after a while. In fact, I was shocked to find that it's possible to get into the bloody pattern yourself. You find yourself calling everyone 'Darling', which is a joke as far as I'm concerned, because all my life, I've only ever called sheilas 'Love'. For a while though, I found this world exciting. I even went upmarket with my car; I went from a Holden ute, bought second-hand from the County Council, to a stationwagon sedan.

It was frantic at times, trying to keep up with the children – to be at football, speech nights and the rest. At home, we were running out of space; with the girls growing up, they all wanted their own rooms, so Jean and I set to, and I used my bricklaying skills to make extensions.

As I mentioned earlier, seven years after Sharon was born, Jean had announced she was pregnant, which was a bit of a shock. Our second son was born at St Margaret's Hospital on St Patrick's Day, 1971. I had insisted that if the baby were a boy, he would be called Reef, but when I went in to see Jean, the Mother Superior said to me in her broad Irish accent, 'I talked your wife out of calling him Reef. Being born on St Patrick's Day, his name is now Shaun. With a name like Doyle, that's what he deserves; so he's now registered as Shaun Doyle.' And that's how Shaun Reef Doyle got his name.

When Shaun was still very small I decided in a fit of something or other, to stand for my local council (Randwick). I have always been passionate about right and wrong and I was delighted to be elected an alderman. Alas, the euphoria did not last long. I rode up to the Council Chambers on a white horse and in a suit of armour. I had arrived; I would save the municipality from those mismanaging people, but it wasn't long before the suit of armour became rusty and the white horse died under me.

It turned out that you can't beat City Hall after all. Bureaucracy did me in; naively, I had had no idea how powerful the unwritten law of 'I'll scratch your back and you scratch mine' was. The entrenched public servants who had been there for a thousand years weren't going to bend. They'd give the nod to any project they agreed with, but if they didn't want to do it, they'd shelve or shuffle it, and then your term would be up and you would be out.

I spent one term as an independent, as a member of the Rate Payers' Association, during which time I worked my way up to Deputy Mayor. Having been on the Council for three years taught me that there's always a hidden agenda, that the first agenda they give you is not the real one. There's always someone trying to float a lurk or a scheme they'll benefit from; there are very few who are genuine first-up. I'm glad my career in internal politics ended there, because it gave me more freedom to pursue business and family interests. You can't build an empire without hard work. Thankfully I wasn't a golfer, so golf wasn't a distraction. Gardening was my relaxation and pleasure, second only to fishing. If I had a spare moment, I'd hop aboard the *Alice Eva*, the cruiser we now owned, and take off. My brothers were very understanding when I needed a bit of time off.

Yet despite the pace of my life, once I'd left the Council, I was still looking for an outside interest. This was when I became involved with government fisheries boards. My love for fishermen was – and still is – so strong that I was fast becoming their spokesman. I'd always believed that if I had to go into the trenches, I'd go with the men of the sea. These were the people I knew best, and together we had put up a helluva fight over the years. So I was invited onto various government boards, I was in charge of the fishermen's training committee, I was overseeing the formation of a new quota system and new licensing laws, and watching over a whole host of other problems and solutions, as the fishing industry grappled with the second half of the twentieth century.

Closer to home, I was emerging as a spokesman for my family. I'd pushed my way in, with no resistance from the others, and I was very comfortable with the role. Initially I stuck to matters to do with seafood, because Alice, as matriarch, had always been the one to speak up on certain matters. After a while, as my confidence increased, I was being sought out for quotes on a wide range of subjects; my past was catching up with me, I, who left school at thirteen, with little education, was now being invited to talk to big gatherings.

I realised I'd have to do a course on public speaking, which I undertook over twelve Monday nights. It taught me to be sure my tie was straight and not to hunch my shoulders – for which my mum has often criticised me – and to be more positive in my delivery. I didn't need any more help on the latter, because I had always been a person to go for the jugular.

That may surprise my acquaintances, as I seem placid, but underneath I'm tough, and I have a short fuse. I've had many a fiery go at employees and those I deal with in business; I've really exploded.

Occasionally I would be asked to speak on television. One of the first interviews I ever did was with Katrina Lee (it was also her first interview) on the beach at Watsons Bay. It was in the mid-1970s when we were fighting the council about outdoor seating, which became a tremendous problem for us. The publicity generated was enormous, as the Woollahra Council campaigned to force us off the parade, and the press had taken up this issue.

The old restaurant that Mum and Dad had on the beach had always had outside tables and chairs, and as the years went by, the tables and chairs increased, so we bought the boatshed next door. The place was becoming very famous, as here we were pioneering outdoor eating in Australia.

For years, the ordinance was that you couldn't eat outdoors because a horse would poop up the road and the poop would dry and the wind would blow it on your food. I don't know how the Europeans managed – they must have been dying in their thousands, eating horse shit in the streets of Paris. Up to this time, European migration had filled this country with people who were used to eating out, and eating out, generally, was becoming more popular. Australia was changing and we were shedding the Anglo-Celtic seriousness that had gone before.

Australians now viewed eating outdoors as their right, and couldn't understand the obstructive bureaucracy. Huge changes were sweeping through, and Woollahra Council was fighting us in the courts and ordering us off the footpath. We had offered them rent on the exterior tables and chairs, but no, this wasn't good enough. Their objection was lodged by a few aldermen on the basis that it was against the law to have tables and chairs on the footpath and that the law must be upheld at all costs. Bugger tourism and bugger what happens in the rest of the world; we must comply with this ancient by-law. What if a horse came down the parade? What if the milkman wanted to start up again with a horse and cart?

So the press leapt on this and I was appearing on TV left, right and centre, and was becoming quite a personality.

There were no frills with my speaking; all of a sudden I was being recognised, I was famous. People were stopping me in the street to have a chat, and I got the feeling that they were pointing me out and saying, 'Who's that bloke there?'

A good friend of mine had been to America and bought me a Mickey Mouse watch, which I still wear. He said, 'I brought you back a Mickey Mouse watch', and I thought, 'Here I am, dressed in Gucci shoes and I have moved out of my Fletcher Jones pants. To wear this watch just isn't good enough', so I put it in the drawer. Shortly after that, I was having lunch with some people at the beach and garbagemen I knew came along, and I didn't say 'G'day' to them. I realised I had always said 'G'day' to everybody in my life, and I needed to wear that Mickey Mouse watch.

I learnt my lesson, and thank God it came early.

# CHAPTER 12

# RICH AND FAMOUS

The first film star I met was Betty Hutton. She was in Sydney, not long after having finished *Annie Get Your Gun*, and was brought to the restaurant by the king of radio, Jack Davey. It was a Saturday, and crowds gathered on the beach to look at her. Mum and Dad were introduced first, and I stood there goggle-eyed, barely able to utter a greeting. I think I saw the movie fifty times when it came out.

That was the early days, the 1950s, and from then on, I have crossed paths with hundreds of celebrities, getting to know many of them quite well. I have found that the multi-millionaires who have really made it are the quiet ones; in fact, you wouldn't know if they had two bob to rub together. Half the time they'd have a pair of old shorts on if they came to the restaurant, yet they might have more wealth than you could jump over. They are the antithesis of the Bonds and the Skases.

The one I admired most was the British engineering whiz, Sir David Brown. Like many of my friendships, this one began with an encounter in the kitchen. I was cooking on a busy Saturday at Watsons Bay when a woman came in and said, 'I'm Sir David Brown's secretary.' 'Oh yes,' I said, never having heard of him. 'He'd like to meet you,' she continued, to which I replied, 'Fine', still having no idea who he was. I went out into the dining area and here's this short, nuggety chap in his late seventies. By the sound of him as he greeted me, he was a Yorkshireman. I introduced myself and he told me, 'I come to eat here every year when I'm in Sydney and I always enjoy the food. I have a feeling you'd be interested in boats; would you like to look at a photograph of my new boat?'

He kept his magnificent yacht – about three days long – moored in Monte Carlo. Its name was *Flying Cloud*. I said, 'It's beautiful', and he smiled. 'Any time you come to Monte Carlo, you must come and stay on the boat with me.' I thought to myself, Oh yeah, because in my game, you hear all these amazing offers, but they rarely come off. The poseurs will plead for you to stay with them in their Arabian tent or at their chalet in the Alps, but you know they're saying to themselves, 'I hope the bugger doesn't turn up.'

In the case of Sir David, I have no idea why he saw the potential for friendship with a rough diamond like me, but he did. The next year, 1980, I was invited by Len Evans and his business partner, Peter Fox, to go to Bordeaux to visit their two chateaux and to pick grapes. Here was my chance to go to France and hob hob with the glitterati.

Len, Peter and I began with an hilarious time in London, from where we flew down to Bordeaux. It felt like the middle of winter as we were picking sauterne grapes; it was actually autumn, but it was so cold and wet that my fingers were nearly falling off. I said out loud, 'Jesus, there must be an easier way to make a quid than this.' My hands were as cold as buggery and here I was, working out in the field with the gypsies.

Serious partying every night took the pain of the day away. Evans was so proud of Australian wines, which he brought over in vast quantities to show them off. I think I met every count and would-be count in France, as well as the American, James Dupont, heir to the family chemical and plastics company which invented nylon, who lived in a chateau around the corner with about one hundred bedrooms.

The day we had arrived at Len and Peter's Chateau Rouhl, Fred Williams, the painter, and Rudy Komon were packing up their Volvo, getting ready to leave. Len said, 'We've just arrived and you're leaving!' Rudy nodded. 'Yes. There's nothing to drink.' 'What do you mean there's nothing to drink? When I left the chateau it was full of champagne and wine', to which Rudy replied, 'We've drunk it all and we're going.' With that, it was handshakes and pats on the back all around and they disappeared. The only beverage left in the joint was half a pot of tea, and Len's wines weren't arriving for two or three days. I found that highly amusing.

Thank God the new supplies arrived without a hitch and I had two crazy weeks with Len, after which I made my way down to Monte Carlo. On arrival, I rang Sir David Brown, who was very bright on the other end of the phone. 'Come and stay with me on the yacht for a few days,' he said. Wow, I thought, I've made the big time, I've crashed through. I had one of the best holidays of my life, cruising around the Mediterranean with this unusual man and his gorgeous young wife, Paula.

His own story is worth telling, and it's one I find endlessly inspiring. David started off with nothing, being originally employed by his father in a small engineering concern. Then he made gears for aircraft during the war, and as the war was winding down, a chap came to see him and said, 'Do you think you could build a gear box for a tractor?' David replied, 'Yes, I could do that. What's your name?' His name was Ferguson, which of course was the beginning of the world-renowned Ferguson tractor.

David was doing very well out of that and then Ford came along and bought the Ferguson company and David was out of business, so he decided to build his own tractor, the David Brown, which became famous. What he initially did was to make one mock-up and take it around to country fairs. This way, he was able to sell hundreds in the first year, without it even being made. He opened factories in Canada and Malaysia, eventually selling out to Case, the American combine.

Following that, David was at a loose end in London, when someone said to him, 'Why don't you buy Aston Martin?', which was having a rough trot. Fortuitously, the next thing that happened was he was invited to have lunch at a gentlemen's club. He told me, 'Well, I thought, at least it's a free meal.' He was a typical Yorkshireman; tough as steel.

At lunch, he was introduced by his hosts (who were making a James Bond movie) to the author, Ian Fleming. There was talk of the need to have a special car for Bond, so David pricked up his ears and said, 'I've got just the car for you. I'll supply two cars, plus mechanics, but I'll require certain percentages.' And with that, he went straight out and bought Aston Martin. Ford own that car company today, but I understand that David Brown's initials continue to appear in every car made.

This man never stopped thinking for one minute. He believed that in business you just keep going.

*Above* My best mate, Albie George, on Lake Pedder in 1970, on holidays. He caught a big trout, I wasn't so lucky that day.

*Below* Michael and Peter Kailis. 'Brotherly love: the next fish that gets on the lure, I'll let you pull it in!'

*Above* The proud owner on board the *Alice Eva* in Sugar Loaf Bay in 1985.

*Below* Hawkey and the boys (bodyguards) in 1985, in Exmouth Gulf, WA. Hawkey with the one that didn't get away, a red emperor.

*Above* The most boring dinner I ever went to. The night was saved by winemaker Murray Tyrrell (in the middle) who brought along a special wine for Malcolm Fraser and me.

*Right* Some of the gang on one of our WA fishing expeditions in 1985, including Richo (in hat) and Laurie Brereton standing behind me.

*Left* Len Evans and my good self at the Lords' Taverners' Ball, mid-1980s. (Courtesy Fairfax Photo Library)

*Below* 'The house' in Watsons Bay. (Courtesy Fairfax Photo Library)

Posing with some of our team at the fish market in 1985. Jimmy Doyle, my brother Michael's son, is to my right, and Robert, Robyn's husband, is to my left.

*Above* Doyles Restaurant at Watsons Bay, showing the outdoor seating.

*Below* Teaching Peter Junior to sharpen knives at the fish market. His brother Sean turned out to be the better fish cleaner. (Courtesy Fairfax Photo Library)

*Above* Jean and myself by the pool with daughter Rob, her son Christopher, Pete Junior, his wife Fiona, and their daughter, Alexandria. (I like to tell young kids that we have a shark in our pool). (Courtesy Fairfax Photo Library)

*Right* Jean and I playing host at our annual Boxing Day party, 1990. It's a fun day, although Jean and I work harder than the crews on the Sydney to Hobart race!

A reflective moment.

He and Paula came to Australia annually. They'd take a suite in a city hotel for a month, as David had a factory, David Brown Gears, in Wollongong.

Our finest hour together was in 1993 when, at the age of eighty-six, he designed a new yacht and had it built to his specifications in South Africa. David had bought a boatyard there, especially to build the boat of his dreams. The boat was of a catamaran style and very large, slightly bigger even than the ones which run across the harbour between Sydney and Manly. It had four staterooms and a master suite, and was very powerful.

He wanted it to do forty knots, so he invited me to stay in Monte Carlo to test it out. Originally, we were going to meet up in South Africa and sail her up, but David decided that was a waste of time. I suspect that in his heart he knew his days were numbered, so he had it delivered and we played with it in the Mediterranean. I took along a great mate of mine, Mickey Sergis, who's a fish buyer. Here we were, each with our own stateroom and a full crew to look after our needs, while the Browns were living ashore. The high life began.

We decided to cruise to St Tropez. It was as calm as could be, but the next day a terrible storm blew up, causing havoc all along the coast. I wouldn't have imagined they could get such big seas in the Mediterranean, and I got the shock of my life. Talking later to the local skippers, I found out that it can get as rough as, or worse than, anywhere else in the world.

All the luxury yachts were pretty much port-bound (you're talking about 100–120 footers) but David wanted to try the new boat out in the raging sea, even though the harbour master and everyone else told him he was mad. So off we set, the only ship out there.

Poor Mickey had gone green only seconds after we cleared the port and was hanging on to the stanchion down aft; meanwhile, Paula had locked herself in the master suite, as the ship was lurching like crazy. She was literally falling off waves, with the water smashing all over us – incredible.

I went up to the bridge and here's David with his captain, an Englishman. David said to me, 'What do you think?' and I told him, 'The way we're going, falling into these seas at half speed, this bloody thing's going to sink.'

He said, 'What do you think we should do?', and as I was thrown to the floor I called out, 'Open the bastard up; she's supposed to do forty knots. You designed her to do that, so one of two things will happen: either we'll go through it like butter – or we'll sink.'

With that, David said to his skipper, 'Open her up', and we took off like a rocket, slicing through these big, tall waves, much to the delight of David and myself. It was fantastic – we were doing thirty-eight knots, although I knew that if the seas kept battering us like they were, the boat could fall in half.

We got through it and had a remarkable day. When we returned to Monte Carlo we devoured a few thousand champagnes which didn't touch the sides. As usual, the Browns went back to their place in town that night, leaving Mickey and me to ourselves, with the chef and stewardesses to look after us. We sat on the deck looking over at the Sheik of something-or-other, who was moored alongside. The luxury of these boats was unbelievable; some had grand pianos – others even had Ferraris in the stern. Mickey, a Greek, turned to me and smiled, 'Now I know what Onassis had to go through.'

David came out to Sydney the next year and begged me to come back for the notification of the Olympic Games in Monte

Carlo. 'The boat is available to the Australian delegation, and I want you to come over.' Unfortunately David took gravely ill two weeks before the announcement, and died. When I heard the news, so many fine memories came flooding back: of my first time on his boat, and how beautiful girls, always topless, would cruise around the big yachts selling icecream from their dinghies. David had an eye for the ladies and he would insist they come aboard so he could closely inspect the various ice-creams. Then, as he did every morning, he'd swim around his boat. Even though David was English by birth, he was very much an Australian at heart.

My first encounter with June Allyson was a classic. I was interviewed by the *Australian Women's Weekly*, and asked who my pin-up girl was. I told them, 'I used to be madly in love with June Allyson, and I'm heartbroken, because I've never met her.' I added that even though my affections now also stretch out to Kim Basinger, I will always adore June.

I never thought any more about it until one winter's day, I was upstairs in the office over the restaurant when one of the staff came up and said, 'There's a lady downstairs who wants to see you.' Down I go, and here's this small lady rugged up in a scarf and a beanie. I said, 'Yes?', and in a husky voice she purrs, 'I don't believe you love me any more.' I just looked at her, and she took off the dark glasses and it was June Allyson. I was flabbergasted.

She had come out on a cruise ship, and by chance had picked up an old *Women's Weekly*, read the story and decided to come and meet me. I took her around the harbour in my boat.

I must admit I still worship her. And I've given Kim Basinger the flick. At least until she turns up in the flesh.

Michael Parkinson is a funny man, as is Dave Allen. In fact, Dave came up with one of the all-time brilliant lines during an outing on my boat. I had a big crowd, including Dave, Lynne Redgrave, her husband John and their two obnoxious children. We'd cruised over to Quarantine Bay, which is a dicey place to swim, yet despite my warning, Lynne's kids jumped in. I called out, 'Don't swim in there,' and they yelled back, 'Oh, yeah', giving me cheek. Dave Allen looked over the side of the boat as they swam and said, 'There's never a shark around when you want one.'

Pick a name and I've probably met them: Princess Anne, Michael Caine, Liberace, Tommy Steele, Elton John many a time, and Charlton Heston, who's about the only one who looks as big as he does on screen. A star I became extremely fond of was horror actor, Vincent Price. I loved him greatly. The funny thing was that he always ate with his back to the view. He'd say, 'I come here for the fish; not the view.'

Lee Marvin was a valued customer, but oh, the way he used to iron himself out – he'd end up sliding off his chair and under the table. In 1979, John Travolta visited, at the height of Travolta mania, and I was asked to take him out on my boat. I said, 'Certainly', and it was arranged that I would collect him from the Man o' War Steps at the Opera House. As I pulled in, a strange-looking character approached me; I thought he was peculiar. It was a sunny day and he was wearing a long trench-coat with the collar turned up. 'I'm Mr Travolta's bodyguard,' he said, showing me his revolver. I instantly christened him Columbo. I took my teenage daughter Sharon along, who cornered John Travolta and told him she was in love with him. I'm not sure what *he* made of it, but I thought it was a scream.

I once enjoyed sharing a hazy harbour cruise with Ringo Starr and his sexy wife, Barbara Bach, although I had to laugh when we got back to the restaurant. Ringo looked at the crowd still there at the end of lunch and said, 'I can't walk through that lot – they'll mob me.' I grabbed him and Barbara and told them, 'Well, we'll go in the back way, through the kitchen.' As we walked into the kitchen, I heard one of the staff say to another, 'Who's he?'

A fine singer from an earlier generation was Nelson Eddy, who was in the line one night when Mum spotted him. She sidled up and said, 'If you'll sing "Rose Marie" [his signature tune] with me, I'll allow you to jump the queue.' They did a fine duet and Alice gave him a table straight away.

Not so fortunate was the King of Norway, who queued up; this was prior to the days when we began taking bookings. One of the people from the Norwegian Embassy came up to the waiter and said, 'We've got the King here', to which the waiter replied, 'So what? He'll have to stay in line like everyone else.'

Alice was at her best the night a visiting Yank, waiting impatiently in the queue, had a go at her. 'Do you know who I am? I'm the head of Kelloggs.' Alice shrugged, 'Sorry, you still can't have a table before it's your turn.' The bloke stormed off, saying, 'Well, you know what you can do with your restaurant.' But Alice had the last word, 'And you know what you can do with your Corn Flakes – and don't forget the banana.'

Many local stars have been regulars, going right back to the quintessential Aussie actor, Chips Rafferty. He was a real fish and chips man, and when he'd just done a film and was in the money, he'd always order prawns. It was easy to tell if Chips was in the money.

Of all the great Australians who have graced our doors, my all-time pick is Dawn Fraser. She's a marvellous human being and a fine ambassador; in any other country, if someone had achieved what she has achieved, they'd have built a statue to her a long time ago.

The world was starting to open up for me, and I went to France for the second time in the early 1980s. Because Doyles was one of the biggest sellers of champagne, I was invited by several of the champagne houses to stay with them in Epernay and Rheims. I had the time of my life, despite my frequent social gaffes. You can take the boy out of Watsons Bay... I was entertained by the Bollinger family, who still retain a firm control of their product and live in a magnificent chateau. Then I went on to stop with the Möet et Chandon people at their chateau, where my room was about as big as my house. And the bath! I could have emptied about four dams to fill it up.

If I had stayed more than two days, I would have ended up in an alcoholic ward somewhere to dry out. Champagne morning, noon and night, in fact I was itching to get into the village for a beer. Champagne's a magic drop, but if you're not born to it, there's a point at which you long for a stubbie.

I stopped in London on the same trip, at a chic hotel called The Capitol, in Basil Street. It's right near Harrods, and I'm a Harrods fan. The first two mornings, I got there at half an hour before they open, and was picked up by the security people wondering what I was doing. I explained, and they gave me a tour of the workings of Harrods.

Another great bloke I know through the business is Sir Alistair McAlpine, this portly Englishman of thirty or thirty-five, who was coming into Rose Bay on a daily basis at one stage. He told me of his plan to build Sydney's Inter-Continental Hotel, which he did. From there he went to Perth and later onto Broome. I visited him up there on several occasions and had the most fantastic fun. The trip to end all trips was the one that began when Alistair, by now a Lord, flew down to Exmouth to collect me and the West's Mr Fish, Michael Kailis.

We got on board, with me knowing that Alistair only ever drank Dom Perignon or Grange Hermitage, although at this time, he was off the grog. His butler said, 'Would you care for some Dom Perignon?' Michael, who was not a small plane flyer, replied, 'I'll pass', but I said, 'Sure.' I figured that if the plane crashes into crocodile-infested waters, it's better to go down with a stomach full of Dom Perignon than nothing.

Alistair told us, 'I won't be having any; my butler is making me tea.' Then he turned to Michael. 'Are you sure you won't have a champagne? No? Well, that's rather a pity, because it's a two-hour flight, and the loo is broken. I'm counting on a few empty Dom bottles so we have something to pee into.' A bit later, Michael gave in and had a drink, and there wasn't much left when we landed, as I'd given it a heck of a polish. I disembarked carrying a champagne bottle full of pee!

We stayed at his new development, the Cable Beach Club. The next night we were invited to dine at Alistair's place, an old prawning master's house, in the heart of Broome. It had a verandah all the way around and pretty shutters on the windows. The focal point was a big yard, with a mango tree growing in the centre and a carpet of crushed pearl shells on the ground. He'd made additions at the back and there was also a guest cottage, where Sidney Nolan was staying on a painting trip.

As we walked in, at dusk, we saw that a long trestle table had been laid with exquisite crystal, silver and china. We were introduced to the other guests, who included Lord Wedgwood, Margaret Thatcher's first secretary, the secretary's private secretary, and Prince Peter of Yugoslavia, with his aristocratic Greek-born wife.

When we sat down in the director's chairs, I noticed a three-legged cattle dog, plus three other dogs, playing around the table. Alistair was a great believer that if dogs wandered in, you didn't kick 'em out.

It was an extraordinarily beautiful tropical evening, with Dom Perignon and Grange flowing like water. The food was cooked by a leading chef, flown in from somewhere or other. I was getting pretty fuzzy trying to remember names, which has never been my strong point. It's usually either 'Mate' or 'Love'.

I didn't know who King Peter of Yugoslavia was, and I got Michael Kailis, who was sitting next to the king's wife, to ask her out loud, 'Peter Doyle wants to know what your old man does for a living?' She looked embarrassed, and said, 'He's a king.' Michael relayed all of this to me, then he turned back to her and said, 'Peter wants to know if your husband is any relation to George King in Exmouth?' The King and I. Not bad going for the kid who had the Barracks' paper round all those years ago!

As the night progressed (if that's the word), Michael

became very thick with the prince and his missus. Michael was saying what a terrible thing it was that they had lost their land and everything, so we decided we'd go and get one of the fishing trawlers and set sail to claim back what was rightfully theirs. I was all for it and so was Michael, and we had to be restrained by the few sober ones at the table. Next morning, I wished I had the rights to manufacture Panadol.

When you rub shoulders with the rich and famous, you end up refelecting on your own life, and wonder how you got there. At times you ask yourself , 'Is it all a dream? Is it going to stop tomorrow?' But you realise that you didn't force your way in, they invited you, that they respect you because you got there by hard work. And you remember what you've known all along, deep down: that you've got just as much right as any of them to be there.

# CHAPTER 13
## THE QUEEN AND I, AND MUM CAME TOO

Back home, the business was going really well, and we were getting busier and busier. With this came the double-edged sword of expansion. I often said to my brothers, 'I don't think we'll ever see the day when we actually have a pool of money; we always seem to be paying out.' We were constantly at the mercy of the banks, what with remodelling the place on the beach, which involved buying the adjoining property, taking over the lease of the Watsons Bay Hotel, as well as redoing our restaurant on the wharf.

We four sons all had families, and we would like to have been able to put away a nest egg for our children, instead of depending on the banks, but if you want to expand, that's the way it has to be. When we did get the odd quid, the temptation was to splurge – I know I did. My wild extravagance was lashing out on a Jaguar with customised number plates, which had just come in, so I chose FISHO. I guess it was an act of bravado, to show that a fisherman could own a Jag.

But what a dog of a car it was; as soon as it got hot, it'd fade out. It just couldn't stand the Australian heat. Sensibly, I kept my ute, reserving the Jag as a symbol, something to drive when I got dressed up to go to a party. It had its uses though; I found that if I drove into one of the flash hotels, the doorman looked after me better than if I arrived in the ute. I've done both, and believe me, it works.

It was at about this time that John and Tim decided to go out to do their own thing. Johnny had an affinity with the land – we all did, going right back to the Crookwell days – and took up a property out west, at Yeovil. Tim already had a sheep property at Crookwell, and they both became full-time farmers. It's the old saying about how the sailor comes home from the sea to build a garden.

It was a blow to lose them, and it also meant that Mick, me and Mum and Dad had to manage the extra workload. We weren't big on employing managers, partly because we expected too much of them – and we'd ask them to work as hard as us. And being tough buggers, we didn't want to pay huge wages.

I was doing the buying at the fish market and then rushing back to cook at Rose Bay. There was barely a spare second to scratch myself. Our restaurants were always packed out – but public holidays were even more frantic. On New Year's Day 1978 I was held up at gunpoint at the Pier.

We had had eight hundred customers through, and come evening, there was only Bobby the cleaner and myself left in the place. I was counting the takings and putting them in a nightsafe wallet. There was over $6000 in cash. When I was done, I stashed the wallet into an old pair of shorts near the counter. Bobby was hosing down the kitchen, and as I walked to the door, carrying the money, I looked out and noticed a car parked outside, out of which climbed two men – one of whom had a rifle. They hadn't seen me, because of the darkness inside, so I raced back in, yelling to Bobby to lock the back door. Next I grabbed the kitchen phone and called the Rose Bay Police, grateful that we had their number up on the wall. I finally got through, only to be told, 'Rose Bay Police; hold the line.'

I'm screaming out, 'Hold up! Hold up!' and next thing I know there's a gun in the back of my neck, and I'm told in no uncertain terms to drop the phone. I'd planted the money on a shelf on my sprint to the phone, so when they said, 'Give us the money', I told them, 'The money's gone.' One of them growled at me, 'Bullshit it's gone', and with that, went straight to the shelf and my hiding place. Immediately I knew it was an inside job.

They laid Bobby and me on the floor, face down, with the water still running – I thought we were going to drown in the fish water. The one with the gun announced firmly, 'If you move, I'll blow your fuckin' head off.' They made a bolt for it and got away. I picked up the phone, which I had deliberately left swinging, and the officer said, 'What do you want?' I sighed, 'I wanted bloody help – but it's too late now.'

The robbers were eventually caught, and we found out that they were in cohoots with a policeman. That was the second time I've been held up by gunmen. I'm getting a bit worried, waiting for the third attack.

Ah, the joys of selling fish and chips in the city.

In 1975, I decided that I'd like to return to Watsons Bay, to live, as a rambling house I'd admired all my life had come on the market. It's the oldest dwelling in the Bay, and at that stage, was surrounded by large trees and a high fence, so you wouldn't even have known it was there. I delivered papers to this house as a boy, which was almost my undoing on one occasion. I was on my rounds, and I lent out the back of the car and hit my head on a telegraph pole outside this house. The ambulance was called, and as I lay, covered in blood, waiting for it to arrive, the lady came out the front, and I heard her say, 'Is he dead?'

And now the old place was up for sale. As it happened, Jean was overseas on her first big trip; not wanting to miss out, I went ahead and bought it. But boy, did it need some restoring – a prospect which was doubly daunting, considering we had broken our backs working on Maroubra.

The morning of Jean's return arrived, and me and the five kids were waiting for her to clear Customs. Before I could say a thing, they yelled in unison, 'Dad's bought a new house.' Jean's eyes lit up. 'That's marvellous – a new house; that means it won't need anything done to it.' I wasn't the most popular husband in the world when she saw it.

We were taking on a big job, but for me, that was a small price to pay for coming back to my roots, and I wanted our children to have the same experiences I had had while they could. It wasn't long before Robyn left home to go teaching in Griffith, in the Riverina district of New South Wales, and Gayle was due to leave for overseas shortly after, to do a postgraduate nursing course.

The line-up at home may have been shrinking, but professionally, the Doyles were once again looking at expanding. The time had come to let out the seams of the original restaurant on the beach. Naturally enough, the authorities were determined to make it as difficult as possible for us. For starters, there was our ongoing battle with Woollahra Council over outdoor seating.

I'm nothing if not a fighter, and I had made an appointment to see the then-Premier, Neville Wran, whom I liked instantly. He said to me, 'I've been reading how you're having a few problems. Come over here to the window, I want to show you something. See the Botanic Gardens there? See the fence running around it? I decided it would be a good idea if people could come into town and hang paintings on the rails, and others could sell icecreams and hot dogs, or whatever, around it. I put the proposition up to the Trustees of the Gardens, and they said it was not allowed.' I asked the Premier what he did next and he smiled. 'I invited them for morning tea, to meet their new Chairman – me. I told them, "Now your problem of seating on the footpath will be looked after".' And of course the Labor Government did bring in the law that permits sitting on the footpath. You had to pay rent, but what's wrong with that?

Another battle we had was over Sunday drinking, which hit us hard when we leased the pub. What you had to do to get a drink was go twenty-odd miles and sign yourself in at a hotel as a traveller. It didn't matter how drunk you got, driving back from, say, Camden or Liverpool, killing as many as you wanted on the road, as long as you got drunk a certain number of miles from your home.

The churches no doubt had an influence over the 'never on Sunday' approach to living we were saddled with, including no movies or fresh bread. In the 1960s, you couldn't sell a can of baked beans out of a small grocery store after 6 pm at which time they had to put up the shutters, and you could then only buy day-old bread and other essentials.

It was crazy. Australia was so downtrodden, controlled by the churches and parliamentarians, who couldn't see further than their hands. Then there were the unions, whom we had to thank for the 'No weekend shopping after Saturday afternoon' law. This meant that if your roof blew off on a Sunday, you couldn't buy any nails to nail it back on again.

Our eventual triumph with the pub came about this way: we began having a smorgasbord in the dining room of a Sunday, and drinks could be served with the meal. After a while, Tim and Dad said, 'Why don't we turn the beer garden into a dining room?' This idea was most logical, yet when we put the proposition up to the Licensing Court the police, as usual, objected. We took the matter to the full Licensing Bench, which ruled in our favour. After all, what is a dining room but a place to eat? As a result, Sunday drinking came in through this amendment to the Act, and within weeks of our win in 1979, most hotels were on the bandwagon. The AHA had spent millions on their campaign, but they gave us nothing towards the cost of our successful court case.

We leased the Tooheys pub for three years in the 1970s from Tooheys, the brewery giant, and every time we made some improvement, the rent went up. Several of our offers to buy the freehold were unsuccessful, so we decided, for now, to get out of the hotel business. Tim was running the pub, and it was after we made our decision not to renew the lease that he left for a life in the country. The hotel was next bought by the Bond Corporation.

One windy day, Alan Bond came to see me, and in a fairly gruff voice asked, 'Which Doyle are you?' I replied, 'Peter Doyle.' He nodded, 'I just want you to know I've bought the pub next door and I'm going to give you a bit of opposition in the dining room.' 'That's fine,' I said, 'I wish you well, but you won't be any opposition to us.'

I next saw him several years later, after he'd gone through various battles. He was sitting outside the then Australian Airlines terminal, and I went up and said, 'You don't know me.

My name's Peter Doyle and I just want you to know that I bought the pub you used to own at Watsons Bay.' I could have been sarcastic and said, 'I was right when I told you that you weren't going to be any opposition to us', but I didn't. When a man's down and out, you don't want to kick him to death.

That was 1992, and we paid in excess of $6 million dollars for the hotel; brother John became licensee. I had suggested to brother Mick we should buy it when it became available, and he said, 'Back into debt again; we never seem to be out of it. Sooner or later, there must be light at the end of the tunnel.' I stressed my point. 'We've got to buy it; that way we'll have a toehold that will give us a huge chunk of the beachfront.'

Before this happened, John had left his farm and returned to the city, where he had opened up his own restaurant called The Fish King, in King Street. There was a bit of aggro between him and the rest of us, but it wasn't heavy enough to stop us helping him with product. After all, family is family and blood is thicker than water at any stage of the game. Others have found our close bond too good to be true at times, but I can assure you, this is how it is. The building where John had his restaurant was eventually demolished and he and his family moved to Tweed Heads to start a fish place there. Then when we bought the pub, we invited John back in with us, because we always felt the business was Mum and Dad and the four sons.

Tim's time on the land was ruined by the terrible drought of the 1980s; it had a devastating effect and wiped him out. Like so many others, he just walked off his property. He then opened a fish shop at Gosford, an hour north of Sydney, but fortunately, we were able to coax him back into the business to manage our new operation at Circular Quay, which opened in 1988. We'd taken up a lease there for redevelopment of the old rope locker at the Overseas Terminal. It became Doyles at the Quay.

In 1980, after the prolonged fight with the Council on our proposed expansion at Watsons Bay, we had bought the boatshed next door and the net shed alongside that. The court battle almost broke us, but we were finally allowed to extend the restaurant site. We picked an ace builder – 18-foot sailing champion, Cliffie Monkhouse. I started to imagine that he was building a boat and not a restaurant, as the place has very nautical lines. We all agreed we didn't like the new modern style of architecture bobbing up everywhere, so we felt that Doyles on the Beach should be inspired by what our grandfather had built all those years earlier. We went for iron lace and heavy timbers, and the result fits into the landscape beautifully.

Once completed, we were able to triple our seating to four hundred, which meant that by turning over the tables once, we could turn over eight hundred people at each meal. (There were many occasions when we could have done with an extra four hundred seats.) The Premier, Neville Wran, did the official honours in 1982, and you'd think we'd then be off and running, with no looking back, but that Doyle luck played yet another trick on us ... we desperately needed cashflow to start repaying the loan, but the week we opened, the drought that had forced Tim off the land came to an end. It never stopped raining.

At one stage, we had over twenty-five wet weekends in a row and it's the closest we ever came to going out the back door. Banks don't have any sympathy; they want not only your blood, but your personal property too. We had laid everything on the line, and we only hung on by the skin of our teeth.

Doyles went on to win numerous overseas awards as the best restaurant in the world. We've had more publicity internationally than we have had here – not that we ever wanted to be known for anything other than selling fresh fish and chips. We're a nation of terrible knockers: we knock anyone who battles up, and I don't know what the psychologists would make of it. And as for the food critics! For some reason they single us out at Doyles – especially the ones who go overseas and eat in three-star establishments in France. They don't take into account that these restaurants seat no more than forty or fifty people, that their menu might be only three set courses and that they have fifteen or sixteen staff in the kitchen, and as many out front. They charge like wounded bulls (if you pay by credit card, the card melts). These critics come back to Australia and judge us, who seat four hundred twice over, on what one of these fifty-seat restaurants is doing.

I've never minded being judged, but let it be by critics who have actually done what I've done – cooked the same way and faced up to the same problems of a big restaurant. How many of them have done that? I can name one, Malcolm Weatherup, who had a restaurant in Surry Hills, which went broke within a matter of months.

I'm now seeing that some restaurants are buying the cheaper seafood lines that we once shovelled overboard; we thought they were inedible, but as my old dad says, 'You can cover a turd with sauce and people will eat it and think it's marvellous.'

We've grown into the biggest seafood restaurant in Australia, and we have one of the biggest liquor licences. Between our restaurants and the pub, we'd serve in excess of five thousand meals a week. We've employed many married women in the lunch trade, and we've watched their kids grow up. Over the years we've also been a matrimonial agency.

A lot of the staff have come to me for advice, particularly in the early days with the Portuguese, who had problems with language, immigration and banking. I've been godfather to some of these children – it's our style to bring people into the family. And it's been our style to let our staff see us work hard because if you're there with sweat pouring off you and under tremendous pressure with customers screaming, they'll work hard too. But if you're someone who says to the staff, 'The fish are biting' or 'I'm off to golf, goodbye', then that's what will happen to your business – goodbye.

Mum had to give up being front of house by the time she was sixty-five, but like any old warhorse, she still rises to the occasion and visits the restaurants as often as she can. She sweeps through majestically, asking everybody how they're doing and remembering names and faces, flogging her cookbook, which, after the Bible, is the only book in the world as far as she's concerned. She's right to be proud: it's into its seventh reprint and Dad is the best salesman she could possibly have. He regularly checks with the restaurants to make sure they're not short of books; if they are, then he delivers them.

At almost eighty-eight, Jack leads a busy life, working in the office every day. And God help anyone who's short of money on the dockets; they're in big trouble. When he and Mum gave up the reins about twenty years ago, they did it so graciously. There was no 'You'll take over now'; they simply handed over the deeds to their sons. We still ask their advice on a new project; they're never isolated, although we don't draw them in on money problems (we prefer to put on a brave face in that department).

Mum more than anyone has been the great leveller in my life; with her around, I'll never get a big head. It takes a lot to impress Alice, but I have to say that, being the diehard royalist she is, I did win a few points by introducing her to the Queen, and giving her the opportunity to meet Charles and Di. I occasionally receive invitations from government bodies to meet visiting royals and other dignitaries, and on the occasion I was due to attend a reception for the Prince and Princess of Wales, Jean and I were unable to make it, so I asked Mum and Dad to represent us.

Alice arrived, carrying a copy of her trusty cookbook, signed for Charles. He stopped right in front of her, so Alice grabbed him, gave him the book, with instructions that the recipes can be converted for English fish. She added, 'If you have any trouble, just give me a call and I'll set you straight.'

She came back very happy, having met the future King. You have to understand that she has always had a picture of the Queen and her corgis hanging in the restaurant. Never the Queen and the Duke. She was shattered when she learnt of my republican leanings.

In February 1992, when I was still Chairman of the National Maritime Museum, I had the opportunity to receive the Queen and the Duke, and I wangled it so my parents and grandchildren could be there as well. My granddaughter, Kimberley, had been made a lovely dress, and was practising curtseying as we came around the corner. I had placed Mum and Dad right next to Kimberley, who must have done about two hundred and ten curtsies; she was going up and down like a yo-yo. The Duke, who had been watching her, said, 'Isn't she getting tired yet?' I introduced Mum and Dad, and Mum stepped forward and said to the Queen, 'I've got something for you, my cookbook. I gave a copy to Charlie when he was last here, and I'd like to know if he's tried any of the recipes.'

The Queen was understandably taken aback, and with that, her lady-in-waiting moved in to take the book – but Alice was too quick for her. She said, pressing the gift into Her Majesty's arms, 'No, it's not for you – it's for the Queen.'

She wasn't done yet. 'And another thing – if you have trouble with any of the recipes, just give me a ring. I told Charlie the same thing. And I think you're gorgeous,' she told the Queen, then turning to Dad, 'I'm always talking about her, aren't I, Jack? By the way, this is my husband, Jack.'

The Queen got the message loud and clear, because for the rest of the tour of the Museum, I saw that she had it tucked firmly under her arm. Maybe she was terrified of bumping into Alice later at the luncheon.

Alice Doyle is an unusual mixture of being soft and homey, yet possessing a powerful personality that leaves its mark on all who meet her. Every day, she bakes cakes for Jack to bring in for morning tea in the office. That's one side. On the other, she still gives her boys and the grandchildren lectures on where we're going wrong. Her mind is as sharp as the day she was born.

I hope she's around for a long while to keep giving us boys a dressing down. I think that at times we all need it.

## Alice Doyle's Tips on How to Get Kids to Eat Fish

As mother of four, grandmother of twenty and great-grandmother of fifteen, I have some experience at this, and my secret weapon is to batter and fry cocktail-sized pieces of fish and wrap each serving up in butcher paper – just like they'd get it from a fish shop, and let them eat it anywhere they want – even in front of their computer. Needless to say, add lashings of tomato sauce.

These days, kids are so occupied with computers, and various other electronic games, in their bedrooms, and I think it's unrealistic to expect the whole family to sit down together every meal time. So take the food to them.

I suggest cutting up a big jewfish – that's the best of the lot for this purpose, although mullet's fine too and it's cheap. My other tip is to say, 'If you eat all the fish, you can have ice-cream with flavouring on it afterwards.'

Do whatever it takes to get them to eat fish – it's so healthy. My mother, who lived to be eighty-four, ate fish every day and she was hardly ever sick.

Most kids love chips, although myself, I'm addicted to Smith's Crisps. But for chips at home, parboil your Desiree potatoes, dry them, cut them up then deep-fry in a mixture of butter and peanut oil. I know it's not fashionable to cook with butter, but I find they taste wonderful when done this way. Use a deep-fryer if you can; every home should have one, and they do cocktail fish pieces beautifully.

# CHAPTER 14
## GONE FISHIN'

I can live without the rich and famous, but I can't live without the sea, its smell and everything that comes out of it. I need to hear the sound of waves pounding on the beach. I still go to sea and get the same charge out of it, but my companions now come from all walks – politicians included.

The people around me have changed; it would be ridiculous to pretend that wasn't so. From my mid-fifties on, I got heavily caught up with duties that took me even further away from the simple life, such as heading the National Maritime Museum, bringing my dream of the new Sydney Fish Market to fruition and being named NSW's Father of the Year in 1990. I must admit that when the blokes at the fish market told me I'd won, I figured they must have been joking.

The first prime minister to eat at Doyles was Harold Holt, back in the 1960s. He and some of his staffers spent a pleasant lunch at the Bay, made unforgettable by the PM's brush with a few ladies of the night. As Holt was leaving, two workers from a certain Kings Cross establishment noticed half a bottle of wine was being left behind. One of them grabbed Holt by the arm and asked whether she could have it. Holt graciously went back and got the bottle to give her. In return, one of the ladies insisted the Prime Minister accept her business card, promising that if he ever dropped in, she'd make sure he had a good time.

'D'you know,' she remarked to me an hour later, 'I'm sure I've seen that bloke somewhere before.'

Despite being fond of that story about the then-Liberal leader, I have to say that I've always had a leaning towards Labor politicians. In the 1970s, I got to know the Labor Cabinet Minister, the late Mick Young, and we clicked straightaway. Then, through Mick, I met Graham Richardson and Laurie Brereton, whom I instantly felt comfortable with.

One day, Laurie and Richo brought Hawkey out fishing on the *Alice Eva*. He was already Prime Minister, and seemed to enjoy the relaxing outing, where he could just be himself. Our next expedition took us out to sea, and I could see straightaway what an aggressive fisherman Hawkey was; competitive and very good, whereas Richo couldn't catch a goldfish in a glass bowl.

As time went on, Bob and Hazel became important to our family. Jean and I went to Kirribilli House on many occasions, sometimes listening to Hazel play the piano. Each New Year's Eve, Jack and Alice would watch the fireworks with the Hawkes from Kirribilli.

My mateship with Hawkey was cemented when we included him in an annual adventure a group of us had started up around 1980, fishing off the north coast of Western Australia. First we went up to Carnarvon, six hundred miles north of Perth, to fish off the *Julie Ken*, owned by Charlie Firns and his son Ken. Charlie had said, 'You haven't seen fishing until you've seen it up this way', and he was right.

One day we caught a thousand kilos of fish in an hour, and we were bringing in three schnapper at a time on the line. Before the fishing became regulated, we'd steam for four hours out from Carnarvon to get to the breeding grounds. Ninety per cent of what we caught was schnapper, which only come in for eight weeks a year.

My introduction to this *Boys' Own* adventure was through my friend of thirty years, Michael Kailis. He and his wife, Sophie, and their whole family are the most generous human beings. Michael and his brothers, Peter and Theo, when I was appointed Chairman of the Maritime Museum in 1991, had at a great cost designed and made a coat of arms for me, which hangs there today.

We fished at Carnarvon for four years, and Laurie Brereton was the first of the visitors to join us. After that, we ventured further north to Exmouth, to fish off a boat owned by charter operator George King. Hawkey started coming along too.We all stayed at a motel owned by George, designed to withstand the typhoons. There were two penthouses, each with two bedrooms. Hawkey and his private secretary would be in the first penthouse and me and Michael Kailis would be in the second. The rest of the Prime Minister's staff bunked down in a nearby chalet. It was all terribly casual. We'd have breakfast early, then go down to the local bakery at 6 am. We'd buy four dozen bread rolls and a few cooked chooks. They also sold lamingtons, and we have been known to buy a whole tray to take out on the boat.

There was a day when the weather was too rough to go to sea, so we decided to take the food and have a picnic at a remote beach George King knew of, that could only be reached by four-wheel drive. When we arrived, we noticed a couple of young girls sunbaking further along the sand. They quickly put their tops on, and we left them alone. Then later in the morning, one of our lot, just for a laugh, asked them if they recognised Michael Kailis. They shook their heads, so the bloke said, 'He's the king of fishing – he can get you anything you want.' They looked only slightly impressed when Michael chimed in, 'If you believe that, you'd believe that scrawny little feller over there is Bob Hawke.' They glanced over at Hawkey and one said, 'Gawd, it looks like him.' Kailis grinned, 'Yeah, everyone tells him that.'

Michael thought Hawkey hadn't heard him, but he had, and he came over, pretending to be annoyed. 'One of these days, Kailis, somewhere, sometime, you're going to need a licence. Don't bother applying.'

This was back when Bob said he wasn't drinking, and for the record, I can tell you he never touched a drop. In fact, he was on a real health kick, starting off with uncooked muesli. Just once he weakened, devouring a plate of my porridge, saying first, 'Don't tell Hazel.'

What is it about men together, without women? We all got on so well. The companionship experienced on these excursions will stay with me forever.

Another member of our crazy band was Len Evans, who, being an excellent cook, treated us to some fine meals. And therein lies a sorry tale of a bouillabaisse gone horribly wrong.

Len announced he was to make this interesting seafood dish which originated in Marseilles. He had brought the special ingredients from Sydney, and set about throwing himself into the project with typcial Evans enthusiasm. He started making the soup one afternoon, and during a marathon cardplaying session with Michael Kailis that went on until 5 am, he kept getting up to do something extra to this precious concoction. After a brief sleep, he was up before the rest of us, tending to the next stage, singing 'Oh, What a Beautiful Morning' at the top of his lungs, with us screaming out, 'Shut up!'

Len finally strained the bouillabaisse, putting it in another saucepan on the stove. 'We'll leave it to set,' he said, satisfied with the result. 'I'll add the scallops when we come back this afternoon; it will be second to none.' Well, you wouldn't want to know ... when we got back from fishing, he turned to Michael and said sharply, 'Kailis, what have you done with the soup?' Michael looked as puzzled as Len, 'I haven't touched it.' After much checking, we found out the awful truth: the housemaid had thought it was dirty water and thrown it out.

Len was not impressed.

Every year, there was no shortage of not-too-serious arguments, either over who cooked the best meal or, later in the evening, when the rest of us would get stuck into Hawkey, Richo and Laurie, telling them how to run the bloody country.

Richo is the best politician in living memory, largely because, in my experience, he always keeps his word. He's a great man and has this country at heart. Keating? I've got a certain amount of regard for him, because of his ability to stay cool. He's a bloody aggressive man behind the helm of a boat – I can tell you that. Once he ran me up onto a sandbank and he never flinched. I was very impressed with that. And then there's Laurie Brereton. He's the most maligned man in the country, yet he'd be my choice for prime minister. Why? Because he's strong, and he takes on hard jobs that no one else will touch, and does them well.

I'm no Rhodes Scholar, that's for sure, but I figure that at sixty-plus, I'm allowed an opinon or two on the state of the nation, so here goes:

- If I were prime minister, the first thing I'd do is bring in a rule that said if politicians lied, there would be no rewards. We can't keep having this system where children see that lying pays off.
- I'd abolish the Family Law Act, so that kids can no longer be given money to leave home.
- I'm pro republic – much to the disgust of my mother. I just happen to think the time has come, and we need to stand up and be counted.
- The older I get, the more convinced I am that our youngsters need discipline in their lives.
- Before it's too late, kids must be made aware of the devastation brought upon us by various kinds of pollution. I cry when I think of the state of our rivers, creeks and lagoons. Let the Federal Government set up a Green Army. Like National Service, it would be compulsory for kids, say at the ages fourteen or fifteen, to do a three-month stint. This opportunity would see them travelling around, inspecting the damage, and then helping to clean up the mess. No guns, just shovels, as young boys and girls make a difference to our national heritage, as well as working on their own self-discipline.

Anyhow, for what they're worth, these are a few of the thoughts I have tossed into the ring when I've been out on the high seas with Hawkey, Richo and co.

If you think politicians sound like an outrageous lot to go fishing with en masse, you should try cricketers. I'm a big fan of the game, and like nothing more than taking the lads out on the harbour on the *Alice Eva*, then drifting into Watsons Bay about lunchtime, where we party on until all hours.

Funny thing, but I've noticed that the next day, the English side never seems to do any good. I became known as the secret weapon for the Aussies, so the Poms tell me they're now banned from having any contact with me on their days off.

I'm proud to say I've won more matches for our side than anyone can count, the only trouble is that I'm always too sick myself to watch them!

## Len Evans's Western Australian Pot Luck

This is my rough and ready version of bouillabaisse, as thrown together on the annual fishing trips to Carnarvon and Exmouth, with Doyley and the others.

I got by using whatever was there in the kitchen, which was often not a lot.

Chuck into a big pot a pile of fish heads and bones, shells, etc., along with a large onion, a large ox-heart tomato and a good slurp of the best white wine you have available. Cover, bring to the boil and then simmer for three or four hours – which in my case, was just long enough for a few noisy hands of cards.

Next, strain the liquid and then leave it to cool overnight. In the morning, scoop out the precious jelly that has formed on the top and keep it until you are ready to repeat the procedure, this time adding the jelly from the previous day, so the end result is more concentrated.

Do this a third time, then after simmering this lot of bones and shells, strain again. Into the reduced triple-concentrate stock, toss whatever seafood you have, such as fish, prawns, squid, mussels (the mussels go in last as they cook quicker), and another slurp of wine. Boil rapidly for ten minutes, without totally covering the seafood with liquid.

As I said, this is a rough version, but it goes down well after a hard day's fishing, especially when served with crusty bread and a bottle of whatever's handy.

I'd like to finish off by telling you something funny that happened one night when a local fisherman called in and shared a bowl of this soup with us. 'Jesus Christ,' he said, 'This is bloody good. Who made it?' They all pointed at me.

We realised he must have thought I was the paid cook, because he lent over and asked if I'd consider working for him next season. 'How much do you earn here?' he asked. 'Sixty dollars a day,' I told him, which nearly gave him a heart attack.

'Christ, you'll need to give a hand with the nets for that!'

# CHAPTER 15
## THE COUNTRY SQUIRE

I've lived every second of every hour of every day, all too aware that we are only here for a limited amount of time and that we should try to achieve something. My thirst and hunger for knowledge increased as I got older. I was terribly busy doing the markets, coming back to the restaurant and cooking, participating on committees, and talking to the media, who had turned me into an expert on the fisheries scene.

My life was complicated and sophisticated but I still had a craving to be close to the land. This feeling – that I had to grow things – was as basic to me as the need to eat. From the late 1970s, Len Evans was inviting me up to the Hunter Valley, where he was a prominent figure. I had developed a taste for wines, and in Evans's company, I had many a night that caused me to wake up the next morning wishing I had never *heard* of wine. I fear I was not a great pupil; the only thing I knew for sure was that if you drink cardboard, you end up like cardboard the following day.

In my travels around Australia buying seafood, I'd try to organise a day in the wineries when in South Australia or Western Australia; hard work became a fun trip after a while. It also helped to have a licensed restaurant as I was very well looked after by the wineries when I called in.

Eventually, I decided I wouldn't mind growing some grapes in the Hunter, trying my hand at what I thought looked like an easy job. I purchased a vacant plot and got Tyrrells to plant eight acres of chardonnay grapes for me. I'd then go up and work among the vines, learning as much as I could.

I liked the spot, yet I never ached to be there when I was back in Sydney – and that's the acid test. Then in 1985, I was notified that there was a beautiful piece of land being sold behind McWilliams, on Mount View. A friend had described it as the best block in the Hunter. That, plus the lovely photographs I saw, were enough for me. I only heard about it on the Wednesday and, sight unseen, went to the auction that same day and bought it. A hundred acres of virgin land. I got it for $120,000, which was so cheap that even if I did nothing more than keep mountain goats on it, I couldn't lose on the deal.

I set sail to see what I owned, figuring that now I was a rich landowner, I should drive up in the Jag. Naturally it broke down halfway and I had to get it towed into the town of Cessnock, so I didn't make it up until the next day. When I arrived, there was only a rough track – highly unsuitable for Jaguars – my car sighed and wouldn't go any further, so I had to walk up on foot.

I fell in love instantly, as I climbed to where I knew straightaway I would build our house. The sun was shining, the bellbirds were deafening, and the lantana and blackberries abounded. Scattered around were a few grazing cows. I couldn't leave for hours; I sat there, delighted.

Soon after, I brought Jean up and we walked around the whole property. She loved it, being a country girl at heart. Her family, pioneers in the Northern Territory, had travelled overland from South Australia in a bullock dray, and taken up large areas of land. Her grandfather, Tim Wickham, was a well-known bushman, very much written about, partly because he spent a bit of time in Fanny Bay Jail for cattle duffing. Jean's grandmother told me colourful stories of the Territory in those days, and of how she wore a revolver on her hip and carried a Schneider rifle to protect her children.

Jean and I would go up to the Hunter, clearing and burning and slashing the lantana and blackberries, and it wasn't long before our kids started driving me mad as to what kind of house I was going to put up. I got moving and had a perfect two-storey bush dwelling, with four bedrooms built. Meanwhile, we began putting in grapes – chardonnay and pinot at first. I was ever hungry to have more acres under vine.

I came to believe that pinot doesn't belong in the Hunter, so I pulled it out and planted semillon and merlot, and eventually had fifteen acres under vine at my property, which I named Endless Summer. The wine is made locally by my friend, Newton Potter; Phil Ryan from McWilliams helps out too. Initially we made a few hundred dozen, which later became five hundred dozen. I sell the other grapes, the merlot and the semillon, as a cash crop to the wineries, and concentrate on the chardonnay, which bears the label Endless Summer.

You soon learn what the soil will yield, and that certain paddocks give a different flavour and yield. I pick the best of the chardonnay from each paddock to make Endless Summer, the best of which I sell through our own outlets; the rest I sell or have bottled off as a secondary wine, labelled Doyles Fisherman's Dry White, which has become most successful.

I have always loved gardening at the farm, and it wasn't long before I'd put in hundreds of rose bushes. The downside was – and remains – that when the black spot comes, I'm kept very busy spraying. You see period movies set in the American Deep South, where the plantation owner sits on the verandah and the slave comes up, doffs his hat and says, 'What will I do now, sir?' That never happens to me.

I never tire of being outdoors in the country. We need nature around us. I've planted as many trees as I can. It always saddens me to see a tree struck by lightning, but as that's the way nature works, I just chop it up for firewood. I am passionate about being in the bush. It calls me – as does the sea. When I have a problem, I go to the sea alone, or take a long walk on the property. The solitude does the trick, and the answers come quickly. I like nothing better of a morning than to get up and go for a walk. I love people, but when you can enjoy your inner thoughts without being interrupted, you make better assessments, and you can be more rational.

Up at Endless Summer, I get enormous pleasure watching plants and trees grow. I try to teach my kids to do the same; the simplest achievement is to grow something. You don't have to build skyscrapers to make your mark; being responsible for a flower enhances the world too. I take my six grandchildren up there as much as possible. I have a collection of ponies for them, although I notice that the boys now want trail bikes. The roar of them shatters the stillness and disturbs the bellbirds, but it's also nice to see the kids having fun.

Whether it's family or mates, the Hunter has become a great social arena. I've taken up everyone from ambassadors to fishing pals, and hundreds of overseas visitors, to show them the beauty of the region. Regulars know they'll be put to work: they call it Doyles' Cheap Labour Force. It's not as cruel as it sounds, because the city folk actually love to be out there, doing something in the soil with their hands.

A typical project was when we built the fowl house, which was the biggest and costliest project I have ever attempted. It took us six weekends, and given the astronomical grog bill, I could have done it for one-third of the cost by getting in professionals. Some of this mob have participated in my annual Clayton's assault on the mountain beind the house. It is staged every Australia Day; we plot our adventure as we consume lashings of Endless Summer chardonnay. Somehow, we never seem to get around to leaving the front verandah.

The original house began to stretch at the seams as the grandchildren grew and more space was required. As it was, my bedroom was directly under the double bunks, and I wasn't getting much sleep with the boys fighting. Also, I'm a light sleeper and guests would come down to make a cup of tea at all hours and, being near the kitchen, I'd invariably be woken. Extensions were called for.

Endless Summer is situated on one of the highest points in the Hunter, at the start of the Brokenback Range. It's nestled in amongst the trees, in the most idyllic spot on earth. I get to what I call 'the home gate' and look along the road which snakes up to the homestead, and I smile at the change in the trees I've planted along the drive; in spring, the blossoms give off a heavenly scent. If it's coming on dark, the lights twinkle from the house on the hill – my special hideaway, set in this magical forest.

So you can see that it was important to get the extensions just right, so as not to ruin the ambience. I decided to have it all done in galvanised iron, which everyone boo-hooed. 'You're mad,' they told me. But I wanted so much to recreate something that has stayed with me since childhood, when I'd go to have a couple of days with the Mills family near Crookwell. They had a hut on the river, made of white-washed wattle mud and lined with newspapers and a hessian ceiling.

Ever since, I've dreamt of having a place made of galvanised iron. People who lie under tiled roofs miss out on one of life's great joys; listening to rain on a tin roof, which gives you comfort and sends you to sleep.

I settled on bush-green iron, to blend in with the trees, and lined it all with white corrugated iron. This is my wing, built on a pole frame, because it's up high and drops away steeply on one side. I live there in harmony with the possums and the birds.

If I hadn't found my way to the Hunter, I would have ended up at Crookwell and bought into my brother's property; to this day, I go there to fish the stream for trout and to shoot a rabbit. It's not just the landscape that draws me to the bush: rural Australia is made up of men and women who remind me of the genuine characters I grew up with. Their openness and hospitality is still one of the wonders of this country.

When I'm at Endless Summer, I talk to my neighbours down the road, the Tinkler family, and to the Ryans, who make wine at the bottom of the hill; they have been true friends and have given me plenty of good advice. They allow me to feel like a real farmer, which is a big buzz. I take the tractor out and do a bit of work, which is very rewarding, as is watching my citrus trees bear fruit and seeing the rose garden bloom.

I treasure my breaks up there, and in many respects, I think how lucky I am to be able to get up and walk away from the business for a day or two – but then, luck is what you make it. As has been said a million times by others, the harder you work, the luckier you get. Okay, so I now own a vineyard and an expensive car to get me there, but don't imagine my brothers and I have lost the hunger necessary to hang on to the winning edge. The hunger's still there and, in some ways, we still think like poor people.

# CHAPTER 16

## I'M NOT SUPERMAN AFTER ALL

In 1993, something made me take stock. I was overweight and unfit. I set about fixing it by easing up on drinking and eating and by getting serious about daily exercise. The conscious part of my brain could not have known the challenges that lay ahead, but I suspect my unconscious had a sense of foreboding, which spurred me to go into training for the fight of a lifetime.

As far back as 1992 I was suffering middle ear problems – it was as though I was seasick all the time. In 1993 I had a skin cancer removed from my head, but I was given no reason to be anxious on that score. Twelve months came and went, and in October 1994, I was diagnosed with secondaries in the lymph glands, and I promptly had those glands removed in St Vincent's Hospital. I had never been ill – apart from having my tonsils out – and here I was, discovering I wasn't bombproof. It was a terrible shock.

Next came a course of radiation therapy, and while that was going on, I agreed to go public about the cancer. I didn't do it for personal publicity, as that was the last thing I needed, but to help get the message out to kids about the lethal effects of the sun. The interview was run on the front page of several papers around Australia, which I think must have helped sell a million hats. I hope so. People everywhere were stunned that I'd been struck down, but no more than I was. I had always imagined I was indestructible, and when Superman falls, the rest of the world is in trouble. I had intended to die with a sword in my hand; I thought I'd go out in a blaze of glory, like a *Boys' Own* hero. Cancer was never in my plans.

I resigned from the business as soon as I got the first diagnosis. There are so many able people in the family, and it was time they had their chance. I no longer had anything left to prove. I had no education and went on to do all that I've done. I wanted to make a point: you don't have to be the greatest scholar in order to become somebody. Anyone can achieve, as long as they are disciplined and can apply their mind to it.

As I lay in St Vincent's, wondering about my future, I saw clearly what my role would be. There was so much I wanted to tell kids, such as it's just as important to speak respectfully to a street sweeper as it is to a prime minister. I pledged that with the rest of my life, however long that turned out to be, I wanted to help others. I thought a lot about smelling the roses – figuratively speaking, as well as the real thing. During a break in the radiotherapy, one of my brothers drove me up to Endless Summer. I hadn't been for a while, and when we reached the home gate, I got out and breathed in the smell of the dirt. It smelt so good.

During that visit, I would wake up real early and sit on the verandah, listening to the bellbirds, and I'd have a quiet weep. I'm not frightened of death, just sad that I mightn't see my grandchildren grow up, and I think of the little ones to come that I'll never meet.

When I returned to Sydney in late November, I happened to hear a beautiful interview on radio with Jose Carreras, the world-famous opera singer who fought leukemia and won. He spoke of being told by doctors that he only had one chance in a million of pulling through, and he said, 'Well that's the chance I'll take.' I was inspired by the words and took his powerful sentiment to heart. I felt I was making the decision not to let my own cancer back in, so it was a bitter blow in December when it returned, this time in the neck.

The prognosis was pretty grim, and it was then I decided to transfer to the Melanoma Unit at Royal Prince Alfred Hospital, headed by a remarkable man, Professor Bill McCarthy, the world's foremost expert on melanoma. I'd like to mention here my advice to others in the same boat: go and get a second and third opinion. Don't worry about hurting doctors' feelings. There's too much at stake.

I had radical surgery there, followed by two months of chemotherapy, which brought me to my knees. It seemed that each day I was going through a revolving door, and each time I came through, I was hit by a cricket bat. I didn't complain at the time, as they saved my life and I was grateful for that.

There's a laugh to be had in even the most serious situations, and my family and I had the occasional giggle about the mountain of cancer cure books that well-meaning friends and strangers alike began bombarding me with. I appreciated their kindness, but an alarming number of them suggested reclining under a banyan tree, chanting Himalayan dances, or some such madness. I was also a sitting duck for every home-made cure ever invented. The classic was shark cartilage. I tried it once, and I'll tell you what: the cure was bloody worse than the disease! I chose instead to concentrate on positive thinking; one's mental outlook counts for so much, and I was going to give it one hundred per cent.

When Jean drove me home from the hospital, after they told me I had cancer again, I went straight to my bedroom and said a prayer. I wanted to recite the Lord's Prayer, but I couldn't remember all the words. Then I cut a deal with God, asking him to save me. In the days afterwards, I found myself asking, 'Why me?', but deep down, I knew I deserved a kick for some of the things I'd done in my life.

As the months went on, I could see I was becoming increasingly tolerant, and I was beginning to look more at the big picture. I was thinking a great deal about this wonderful country of ours, and of the boundless opportunities it offers anyone who'll have a go. The chance is there to become a multimillionaire, and then you can lose it all; it's up to you. Just know this: don't believe that hard work won't kill you. That line was invented by the bosses – of course hard work can kill you.

By the middle of 1995, I took off to Port Douglas for a break, in the company of my long-time mates, Albie George, Jimmy Saul and our better halves, as well as Mickey Sergis. I was all right some days, but others saw me as weak as a kitten. One morning I caught a barramundi and I didn't have the strength to take the bloody fish off the hook.

Once in Port Douglas and twice in the three months afterwards, I had a bad turn, during which I felt extremely unwell while one side of my face would go bright red. Each episode only lasted a matter of minutes and then passed.

They were warnings of what was to come on 19 October.

# CHAPTER 17

## KINDS OF LOVING

For the first time in my entire life, I now found myself with hours at a stretch where I didn't have to be anywhere or do anything. I had no energy to do it with anyway. A spin-off of my new, less-hurried circumstances has been that I've had a chance to think about a whole lot of stuff that had previously passed me by. Here's one: the nature of love. Love's a funny thing, isn't it? You get blokes who will literally kill for it, and others who would cross the road to avoid intimacy with the opposite sex.

Having married young, I'm no expert, but from what I can see, most people fall in love anywhere between one and ten times in their lives. And it seems that for many, the big one, that grand passion, only comes along once. Society is so bombarded with pulp fiction and movies which give them an unrealistic expectation of what relationships will be like that people consequently don't have a clue of how much give and take is involved to make these things work – and of how much heartache probably lies ahead for them.

My generation was fed all this fantasy rubbish, too, with those 1940s happy-ending films, but I don't think we turned out that bad. Thinking of the generation before mine, I've met some wonderful elderly people who married young and have had a beautiful life together, which is a joy to see. It *can* happen. In fact, I don't have to go any further than Mum and Dad as a perfect example.

Alice is such a dominant and fun-loving person, that she's just the right partner for Jack. Certainly luck came into it – luck's everything in life. As I said earlier: The harder you work, the luckier you get, and I guess that applies to love, too. No doubt they have worked at their marriage, at making it as good as it can possibly be – but don't for a minute think they're absolutely perfect – how boring that would be!

They have such *fun* together, which is a lesson in itself. No matter what they do or where they go, they'll often as not end up with an entertaining tale to tell afterwards, such as when they head off on an occasional ocean cruise. They go about their travel arrangements with a novel approach: Alice has a theory that if you leave it until the day before the ship is sailing, there'll be cancellations and then she and Jack will get their tickets for a discount. And you know what? They usually do, which then entails their packing in a hurry.

Their farewells are hilarious, such as the year they were about to sail on the *Canberra* to go to England, and we four boys went up to the point to wave them off. Now this was the days when fireworks were banned, so Johnny went to Chinatown and bribed a bloke and brought back a pile of rockets and we fired them all off at South Head as Mum and Dad sailed past. The trouble was that the passengers who saw our display thought the bloody ship had run aground, and there was absolute panic on board.

On another trip, Mum put a message in a bottle and threw it over the side of the ship. I met a man in Perth some years later who, on hearing my name, said, 'I know your mother.' When I asked how he had encountered Mum, he told me her bottle had washed up at Albany and he was the one who had found it, and he had then been in touch with her. It would only happen to Alice Doyle! How could Jack not have stayed charmed by a one-off such as Alice?

Over the years I've known many men and women who have married for the second or even third time – but I suspect that they never get over the first. I could be wrong, but this is how it looks to me. Furthermore, I reckon there aren't too many who can live without love.

But what would I know? I don't even like going to weddings; I loathe them to tell you the truth. They're like bloody funerals – you run into people you haven't seen for years and you say to them, 'We must get together', but you never see them, until the next wedding or funeral.

Love is not a topic I'm good at talking about; it kind of embarrasses me. But get me onto the subject of love for my kids, and I'll probably smile and ask, 'How long have you got?'

It's great when youngsters grow up and take on the profession that is truly right for them. I have this theory: that there's a limit on our time. We're only here for a brief while – even if we lead a full life – and we don't know when it will end, so when you leave school, do what you want.

My dad has this old tradition about when you leave school, you should get an apprenticeship, so we all did. I became a bricklayer, Michael a wool classer, John a printer and Timmy a butcher. Dad then said, 'Once you've got a trade, you can do what you like', but I'm a firm believer that you go out there and do what you want to do. If you want to become a brain surgeon, study to become one, if you want to sweep the streets and travel around, do it. If I had my life over tomorrow, I feel the greatest opportunities in this country lie in the north, the developing north, and I'd set sail. The thing to avoid, the trap, is that when you get to these places, you can go native. Don't go troppo.

Rob, our eldest, went into teaching, which never surprised me for a second, because she was good with kids from as far back as I can remember, and teaching was all she ever wanted to do. Gayle, on the other hand, was definitely cut out for nursing, even when she was quite small. If I came home with a cut finger, she'd say, 'Oh Daddy, that's a bad cut', and off she'd go to get me a Band-Aid.

Rob's strength has been a blessing in one particular aspect of her life: she has two fine sons, Tom and Christopher; and Christopher was born deaf, which has been a challenge for them. He was to be one of the first in Australia to receive a cochlea implant. They subsequently moved from Watsons Bay to North Rocks, an outer Sydney suburb, to be near the Garfield Barwick School for deaf children. Christopher has grown into a handsome boy, and is a good rower (maybe taking after Grandad!). He has now joined his brother at The Kings School.

Gayle has a lovely son, Matthew, and I'm proud to say he's a top fisherman. I lend him my boat and he takes it out on his own, which I'm very happy about. Gayle is a great mum, partly by virtue of being so placid, although she does have her moments!

I didn't push any of my children very hard academically because I was such a dud myself at studying. I drove Mum and

Dad to tears in that department, and I think they just about gave up on me at one point.

When it came to educating Sharon, we gave a great deal of thought to finding the right school for her, given she was always very strong-willed. As I had a few bob by this stage, it was decided that Frensham, an exclusive boarding school at Mittagong in the Southern Highlands, would be ideal. It offered an open curriculum and it turned out to be an ideal choice.

After she left, she initially didn't know what she wanted to do, so she came to work for us at the fish market. There she'd be, weighing prawns and fish and selling them; then one day she said to me, 'Dad, I want to study law', and I replied, 'Okay, we'll be behind you.'

First Sharon had to go back and matriculate, and it's been a hard slog – especially as she had her daughter, Victoria, while she was still studying. She eventually graduated, and I'm very thrilled and proud of her.

All my kids are individuals, which makes life interesting. Young Pete is a very caring and intense boy, and full of confidence. He has firm opinions, and is not afraid to air them: he's a very black-and-white guy. Pete and his gorgeous wife Fiona have two beautiful daughters, Kimberley and Alex, and he treasures his life with them. It worries me, though, that he has so much else to do; he puts in terribly long hours in the business, as well as working in the kitchen, which is very demanding and exhausting. I fear that he's doing too much.

He has also grown into a top fisherman, one with great perseverance, who always listens carefully while I explained how to rig up the gear. He's fiercely competitive, but he's just as likely on other occasions to see it as pure relaxation. He's got a Marks-built boat and he takes his family out as often as he can.

To this day, he tosses a line out in front of the restaurant almost every morning, Pete does, which is a break for him. I think it's marvellous he does it, and it pleases me the way the locals stop and have a yarn with him. Not-too-serious arguments break out with the likes of fishing experts Eric Love and Eddie Brooks geeing Pete up a bit, about how many fish he's caught and how he caught them.

Talk about God's own country! Watsons Bay takes the cake as far as I'm concerned. To be out the front of our shop, with a line dangling in the clear water, is to feel instantly revived and glad to be alive.

Out of the five, I'd say that Rob and Pete are the most like me, although I should point out that Pete is very much his own person, and I'm glad about that.

And now I come to Shaun, the youngest, who, of all of them, least conforms to the Doyle mould. I suppose you could say that he listens to a different drummer.

Shaun is a keen fisherman, good on the boats and a keen worker at the market. He's fastidious with fish and won't let any product leave the market for our restaurants unless it's 100 per cent. I suspect he's the least like me of the five, although he has my wild streak; authority doesn't sit well with Shaun. We're the furthest apart in the looks department; he is a good sort and always seems to have a string of girlfriends.

I have often thought about the kind of father I've been to Shaun; the difference here is that I was older when he came along, busier maybe, although I did try to take him fishing from an early age, and to be with him as much as I could. I often think of the time I took Shaun out to catch a shark, which he had longed to snare. He was about eleven, and we went out, wide of Long Reef, on a very rough day, to a ground known as

The Whale, where I knew the big sharks came. No sooner had we moored than a huge shark started circling the boat. Shaun was most uncomfortable. I said, 'Here's the big shark you've been dreaming about', but next minute he took off down below and hopped under a blanket. We left without hooking up the shark, but at least the excursion laid Shaun's obsession well and truly to rest.

All my kids appreciate the joys of fishing, and I couldn't be happier about that. Jean has never been keen on fishing; it always frightened her. I think this goes back to a time in Newcastle when I took her out on the shark boat, with a girlfriend of hers. We ran into a big patch of tuna mackerel, which are a fish that fight very aggressively. Jean got her hands badly cut and never much wanted to go fishing after that.

It was a shame, as that unpleasant experience rather spoilt it for her. Back when she was a girl, we'd row around the harbour, maybe up to Bradleys Head, or off Camp Cove, to see what we could catch. I'd also take her lobster fishing with me. It was Jean's job to keep the boat steady and we'd have awful fights, with me getting mad at her for not keeping it steady enough.

I suspect I'm a rather impatient companion out on the water, especially if I'm with someone who knows less than me about fishing. And as for teaching children the joys of this noblest of pastimes – you need ten fishing lines for each kid, because they get them tangled so easily, and it doesn't take them long to get bored if they don't get a nibble. They're always so impatient that you've barely dropped anchor and they're already saying, 'How long before we'll catch a fish?'

Once, when we lived at Nambucca Heads, we were on a sandbar getting some bait. I threw a line out for Robyn with a yabby on the end, and straightaway, she said, 'Dad, I've got a bite.' I went over, and sure enough, she'd caught a big black fish. She was only three or four, so it was a mighty effort. I hadn't believed her when she first called out to tell me she had something on the line, and when we got home, she made sure she told her mother I had doubted her!

There was never any money for flash holidays in the early days, but that was all right; too much too soon can see a youngster grow into an adult who no longer has the ability to be easily delighted.

There was a scream of a time when Jean and I crammed the kids into the stationwagon and headed down to Adaminaby on the Snowy River, where we stayed in a caravan. After a long journey, with a thousand fights having broken out in the back and constant enquiries about 'When will we get there?', finally we arrived and booked in. We were totally whacked, but no sooner had we got our bags in when a terrible storm broke; it felt as though the caravan was going to take off. It was quite hilarious.

Once the kids left school, and my own horizons had well and truly broadened, I encouraged them to go abroad, on the understanding that if they paid their own way over, I'd always stake them the return fare if needed. Gayle took me up on that offer when she was nursing in London. She rang and said, 'I'd like to come home; will you help me?' I sent the money over, but she and her boyfriend used it to go on a holiday to Gibraltar. She rang again for more money, but this time I was smart: I paid for the air ticket in advance and just told her where to collect it.

I'd like to see schoolchildren go to Asia and India as part of the curriculum, so that they could see how other people live. I have firm ideas on how to give children a sound start, and I can't stress enough how crucial it is not to spoil them. An example of this is that I never held with buying them their own cars. I knew that if they saved up themselves, they'd appreciate it more.

What I did do was buy a Mini Moke to teach them all to drive. It only had a canvas top on it, so that when you were doing twenty-five miles an hour, it felt as though you were doing a hundred, and everything shook. I used to tell 'em that if they drove too fast in it they'd lose their heads. I'm very big on parents teaching their kids to drive and encouraging them to save up for their own car, otherwise it's all too easy for them to end up in some mate's bomb, and perhaps end up injured or killed.

I did my best in the early years to try to get Rob, Gayle, Sharon, Pete and Shaun to keep their rooms tidy; I felt their mother had enough to do without constantly cleaning up after them. It's also a great habit for life, however I didn't have much success. My daughters' bedrooms were always a mess and I despaired. I'd say to them when I came home, 'I see we've had a burglary and your rooms have been ransacked', and they'd run in and have a look, then come back and say, 'No, there hasn't been a robbery Dad; nothing's been moved.'

It is with great pride that we Doyles sit on Marine Parade, soaking up our personal history. I suspect the younger Doyles are too young to truly appreciate our background, and it's hard at times for some of them to live up to the name. When my five meet someone and that person finds out they're my children, the comment will often be, 'Oh, you'll never be like your father.' That's a shocking thing to say, so no wonder the kids might sometimes be tempted not to admit to who they are.

Over the front door of our flagship restaurant is a sign: 'Proprietors: Alice and Jack Doyle, and Sons and Grandchildren.' I'm thrilled that four of my five kids are in the business. My children and grandchildren are my future in this mad bloody world, and they never fail to delight me with their values. Time over, and Jean willing, I'd have had an even bigger family.

I get such joy spending a while out the front of the restuarant in the early mornings, where the scene is enhanced by the big pots of petunias along our section of the parade. Tending them used to be my responsibility, but since I got sick, Pete's taken that over, and he's an excellent gardener, which I like to think he inherited from me.

Since our children have grown into adults, Jean has enjoyed holidaying overseas. As far back as I can remember, she wanted to travel and visit ruins and way-out places and it's marvellous she can now indulge in that.

Unfortunately, when we travel together it never seems to work out that well as we tend to want to see different things. So far, we've covered Australia extensively and we did go to Japan – but usually, we travel separately; me on my own and Jean with her sister, Leonie, or her best friend, Nova. They're like a couple of fabulous Aunty Mames, unleashed on an unsuspecting world.

Jean saves furiously to try to get away every twelve months. She's had some funny experiences over the years, such as the time she went to South America, and I got a call in the dead of night from Bolivia. 'I'm caught in the middle of a revolution,' she sobbed, 'and I want to come home.' The other classic was when she rang me from the Philippines. She had landed in the eye of a typhoon, and in all the chaos, the only place she and her friend could get accommodation was in the red light district. She wanted to come home that time, too.

It's always good to have Jean back from one of her jaunts – partly because she's a terrific cook and I miss that when she's away. My favourites are her casseroles and her banana cake. I hope I show enough appreciation for her culinary efforts – I'll certainly never be as reckless as Dad, in the early days of his marriage to Mum. It seems he took one of her scones from the first batch she made as a young bride, and nailed it to the kitchen table. Alice has never made them for him since. And he loves scones, so Dad learnt an expensive lesson.

At our place, I tend to be the fish cook. I especially like going out in the boat and catching a feed, bringing it back and doing it under the griller with a slice of tomato on top. I'm quite partial to it fried, too – and I make great chips.

It's noisy and wonderful when the whole gang gets together for a meal, with Christmas Day being the noisiest and jolliest occasion. Mind you, it gets crazy with all the grandkids and kids coming up to give advice about lunch when it's being prepared, especially since half of them can't boil water! We went in for a cold lunch for some years at Christmas, but now we've swung back to doing the traditional bit, and it's all the more special by sharing it with assorted mates, including a couple of local pensioners who don't have families to be with.

These days I'll sit on the verandah and recall what happened at all the stages along the way, like when Gayle first wanted to leave home and go flatting with some nursing mates, and I was dead against it. An old pal of mine, who was wiser than me, gave me some sound advice. 'Don't fight it; you'll only get offside with your daughter. Let her go and she'll be back home when she's hungry and her washing's dirty.' How true that was.

Then even further back, when the girls started dating, I laid down the law about what time they had to be home, but tended to nod off before they made it back, because I had to be up so early the next morning, so I never knew whether they did as they had been instructed. To the boys, I always said as they were going out the door, 'Be a gentleman, and get the girl home at the right hour. And no booze.' Once Gayle had a wild party when we were still living at Maroubra. There were gate-crashers, it turned into bedlam, and I had to kick them all out.

I've never lived alone and I wouldn't want to. I guess I'm an organism that does best in a lively environment, so it was no hardship as far as I was concerned that Mum's brother, Uncle Harry Newton, lived with Jean and me as long as he did (and I can't say often enough that Jean was bloody marvellous about having him with us). Harry was good for many a laugh. I still giggle to myself about the night Jean and I were trying to have a romantic candlelit dinner at home to celebrate our twentieth wedding anniversary. We were just sitting down to eat when Harry came through the door, looked at the candles and said, 'Not another bloody blackout!'

It's a wonder Jean didn't hit him on the head with a frying pan, but she's too nice for that. My Jean's a truly kind person, and I've seen it time and again, especially when someone dies; Jean's the first one around there with a cake or a casserole. Since my illness, she's developed a strength that neither of us ever knew she had. I now feel there's nothing she couldn't cope with and, as is the way of life, it has taken this adversity for that strength to surface.

We love our stone house, Jean and I, even though it's as cold as buggery in the winter. There's something about old places that gives you a sense of continuity; you can accept that new people will come along to fill your home after you've gone, just as you took over from the previous occupants, and they from the ones before them. It's like knowing that the rivers will keep flowing once I've moved on. I like that thought.

Jean and I have opposing outlooks when it comes to decorating old houses; we're entirely different on that score. We certainly had a few fights, which I usually won, with Jean just giving up in despair. In the end, I scrounged most of the furniture from my mother and my aunties. I probably prize most a beautiful Australian-made sideboard Mum gave me; it's about one hundred and twenty years old, and Mum values it at millions of dollars, of course!

Our other showpiece is the dining room suite. I bought the antique mahogany table in Tasmania years and years ago. It seats ten, and Jean has done magnificent tapestries to go on the cedar balloon-back chairs.

Every room has a working fireplace and high ceilings, so you easily feel transported back in time. It is a fine house in which to enjoy my new-found quietness – and to think. My favourite spots are the front verandah, with its harbour view and summer breezes, and my office, which is an absolute mess, with junk everywhere. Kinder friends have referred to the jumble as 'organised chaos', but that's far too generous. Let me take you in there: I have model ships and a set of harpoons on the walls, and fishing rods all over the place. It's probably in the interest of public safety that no one is allowed in without a written invitation.

I'm talking about kinds of love; well, okay, I *love* this room, and I love the way my pals have added to my treasured possessions over the years. They bring me things like ships in bottles, which give me more pleasure than I can say.

I've had a go at making one, but it takes great patience – and it's even harder if you've just drunk the contents of the bottle!

I love where I live – which is another sort of affection in life. My love affair with Watsons Bay is as passionate as ever, maybe more so. Not in a patronising way, but I've come to feel sorry for the person who lives in an area which doesn't delight them. How lucky I am: every time I cruise down the hill into the Bay, I smile.

The wonderful souls who enriched my childhood come back to visit me, in spirit anyway, as I revel in this more reflective stage of my journey. By just closing my eyes, I'm back there on the day Pat Kidman was missing, presumed dead, in the 1930s. Old Pat had been a professional pearl diver in Broome, and had retired to live on the Parade, just near Marks' boat-building yard.

Late one night, as the ferry was coming into Watsons Bay, a couple fell overboard, and Pat was urgently sent for, to dive for the missing man and woman. After a while, when Pat had still had no luck, the ferry crew went off to the pub. It wasn't until the next day that they realised no one could remember seeing Pat surface for the last time. Had he drowned? Thankfully, Pat was located, none the worse for wear, and he continued with his pleasant retirement, fishing with Headache and Aspro, and doing a bit of drinking.

I get equally nostalgic imagining I'm back with Tich, as we called him. He was quartermaster sergeant up at South Head, and many's the time I hitched a ride home from school with him, in his horsedrawn wagon, as he made his way (slowly) back from Victoria Barracks. Tich was always merry – perhaps due in part to the convenient way his horse managed to stop at every pub between Victoria Barracks and Watsons Bay. He was a kind man too, old Tich; the only time he ever raised his voice was to his horse.

Usually four or five of us kids would be waiting at the corner of Cambridge Street, hoping to see Tich going our way. If he was thirsty, he'd bring out the whip and the horse knew to speed it up and get him to the Watsons Bay Hotel as quickly as possible.

In recent years, it seems that the whole of Sydney has come to see Watsons Bay for the jewel it is; it has become desirable, chic even, to move here. I laugh to think back on the days when certain locals would say they came from Vaucluse, rather than Watsons Bay, because it sounded better.

Out on my front verandah, I ponder the reality that the Bay is no longer the fishing village of my childhood. Does anything stay the same? The simple fishermen's cottages that I played around as a kid are now much sought after by yuppies and others with healthy wallets. Little houses that were built for a few pounds are now going for hundreds of thousands of dollars.

What would the old families make of this shift? The Newtons, the Farmers, the Farrells, the Grahams, the Wagners, the Voights, the McGanns and the Edwards. Like our family, they all survived in winter by huddling around the fuel stove, stoked with wood and coal collected on the beach. Imagine them peering in through a window of their cottages, to see the present incumbents enjoying central heating, wall-to-wall carpet and state-of-the art kitchen appliances.

My generation has come to equate money in the bank with success, but how valid a measuring stick is that on its own?

The fishermen I longed to be like as often as not got jobs on the net boats and were paid in fish, in lieu of cash for a day's work. They then paid their way by exchanging the fish for their other needs. We operated on the barter system in the Bay, and I fail to see why that isn't an acceptable way to live.

Not often, but some days I can be sitting on my verandah and swear that I hear Charlie, our Chinese fruiterer, who did the rounds with two baskets of produce balancing a wooden pole hanging across his shoulders. He added colour to Watsons Bay, as did the regular rabbito who came around. I miss them all.

There are many of us around my age who query the use of the word 'progress' in the context of modern living – just take our eating habits, which have become far more intricate. Several food critics are so quick to look down their noses at wholesome meals – which they dismiss as 'club' or 'RSL' food – usually very popular with the general population. To serve what they consider old-fashioned dishes is a serious felony. We are seen as major offenders for keeping the old favourite, prawn cocktail, on the menu. What's the point of being at the cutting edge of anything if you fail to give your customers what they want?

My own philosophy is to keep it simple – and, if it ain't broke, don't fix it. A perfect example of that is something from the old days: Nanna's scones and fig jam, which tasted sublime when made on our fuel stove. You just can't improve on that. Oh God, don't get me started on Nanna's scones, because no food I've tasted anywhere in the world has surpassed them. Alice still uses the same recipe, and I like nothing better than to collect a hot batch, kept warm in a tea towel, and hit the road with brother Michael, and drive up to his property at Crookwell (the Wongs' old place, where we lived during the war).

Mick's wife Margaret has done an impressive job restoring the rose garden there. I love to sit on the verandah, looking at the roses, reflecting on the days we'd flop down there with the Wongs, after a hard day of marking lambs. We would then open up the tea towel of scones and smother them in fig jam.

I have much to thank Michael for in buying the Wongs' farm. It allows me the fantasy, and occasionally the reality, of cutting a couple of thick slices of country bread and coating them in fresh butter, to make a sandwich with corned beef and lashings of Mum's green tomato pickles. I take them down to the Bolong River, near the quince orchard, where I fish for trout with my trusty old rod. I boil the billy for a cup of tea, to have with the sandwich, which, like the aforementioned scones, somehow tastes best when wrapped in a tea towel. I'm a lucky bastard. And now you know about yet another reason why I plan to be as healthy as I can, as soon as I can.

Even today, as I fight to get well again, I still go down to join in the loveliest of rituals when I can. I grab a cup of coffee and sit on the beachfront, waiting for pals such as Eddie Brooks and Eric Love, both retired fishermen, and Billy Dunn, who used to have the paper shop. We get together, along with any other lost soul who floats by. Some days we have to move, as we are awash with fish from all the tall tales about big catches of bygone years.

I so love Aussie humour, and worry that it's under threat from the 1990s style of sophistication; we've all got too complicated and swish for our own good. It's so easy to get caught up in the complexities and to miss the sweet moments of pure fun. We all need to get out of the cities from time to time, and into the countryside or to the sea to soak up what is authentically Australian.

Sadly, I feel we've lost the plot in the big smoke.

Here's the sort of nonsensical witticism that breaks me up, but would go down like a lead Zeppelin with the Yanks or in Europe. Jackie Marks, of the distinguished Watsons Bay boatbuilding clan, tells the story of Uncle Wilkie standing out the front of our shop with a bunch of the usual suspects one day. They glance up the harbour and there's a cargo ship coming into view, and she's got a heavy list.

One of the old codgers says to Uncle Willkie, 'What do you reckon her cargo would be, to cause such a lean?' and Uncle Wilkie, quick as a flash, tells him, 'She's got a heavy load of post holes, to build fences out in the country.'

Now that breaks me up to this day. It's true that laughter is the best medicine; that's a wonderful saying and I wish I had said it. I just wish I didn't have such a terrible laugh these days, distorted by all the treatment I've had.

I actually value the fact that we are like no other nation on earth. When I go overseas, I speak ocker to them, and if they're going to like you, it really only comes down to your personality. So I'm all for just being yourself, whether you're in Lapland or Los Angeles.

We've turned into a nation that is embarrassed by eccentricity and poverty, and that's a tragedy in my book. We want everyone to be the same, and speaking just for Watsons Bay, it will never establish its unique charm again if we keep this up.

Only the other day, my nephew Jim, who works at our takeaway shop on the wharf at Watsons Bay, noticed a bearded bloke who looked down on his luck. He had on an old overcoat, and not much else. Jimmy gave him something to eat, and a few locals rang the Council to complain; next thing, an officer comes down and tells him not to do that. Jimmy says to the policeman, 'I'll feed who I like.'

The genuine characters are the main reason I still go to the fish market and the produce markets nearly every morning. I especially love chatting with the Greeks, many of whom come from the island of Castellorizo, and are known as Cazzies. I never cease to be amazed at how, when any Greek in Australia does well, he's made an honorary Castellorizian, but if he goes bad, my Cazzie chums give him the big A and insist he's from the mainland!

I know a very funny Cazzie bloke over in the West. Jack Lekias is his name, and he used to come along on our fishing expeditions up to Carnarvon and Exmouth. When he went back to visit Castellorizo, the Turks captured him and interned him for a couple of weeks. Jack is especially memorable for a couple of reasons, the first being that he's a terrible snorer and some nights, in desperation, and so we could get some bloody sleep, we'd drag him out of bed and stick his head in the cupboard under the kitchen sink. Another time, we took him all the way into the yard and left him there.

Jack's other distinguishing characteristic is that he eats like a horse (on that point, I felt he was in the right game, as he is one of Perth's best known restaurateurs. On one occasion, he and I were driving together from Perth to Exmouth, in convoy with the rest of the gang, and Jack insisted on stopping at a roadhouse, about halfway along the journey. Jack looked at a pile of horrible old cooked sausages festering away under hot lights, and he said to the girl behind the counter, 'Love, I'll have the lot.' Then before she could pick up her tongs, he added, 'And love, while I'm waiting, give me half a dozen pasties,' which he devoured on the spot.

I miss the silliness of those trips and I long to rejoin my good companions over in the west for our annual adventure. I'm not too macho to say that I truly love my friends. At sixty-plus, I now see that affection comes in all sorts of shapes and sizes, and I pray that I have some years ahead of me in which to enjoy my many loved ones.

## Nanna Everitt's Famous Scones

**Ingredients**

1 pound of flour

2 heaped teaspoons of baking powder

pinch of salt

1 tablespoon of butter

a good half pint of milk.

**Method**

Sift the flour, baking powder and salt together. Work in the butter with the fingertips until it is like fine breadcrumbs. Mix in the milk and form into a dough with the blade of a knife. Knead lightly, roll out to about a quarter of an inch thick and cut into circles with a scone cutter. Bake in a quick oven for ten minutes.

## Nanna Everitt's Fig Jam

Peel and cut two pounds of figs in half. To every pound of fruit, add half a pound of white sugar. Put the sugar over the fruit, and let it stand all night. Boil until the figs are clean and the syrup is nice and thick. The juice of a lemon to every two pounds of fruit adds to the flavour.

# CHAPTER 18
# Fighting the Good Fight

As soon as I got back from Port Douglas, I began working on this book with Janise Beaumont, confident my life-threatening sickness had given me a new insight and clarity of mind.

My throat has been damaged by surgery and chemo, so our taping sessions would last no more than two hours. We'd go as long as my raspy voice held out, and then I would usually head for home and my afternoon rest.

Then, one Thursday in October, we had spent an hour on a particular chapter, when Janise suddenly said, 'The sea is such an integral part of your story, and yet we haven't had any of our conversations by the water's edge. Why don't we go right now and sit on a beach somewhere?' The closest beach was Double Bay. We drove down the hill in my four-wheel drive – defiantly purchased only a month before – in readiness for a future filled with reckless adventure.

We sat for an hour or so on a bench, gazing at the yachts and inhaling the familiar marine smells that never fail to energise me. We got talking about what matters in life, and Janise has since told me I had plenty to say about the importance of my family to me.

I left to take my former bank manager to lunch, down at Watsons Bay. I felt off-colour by the time I arrived, and was looking forward to getting home. By mid-afternoon, after I returned home, I flopped onto the bed to read the paper. Shortly after I experienced a terrible pain on the left side of my face, and my head exploded with stars.

I was terrified as I attempted to make it down the stairs to Jean for help; in the state I was in, I ended up falling most of the way and then collapsed on the bathroom floor, bumping my head hard against the toilet. Minutes later, I was in an ambulance going to St Vincent's, our closest hospital.

I awoke there and saw a friend, Brother Dan, standing at the end of the bed. I thought: I can't be dead, or else he'd be at the church waiting for me. It was touch and go whether I'd make it through, but there wasn't a moment when I ever considered packing it in. All I could think of in the early stages was, 'Jesus, not another year in hospital.'

Dying never crossed my mind.

The massive stroke left me paralysed down one side, and unable to swallow, therefore having to be fed by a tube. After a lifetime of action and independence, here I was, unable to walk – or even sip a cup of tea. There were times when I felt very downcast. I get very frustrated with having one side of my body fairly useless. If only my left leg would kick in.

I've been so low as I try to get my brain to co-ordinate with my body. When I have to pee into a bottle, I always seem to miss, and that's mortifying. It's hard to stay determined on the days when I wake up and my memory's not too bright and my words are all jumbled. I feel lonely and inadequate.

My brothers and their wives have been constant companions during this recent illness and I love them for that. Still, even with them, as close as we are, I hate to be seen as helpless. Sometimes I'll say, 'Jesus, I feel so terrible in this wheelchair.'

I tell my knockabout mates, 'Try to remember me as I was at the fish market, throwing around a crate of fish – or being a larrikin with you all.'

Jean has been my rock through a lot this; from the start, she would visit twice a day, morning and night, with Alice and Jack getting a cab in each afternoon at three. The strength I get from all my kids and grandkids lets me know how much they love me, and that's meant the world.

As usual, I've overdone it with the avalanche of friends who have stopped by to wish me well. It got too much on several occasions, leaving me absolutely stuffed – although the arrival of certain pals gave me the boost I needed to keep going; mates like John Brown, the Kailis family, who came all the way from Perth, and even Lady Paula Brown from Monaco.

The flipside is the number of people who claimed to be my friends during the good years, who I have now not seen for dust. But who cares?

While in St Vincent's, I was given a scan, which showed the cancer had not returned. In the midst of uncertainty, this news was a beautiful gift. After four weeks, and our fair share of medical scares, I was deemed well enough to move to the Eastern Suburbs Private Hospital, which specialises in rehabiliation. The hard work was about to begin.

Physiotherapy and speech therapy became part of my daily routine as I began the long and frustrating journey back to independence. I also got on with the book, which was close to completion. Thankfully, my long-term memory is sharp and my short-term memory is getting better all the time.

There have been days when I've been too exhausted to work on the memoirs – especially after a gruelling session of physio. This has given me a new respect for the disabled. The next time you see a person walking with the aid of a frame, go up and pat them on the back; they deserve it. My ego has taken a battering of late, as I come to terms with people who have always looked up to me now towering over me in my wheelchair. Maybe I needed this lesson in humility. I also got to thinking about the remarkable film, *My Left Foot*. It inspired me when I first saw it, and it inspires me now.

Who knows what lies ahead for me, or for anyone else? I now know that there are no guarantees; we're all a minute-to-minute proposition. My plan is to walk out of here, and to have a marvellous holiday overseas. I'll do it, too.

I'm fighting the good fight, convinced I can win. Mind over matter is a big part of my strategy, but by Jeez, you need modern technology too.

And Mr Carreras, I can never thank you enough for pointing out that a chance in a million is a chance worth taking.

# EPILOGUE

As I lie here in my hospital bed, I can see a precious gift on the table beside me. The Thomas family – fishermen and long-time residents of Watsons Bay – have brought me a framed photograph of a lighthouse.

When you're at sea, you keep your eye on the lighthouse and it will save you from harm. I need that guiding light more than ever now. I'm counting on my difficulties passing, then I will be able to go back to sea, out to where you can hear yourself think. *And I've got just the boat, too.*

After years at the top end of town, complicated by board meetings, court battles and creating an empire, I am ready to go back to basics, and I've had Jackie Marks build me a simple wooden fishing boat. It's very plain – inspired by an eighteen-foot open boat I admired as a youngster; in fact, I watched it being built in 1946, and thankfully Jackie remembered it too. It was owned by Jack McGann, who had the boatshed at the end of the Parade.

Jackie Marks put it together in his back yard at Five Dock (we settled on nineteen-and-a-half foot for the length), and I took delivery in February 1995.

It was raining the day we launched her and I was so happy. My cancer seemed to disappear as I drove her back to Watsons Bay with my son Peter, Jackie and his mate who helped with the building. It was a powerful flashback to my youth.

I named her *Coo-ee* and she seats six comfortably. I moored her in the Bay, not far from where McGann's boatshed used to be. Pretty soon, people started coming along and commenting. Eddie Brooks was one, and he's a person whose judgement means something to me. He liked it, as did Ned Abbott, a great fisherman who knows about boats. Next thing I did was teach my children how to work her.

By the time I had finished my chemo in the middle of 1995, I figured I needed a small wheelhouse on my boat to protect me in bad weather, so I got Jackie to put one on. It's just finished and I can't wait to go out in her again. She looks so fine: white timber, with a varnished wheelhouse, and you steer with an old-style rudder.

I have this daydream of taking a bunch of my long-gone heroes on the *Coo-ee*. It would be when the wattle comes out, in the flathead season, and we'd feast on a 'hot lunch', Headache and Aspro-style.

I also fantasise about solo trips, which would give me a chance to clear the cobwebs out of my head and to do some re-evaluating, without interruption.

I keep reminding myself of Joan Collins's philosophy: 'What doesn't kill us, makes us stronger.' She got that one right, although renewed spiritual strength can come at a terrible cost.

As far as regrets go, I reckon that people who say they don't have any are liars. I should have passed more of my knowledge of the sea and the environment on to my children when they were young, but at least I can do it with my grandchildren. Lost opportunties can weigh us down, but I figure they're like the wind; just let them blow out of sight and don't dwell on them.

I now realise that it takes a big person to say 'Sorry' and actually mean it. These are random thoughts, but they are so important to me at this stage of the game, also the notion that maybe simplicity is the key after all. Mum always said that Doyles's secret has been to buy the best seafood available, whatever the price, and give big servings. Could anything that simple be so successful? Yes, yes, yes.

I've thought about the nature of winning, these past months, that you must be prepared to sacrifice, including hurting loved ones, and that's hard. I'd do it all again, but with a different outlook.

My hot tip is: never give up. Plus, you must have determination and an eagerness to work hard, and you should be disciplined – which I'm not. Never feel sorry for yourself and always maintain a sense of humour; combine those two with a bit of luck and you will surely burst through.

Everyone gets lost from time to time. I've learnt that there are a lot of shallow people out there, but overall, most men and women have a terrific streak in them – although it often takes a crisis for it to surface. I know I've gone up the wrong street more than once, but I'm still here. And that's enough of a miracle for now.

Come next November, sweet November, I intend to be well enough to take my little boat out alone. I'll be watching the phases of the moon, and when the time is right, you'll find me moored off Long Reef, catching jewfish and looking at the stars.

# PETER DOYLE BY FRIENDS AND FAMILY

## JOHN BROWN

*One-time Federal Minister for Tourism, Currently Chairman of the Tourism Task Force*

How does one sum up Peter Doyle in a few short sentences? With great difficulty. How can one person be so eclectic in so many ways? How can one person, so humble and self-effacing, also be so influential in so many spheres?

I have had the honour of knowing Peter Doyle and his family for a long time. The more I experience Peter the more I respect him, the more I understand the depth and breadth of his character and the value of his simple wisdom. Peter Doyle epitomises all the distinguishing characteristics which comprise the essential friendly Australian. He possesses all the qualities which make us a unique race.

Doyles restaurant at Watsons Bay has come to symbolise easygoing Australia. We featured it in the original 'shrimp on the barbie' advertisement with Paul Hogan saying to the Yanks

'You'll have to get used to getting a suntan in a restaurant.' Doyles is an icon of Australian tourism. The setting on the harbour at Watsons Bay is of course a magnificent asset, but the biggest attraction by far is the restaurateur. Peter Doyle has more international friends than anyone I know, and his restaurant is a magnet for visitors on each trip to Sydney.

I arranged for Doyles restaurant to be named Australia's Best Tourism Restaurant at the National Tourism Awards in Adelaide in 1986. The pseudo-sophisticates of the food industry were appalled. In my view there was no contest – Doyles is unique. It shrieks of laidback, friendly Australia, which is exactly why tourists love us. In typical style Peter accepted the award with a simple, irreverent but charming speech. 'We're not flash, elaborate, sophisticated or trendy at Doyles – we sell fish and chips and we've been doing it for sixty years.' 'Hooray!' thought I, let's hope you impress all our visitors for another century or more with this typical Australian charm and friendly candour.

Peter Doyle's generosity is legendary. As a host he has no peer. To be invited, as I have been, on so many wonderful occasions to be Peter's guest at a large table of visitors for Sunday lunch at Doyles, is to be entertained royally. The 'stars' whom Peter has 'spoilt' at these lunches would read like a glossary of the world's most interesting characters. Knights of the realm, cabinet ministers, sporting stars, business luminaries, fabled names of stage and screen, international visitors mingled with Peter's old friends from the fish markets, the police, and his huge collection of buddies – both male and female. Such occasions were a joy. Peter Doyle, the concert master would move around the table, sagging under copious supplies of succulent seafood and wonderful wines, and treat old friends of supposed lowly status and world-recognised stars with exactly the same respect and affection. 'Good to have you all here at Doyles,' Peter would say. 'Drink up, eat up and have a good time: Australia is the greatest joint on earth.' 'Amen,' I would say under my breath, and 'Peter Doyle is one great Aussie.'

The last occasion I sat down with Peter at one of these lunches was on a Saturday about two years ago. Peter had just been diagnosed as having a rare form of skin cancer. The diagnosis and the prognosis were far from encouraging. In fact, Peter was facing a very uncertain future with the odds anything but in his favour. So we all arrived, some twenty of his closest mates. Again an eclectic mix. Politicians (all Labor!), policemen, fishermen, old friends from near and far – young men and some far from young.

Peter gave us a little homily to begin with. We all knew of the precarious position regarding his future. I guess we were all harbouring feelings of apprehension and a great deal of sadness – was this to be his last supper? Peter's *joie de vivre* soon dispelled our not-so-well-concealed gloom. 'Now look here you blokes. I've got, as you know, my own special private collection of beaut wines. The executor of my will is my brother-in-law who wouldn't know shit from clay when it comes to wine, so there is no way I'm leaving this stuff for him to bugger about with. We're going to drink half the collection now and the other half when I recover – or if I don't you blokes can drink the other half at my wake.' The gloom dissipated in the face of Peter's little speech. How could mates of his not respond with optimism, hope and good humour in this atmosphere of courage and wonderful good nature?

History shows that Peter, having conquered the cancer, suffered a debilitating stroke. But the same good humour, love of life and rare courage which Peter displayed to his mates at the 'last supper' has pulled him through. I for one look forward with great anticipation to robbing the executor of the governance of the second half of the wine collection by helping to drink it with my mate Peter.

Charitable causes have been Peter's passion. The Doyle family has over the years raised or given millions to deserving causes. As a small example of that commitment, the Christmas Party at Doyles for the Children's Hospital with Miss Alice Jonnies and her girls' choir is a must. Peter was no doubt jubilant when his good friend, Dr John Yu, the Medical Superintendent of the hospital which Peter has helped so generously, was announced Australian of the Year for 1996.

Peter Doyle was made the Founding Chairman of the National Maritime Museum. Nobody could have occupied the position with greater enthusiasm or style. His leadership over many years helped this organisation to achieve its great reputation as a living pageant of Australia's maritime history. Typical of Peter – who had entertained, among others, President Bush of the USA – he arrived at his testimonial send-off dinner, the retiring Chairman replete in dinner suit, on the rear of a motorbike. No arrogant pride of position with Peter – he has always been the humble fisherman with a wonderful sense of self-ridicule and a lack of pomposity.

No one has ever had a more faithful friend than those of us fortunate enough to have earned the appellation of being a mate of Peter's. Fidelity and support have been the hallmarks of Peter's friendship. Several times when I have been involved in some public wrangle over my political career, when true friendship is tested, Peter was always there. And always there is a courageous public defence, not just the private phone call of support – no, not just that gesture. Peter did it the hard way in a manner which put him and his friendship on the public register. The support would appear in the *Sydney Morning Herald* letters column. Unstinting fidelity to a friend on even an unpopular subject signed 'Peter Doyle, Watsons Bay'.

Yes, he's my mate, Peter Doyle, fisherman, restaurateur, family man, raconteur, humorist, homespun philosopher, patriot and wonderful friend. He sure has earned the dual titles, 'Good Bloke' and 'Great Aussie'.

I salute you Peter Doyle, AO.

## Bob Hawke

*Former Prime Minister of Australia*

I have been fortunate in my life to meet a few individuals who reflect the quintessential Australian character. And no one has done this more, to my mind, than Peter Doyle. First of all, just the look of the bloke! Rugged, weatherbeaten, not handsome but attractive, and a face radiating friendliness with the appropriate elements of strength and a healthy sign of cynicism displayed at any evidence of pomposity.

Peter Doyle is, above everything else, a fisherman, and he embodies in his virtues all the best of the characteristics of strength and courage we have come to associate with that profession. I have never seen him daunted by any situation, and perhaps the best way I can put it is that if I had been going over the top at Gallipoli, I can't think of anyone I'd rather have had next to me than Doyley.

By the dint of his labours, together with those of his wider family, Peter has become a wealthy man, but I can't think of any person of means who flaunts his wealth less. His generosity is legend, but it is the generosity of spirit to all his fellows that marks him out from most others.

There are not many better ways of getting to know someone's qualities than being away in some remote spot for a few days with a group on a fishing holiday. I had this pleasure on a couple of occasions with a mixed mob (all males, let me hasten to add) and you simply couldn't ask for a better companion. What Peter doesn't know about fishing isn't worth knowing, and he was always ready to help the rank amateur. He was a neverending source of enjoyment with his stories and down-to-earth humour which was never unfairly aimed at the unfortunate. And he was a bloody good cook!

Peter Doyle is a publicly-spirited citizen, evidenced in so many ways but nowhere more than in his outstanding leadership in the creation and early work of the National Maritime Museum. This will remain a permanent memorial to his vision and commitment to Australia.

I have spoken of Peter's courage and all of us who've seen him and been through his recent illness with him can have had nothing but admiration for his steadfastness in this adversity. We all hope and trust that he is going to have many more years to enjoy life and pass on those incomparable fishing skills to the beloved grandchildren.

In looking back over what I've written I wonder whether people might think I've been writing about a saint. Saint he ain't, but he's about as close as I can think of to the perfect Australian mate.

## Len Evans

*Peter Doyle's Mentor and the Irrepressible Food and Wine Identity*

Ten years ago or so I wrote a cookbook with a difference. Although full of recipes, each chapter had a sort of anecdotal foreword that led to each section of different foods. Not surprisingly, the fish chapter was headed 'Doyle and the Rest'. It contained a number of Peter Doyle stories.

'Peter Doyle, of the famous Sydney fish family, was once a fishing inspector. On an inland posting, he found illegal traps on a section of a river under his jurisdiction. Determined to catch the culprit, he waited for two days and three nights by the traps. All that time he put up with the discomfort of flies and mosquitoes, packed cold food, no hot drink. Finally, at dawn on the third morning a furtive figure slunk to the riverside. Doyles patience was vindicated.

The poacher began hauling in the traps. Doyle quietly crept up behind him and placed a large hand on his shoulder. In complete confusion, the man looked up and shouted, "Who the hell are you?" "I'm the local fisheries inspector", Doyle replied. "Thank God for that," cried the poacher, "I thought you was the bloke that owned the traps."'

I met Doyle through my great mentor, father figure and friend, Rudy Komon. Rudy had insisted on eating some fresh seafood one day, and said there was no place better for it than Doyles, Rose Bay. Marching straight into the kitchen he demanded of the rather hot character who was cooking the chips, 'Do you have any live crays?' 'Yes, mate', replied Peter Doyle, without looking up. 'They're all over the bloody floor.'

We looked down. Sure enough, the sack of live crayfish had come undone, and crays were walking all over the place, under the stoves, in the corners, marching out the door. Completely unfazed by this, Rudy inspected them in turn until he pointed and declared, 'Good, I'll have that one.'

So began a friendship with Doyle which is now over thirty years old. We've had a couple of rows, a hundred or more fishing trips together, and thousands of laughs. Doyle is not a joke teller, but he's a great anecdotist, with a compulsive love of the sea. The kind of fishing mania he possesses is typified by a story he tells of when he was young.

He was live fishing for kingies at night with one of his old uncles from Watsons Bay. The fish were biting, and since other boats were sniffing around, the Doyles kept their lights doused. They were kept busy hauling lines in, throwing the fish under one arm and holding them to the body to get the hooks out. It was a hot night and Doyle was only wearing shorts.

Another big one bit, and Doyle hauled the line in, pulling the large fish into the boat and grabbing it under his left arm. In the dark he didn't realise there was a dreaded blue bottle on the line, and suddenly his body was covered in huge weals. The pain was intense and he nearly blacked out.

The old uncle was a bit of a tippler and had a couple of bottles of sweet sherry on board. Doyle swears he drank about a bottle and a half before he finally passed out. At least the drunken sleep covered the pain.

A couple of hours later, he was awakened by the old salt. Thickheaded, cross-eyed, still hugely puffed out and still in pain, Doyle asked, 'What's up?'

'Pete,' his uncle whispered, 'they're on again.'

Fishermen have their own subculture. At the time when nude beaches had become popular, Doyle took me out in his boat one day. 'I want to show you something', he said, heading for one of the beaches. Frankly, I was rather disappointed that Doyle should not only prove to be a voyeur, but also assume I was one. He passed the beach without a word. 'There,' he said finally, 'see that rock? That's where I caught the biggest bream I've ever seen in my life.'

Doyle, ever one to deflate the pompous and laugh at the ridiculous, claims he was present when there was a big ceremony of some kind at Constitution Dock in Hobart. The wife of the chief official at the function was asked by one of the fishermen present if she would like a cray. 'Yes,' she replied, 'as long as it's a fresh one.' The fishermen dipped his hand into the box and brought out a huge cray, holding it by its back. The cray's tail swished and its head jerked repeatedly as it tried to escape.

'Oh,' cried the woman, 'it's huge. But is it fresh?'

'What the hell, lady', was the reply. 'Do you think I wind the flaming things up?'

Years ago, we went fishing with celebrated American wine man Bob Mondavi, about sixteen kilometres outside the Heads, and we had all the big gear out, trolling. It was a hot still day, and there were not many fish about. Happily, a large tuna hit with some vengeance and Bob had a great time reeling it in. Not long after, Doyle saw something way off, from the flying bridge. It turned out to be an elaborate deckchair, obviously thrown off a passenger liner by some early morning drunks. With some difficulty we hauled the chair aboard. About fifteen minutes later we spotted another. That too was hauled aboard.

'Reel in,' shouted Doyle. 'Get the poppers. Get those lines in.' Why? It was still a lovely day and there was plenty of time. 'We've got two chairs. What I want now is the table to make up the set.' Unfortunately for Doyle and his dreams of sybaritism, it wasn't to be.

Peter Doyle managed the family business for years, with huge success until his troubles. Of course, his parents, Jack and Alice, his son Peter junior, his wife Jean, brother Mick, and daughters, nephews abound, all involved. It is very much a family business, and one cannot escape their warmth and humanity. Yet Peter has been at the forefront and he is known and loved throughout the world. The many times at sea I've shared with him and others mean a great deal to me. A story from my book again. 'One day we were some distance out in his faithful *Grand Banks*, and after seeing whales and a couple of sharks, we found ourselves in a school of porpoises. There must have been over a thousand of them. Soon the bow waves were crowded, and more started playing behind the boat, then by the side, doing jumps in pairs, then counter pairs, with some showoffs leaping far out of the water and falling flat on their backs. "Jeez mate," shouted Doyle, "you wouldn't be dead for quids. But when I do go," he added, "I hope it's pissing down with rain."'

I hope it won't piss down with rain for a good while yet. Since some of those anecdotes were written, I haven't fished as much with Doyle simply because I moved to the Hunter Valley and haven't been so readily available.

(5 am phone call: 'Mate, there's a big batch of kingies around Sow and Pigs and they'll be gone when the wind changes.')

Happily, Doyle started a vineyard and built a house in the

Hunter not far from me, to which he became devoted. 'Stuff the fish, has it rained up there yet? How are my bloody vines? Jeez, it's bloody dry, dry as a wombat's arse.' Nothing changes.

Now Doyle has a fight on his hands. After the melanoma, after the cancer, after the second huge skin graft, he had a stroke. I cried when I saw him soon after, for he seemed to have shrunk by half, and my tough, resilient, resourceful mate was curled up like a refugee child. But the spirit blazed through and it continues to shine and dazzle. I know he has rough times; I know he sometimes despairs. Yet I know also that he is unconquerable, and that his capacity for life and love will keep the rain away.

## Peter Doyle Junior

What does my dad mean to me? As a little boy sitting in the backyard of our Nambucca Heads home he meant warmth and happiness. I remember Dad had brought home a fishing net that he had spread over the grass. I was going through the net finding small fish that had been trapped. It was a warm day and I was with my dad. I felt safe. A wonderful feeling to have and a feeling that I have had with my dad all of my life.

Like anyone there are always regrets. My regret is that from childhood through teens I was unable to spend enough time with my dad. We had spoken many times about it and it is a regret he shares with me. Dad was working seven days a week, leaving early and coming home late. Most people never realise the work my dad, along with his family, put into the business. Dad put in the hard yards, the long slog. He made the sacrifices and has earned the rewards. And through it all, the hard times and the good times, he hasn't changed.

My dad can talk to the street cleaner and talk to a king. What you see is what you get. He has that wonderful ability to be himself, and has no need to make any apology for it. He is, to so many different people on so many different levels, a mate. Dad has the most amazing ability to be able to walk down the street, say 'G'day' and strike up a conversation – no matter who it is. He has that 'everyman' personality.

I have never been afraid to ask my dad for advice. Sometimes it was advice I didn't want to hear. At other times I have been amazed at his perception and understanding. To see through the mist, or more to the point, being able to cut through the bullshit, has brought many people to him for advice. He gives unselfishly of his time, and at times has been taken advantage of. He knows when this happens, but shrugs it off and puts it down to experience. Dad doesn't hold grudges, and he says very often that life is too short. He's right. Why waste the energy?

As I've got older, I have grown much closer to my dad. I never lose sight of the fact that he is the boss and I have learnt so much from him. The greatest thing he has taught me is respect; not only respect for others but respect for oneself. He has also taught me the value of being humble. Dad would go to the fish markets early then be out at the restaurants. He was forever in a pair of stubbies and gumboots. Dad was never guilty of overdressing for work. Dad thinks nothing of picking up a broom or helping with the dishwashing. It's all part of the job.

But above all my dad is a character – bigger than life. He has a wonderful sense of humour and is able to lift the spirits of all those he comes into contact with. He doesn't suffer fools and who can blame him? His work for charity goes very much unnoticed and my Dad can never say no. His work for the fishing industry has been tireless. He has sat on many boards and committees, always giving his time and efforts one hundred per cent. He has never held back and I don't think he ever will.

Dad cannot keep still. He is always active, always on the move. I remember wanting to talk to him one day at the restaurant. He has this terrible habit of walking away as you talk to him. I'm sure he doesn't realise it but he just can't stand keeping still. I told him that I was going to get a nail and hammer and could he wait. He asked me what for. I told him I was going to nail his foot to the floor so that he would stay still while I spoke to him. As I have gotten older I have become a bit more cunning. Now I don't walk behind trying to keep up and trying to talk. I stand still and talk. If he would walk away I wouldn't follow but instead walk in the opposite direction. It must have made him curious to find out what I was saying because he would always search me out and ask me what I wanted.

Fishing is his greatest passion. He could fish every day for the rest of his life and still want more. It's murder though to go fishing with him. I always have the wrong gear, the wrong bait and I've tied the hook the wrong way. If the tailor are running there is always a competition to see who can catch the most. And Dad hates to lose. It's even worse if my brother or cousin or myself has caught fish the day before. He wants to know where, how and why and you can bet your bottom dollar he'll be out there trying to outdo us. To Dad the world stops when he goes fishing. The best time I ever spent with Dad was fishing in Western Australia. We were with friends from WA and stayed in a lodge and ate what we caught. We rose at sun-up (I still don't know why, as we never went fishing till ten) and walked and talked. It was more than being with my dad. It was being with my mate.

When Dad retired as Chairman of the National Maritime Museum, I said a few words and wrote a poem for him. It is more appropriate now than ever. He has been a wonderful father. I could not ask for more.

> An Australian is someone who loves this country. The
> terror, the beauty. An Australian embraces it.
> An Australian doesn't moan or groan or whinge and
> whine.

An Australian is fair dinkum.
An Australian has got mates and says 'G'day'. An Australian is proud of Australia and makes no apologies for being proud.
An Australian, when his back is to the wall, never gives in. An Australian is like the Diggers at Tobruk. They stick by their guns and by their mates.
An Australian is someone you can look up to.
An Australian is my dad.

## Alice Doyle

*Peter's Mother and Matriarch of the Doyle Clan*

I would like to write these few lines about our son, Peter, the eldest of our four sons. At this time of Peter's life, at the age of sixty-three, and with the serious illness he has been through, I think we have been more proud of him than when he told me, 'I am meeting Queen Elizabeth next week, Mum, and I want you both to be at the Maritime Museum and I'll introduce you both to her.'

'Oh, Peter, I'll have to learn to curtsey,' I told him.

I am so proud of Peter because I can honestly, truthfully, say that, he has never once complained to me about his illness, and the problem associated with it. I have said to him, 'Peter, I would like to write to the *Sydney Morning Herald* and tell them you never complain about the suffering, test results, and so on.' But he said, 'Mum, never do that; there are thousands like me.' Other times he'll say, 'I'm going to beat this; I'll get better.' And he will, too.

It was a great life when, as a small child in the 1930s, you could actually live on a quiet beachside part of Sydney Harbour – a small strip of footpath from your bedroom door – the calm waterfront. And right next door to a working public boatshed. That is what Peter would remember as his early childhood.

It was really my childhood lived once again by Peter and his brothers. Peter attended the local public school in Vaucluse, in another lovely part of the area. I am afraid Peter spent more time on Sydney Harbour than at school. Sometimes I used to think that maybe Peter would be better suited to becoming a farmer, because when he was nine or ten, once a month I would take him to Paddy's Market, where he was very interested in poultry and produce. I could only take him to the night market, when Jack would come home from work to be with the other boys at home. I still remember those day-old chicks at the bottom of his bed, and the electric light globe to keep them warm, and his brothers in the same large room complaining about the chicks tweeting.

In 1939, when the war began, there were many housewives in the area who opened up their homes for functions to raise funds for 'comforts abroad', such as knitting socks, scarfs, etc. There was one lovely waterfront home at Watsons Bay in particular, and there would be weekend fetes, and of course, a 'best iced-sponge cake with mock-cream filling' competition.

As Peter then was at an especially hungry age, he would tell me to make a sponge cake. 'Mum, it's for the competition.' I certainly made many sponges for that competition, but to Peter's dismay, I never won a prize. To this day he sings the praises of my sponge-making and still speaks about how he thought he believed I was robbed in never winning a prize.

Peter was a great organiser, forgetting his friends on school holidays to throw a net out on the beachfront to try to catch a big haul of fish. The net was an old parachute someone had given him. He had visions of selling them on a table under the old fisherman's tree, at the wharf. Lots of disappointments for Peter – no big haul of fish, but enough for me to throw in the pan with bread and butter for his fishermen friends so he could sit on the beach and plan a different beachfront in the Watsons Bay of tomorrow.

I remember the night the Jap submarine came into Sydney Harbour; the sirens were screaming, we were all up at my parents' – our sons and I, and Jack was home on military leave. Peter had us all organised with pegs in our mouths, and he was proudly marching around the house with his school-issue first aid kit, which was a large shoulder bag, Army issue, full of bits and pieces, including iodine and torn sheets of household bed linen, a block of chocolate and a water can. Oh boy! Then – and I swear this is all true – Peter took the peg out of his mouth and said the Lord's Prayer!

The next morning the scene in the water out the front of our place was a sad reminder of the depth charges that went off, killing so many sailors on the Kuttabul Navy ship. I remember it was a medium tide and a westerly was blowing as we stared at hundreds of fish breathing their last; they were washing backwards and forwards with the tide. Peter was throwing the fish further out in the water.

Peter had a great life, going out at times with the different big-game fishermen, such as Max Lawson. Naturally, after being apprenticed to a builder and learning to be a bricklayer, he gave that away to become a fishing inspector. Peter really worked hard to achieve what he believed in most.

In this part of his life he met so many interesting people and he said to me one day, 'Mum, remember when you used to say to us at the dinner table, "Sit up straight, use your knife and fork the right way, or you will never get to the Lord Mayor's Party."'

I used to tell my kids that my father would say to me and my brothers and sisters, 'Well, next week I am dining with the Lord Mayor of London', which he actually did.

And I never did myself, but I was fortunate enough to meet

the Lord Mayor of London, one night at our restaurant and I presented him with an inscribed copy of my cookbook. And I have a treasured letter from him to me.

Now I pray to the good Lord for a miracle that Peter could eat a piece of bread and take a drink of water. And I believe in miracles. It's just perhaps not the right time yet.

LOBSTER · PRAWNS · FISH
Doyles
RETAIL MARKET